BANKING LAWS AND REGULATIONS IN NIGERIA

SELECTED THEMES

BANKING LAWS AND REGULATIONS IN NIGERIA

SELECTED THEMES

Dr (Barr) BM Magaji, Fnim, PhD
Associate Professor of Law

malthouse

Malthouse Press Limited

Lagos, Benin, Ibadan, Jos, Port-Harcourt, Zaria

First Published 2024
ISBN 978-978-60012-0-3

Published by Malthouse Press Limited

Lagos   Port Harcourt   Zaria

43 Onitana Street, Off Stadium Hotel Road,
Off Western Avenue, Lagos Mainland
E-mail: malthouselagos@gmail.com
Facebook:@malthouselagos
Twitter:@malthouselagos
Instagram:@malthouselagos
Tel: 0802 600 3203

DEDICATION

This book is dedicated to the cherished and everlasting memory of by beloved mother, Hajiya Hauwa Magaji Birnin Kebbi. She was a loving, caring, religious and above all, disciplined mother, housewife and a community philanthropist in her own modest way. May Allah grant her *Aljannatul Firdausi* for her countless good deeds, *Amin*.

ACKNOWLEDGEMENTS

The contributions of a number of persons made this work a reality. In the course of this work, a number of other works were consulted. Even though they have been mentioned in the reference, they deserve further mentioning here. They include Professor Goldface Iroka of Faculty of Law Ahmadu Bello University, Zaria. Mr. Layi Afolabi's work *Law and Practice of Banking*, provided a further useful source of my work.

My gratitude goes to my colleagues at the Department of Legal Studies Kaduna Polytechnic, who provided the enabling environment for this work to materialize. Mention should be made of the pioneer HOD of Legal Studies Department, Mrs. R. A. Ataguba, who could rightly be called the 'Mother' of my toes by honouring me with her draft thesis to proofread and to jointly write academic papers.

Mrs. Adeniyi "loaned" me a book on *Law and Practice of Banking*, by Milnes Holden to prepare for my first lecture class on banking which later provided the springboard and inspiration for this work. Mallam A. D. Ahmaed and Alh. Barrister N. K. Sani, deserve a special mention and thanks for the constant words of advice and intellectual interactions. Over and above all, my HOD Mallam Barrister Sule Shaibu who's steering of the ship of the department and who always put me on my toes with academic assignments at short notices, he deserves a big thank you. May Allah bless all of you.

A very special mention must be made of the Director of the College of Administrative Studies and Social Sciences (CASSS), Dr. (Mrs.) Asama'u Maikudi who has been a source of inspiration, encouragement and support to me and my colleagues at the Department and the College as a whole. May Allah continue to bless and guide her. The pioneer HOD of Banking and Finance Mallam Musa Mshelia and the pioneering students of the Department deserve a mention for their contribution and particularly their probing questions on Banking Law issues which kept me constantly researching on the legal issues relating to banking.

Over and above all, I thank the management of Kaduna Polytechnic that has over the years, exposed me to access a number of courses including Postgraduate Diploma in Education (PGDE), Master of Laws (LLM) and currently PhD in Law at Ahmadu Bello University, Zaria. This has widened my academic interactions and intellectual horizon.

Daniel S. Kurah and Tunde Louis endured my impatience and typed the manuscripts with a sense of duty and commitment for which I remain grateful. My family provided the home support to enable the work to be accomplished. Above all, all praises are due to Allah, Almighty God who has given me the strength, guidance and resources to undertake this work. To all I say thank you and God bless you all.

PREFACE

It would seem that there is no business more hedged about my laws than the banking industry. Constantly, laws, regulations, new conventions and practices are emerging to meet the dynamics of the changing economic climate both nationally and globally. This work is the result of many years of teaching Business Law and later, Banking Law in the College of Business and Management Studies at various levels in Kaduna Polytechnic. With the introduction of banking and finance course in the programmes of Kaduna Polytechnic. I pioneered the teaching of Banking Law of the programme. The idea of writing this book was mooted after realizing that there is none in the National Board for Technical Education (NBTE) approved syllabus. This work is an attempt to bridge this gap. Although the main targets are the students of banking and finance, banking practitioners, solicitors, financial managers, business executives, and anyone having the one form of relationship or the other with the banking industry, and that means practically everybody, in view of the rapid growth of the banking culture nationwide, will find this book very useful.

Barr. B. M Magaji MNIM
Department of Legal Studies
College of Administrative Studies and Social Science (CASSS),
Kaduna Polytechnic, Kaduna.

FOREWORD

Banks, worldwide, play significant role in socioeconomic life of individual and nations. Apart from their traditional functions of accepting deposits and advancing loans, banks facilitate capital formation, which further stimulate development in all sectors of the economy. For banks to effectively perform the said functions, their activities and conduct need to be guided by laws, rules and regulations. This makes a book on Banking Law and Regulations relevant and timely.

Banking Law and Regulations in Nigeria: Selected Themes essentially deal with the laid down rules or code of conduct meant to control and set standards for banking business. Indeed the main aim of the on-going banking reforms in Nigeria started in 2004, is to ensure banks' conformity to the laid down banking rules and regulations. The eleven-chapter book written by a practising lawyer and academician of repute, Barr. B. M. Magaji, contains vital and rich information on theory and practice of Banking Laws and Regulations in Nigeria. The theoretical aspect of the book written based on the N.B.T.E approved syllabus for National Diploma in Banking and Finance, will tremendously benefit students of the program. The practical aspect of the book will be of immense benefit to bankers, business executives, lawyers, regulators of the banking system, etc.

It is my singular honour and privilege to strongly recommend the book to the aforementioned categories of stakeholders in the banking system and the entire general public. The book is recommended for some reasons. First, the topic covered by the book span the entire syllabus on Banking Law for National Diploma in Banking and Finance. Secondly, the book was written in simple language avoiding or at least minimizing the use of the old-fashioned English Law jargons. Thirdly and lastly, the book is homegrown material on Banking Laws and Regulations and need to be patronize on patriotic basis.

I really congratulate the author. Barr. B. M. Magaji for the job well done! I urge all the sundry to encourage and support the author by means of patronage of the book and where and when necessary constructive criticism for future improvements.

Aliyu Mamman, Ph.D.
Director, College of Business and Management Studies,
Kaduna Polytechnic, Kaduna State, Nigeria.
May, 2011

TABLE OF CASES

Foley *v.* Hill (1848), Green Wood *v.* Martins Bank Ltd (1932) 1 KB 371; 23
Green Wood v. Matins Bank Ltd (932) 1 KB 371; 37
Halifa Union v. Wheelwright (1875); 5
Hardly *v.* Veasey (1968) 17 LT REP 607; 29
Hedley Bryne & Co. Ltd (1964) Ac 465; 33
Holland *v.* Manchester and Liverpool Banking Co, (1999) 25 TLR 386; 28
Houghland *v.* R.R. Low (Luxury Coaches) Ltd (1962) 1 OB 694.698; 35
Ide Cheist *v.* National Bank of Nigeria (1976) NWLR 145; 27
Imersel Chemical v. National Bank of Nigeria (1974); 33
Isokwa v. UBN (1996) 12 SC NJ 445 447; 37
Johnson *v.* Sobaki (1968) ALR COM 24; 31
Lacave *v.* Credit Lyonnais (1897) 1 OB 148; 20
Ladbroke & Fodd (1914) 30 TLR 433; 21
Langtry *v.* Union of Landon (1696) 17 JIB. 338; 36
London Joint Stock Bank Ltd *v.* Macmillan & Arthur (1918) AC 777
Mahmud v. Barclays Bank (1877) NCLR 115; 40
Merchant Bank Limited *v.* Federal Ministry of Finance (1961); 12
Merchant Bank *v.* OnigbanJo (1969) NCLRT; 21
Midland Bank Limited *v.* Seymour (1995) 2 LLOYD's REP 147; 32
Missiri *v.* Bank of West Africa (1967) ALR COMM 427 Mahmud *v.* Barclays Bank (1877) NCLR 115; 41
Mutual Life and Citizens Assurance *v.* Evatte (1971) AC 793; 33
NDIC *v.* Manu & Co. (1997) 2 FBTLR 270, 284; 42
Nsirim *v.* Omuna Const. Ltd (1994) NWLR PT 318, 1.23; 21, 22
National Bank *v.* Fasoro (1971); 26
Odumosu *v.* African Continental Bank (1976) NCLR 53; 42
Official Receiver & Liquidator *v.* Oladipo More (1959) LLR 46, 50; 28, 42
Ojikutu *v.* Agbonmagbe Bank (1966) 2 ALL NLR 279; 17
Pappoe v. Bank of British West Africa (1933); 41
Parry Jones *v.* Law Society (1968) ALL ER 117, 180; 31
Prosperity Limited *v.* Lloyd Bank (1923) TLR 342; 26
Ricketh *v.* Bank of West Africa (1960) 5 FSC 113; 42
Re. *v.* United Service Co. (1870) 6 CH. APP. 212; 36
Re. *v.* Industrial Dispute Tribunal; 5

TABLE OF STATUTES

TABLE OF CONTENTS

Chapter 2: LEGAL REQUIREMENT FOR ESTABLISHING A BANK IN NIGERIA

Chapter 3: THE LEGAL NATURE OF BANKER - CUSTOMER RELATIONSHIP

Chapter 4: CONTRACTUAL OBLIGATIONS OF CUSTOMER

Chapter 5: SECURITIES FOR BANKERS' ADVANCES

Chapter 6: MONEY TRANSMISSION MECHANISMS OR NEGOTIABLE INSTRUMENTS

Chapter 7: TERMINATION OF BANKER-CUSTOMER RELATIONSHIP

Chapter 10: PARTNERSHIP

Chapter 11: FRAUD IN THE BANKING INDUSTRY: IMPERATIVES FOR AN ANTI-FRAUD COURT IN NIGERIA

Chapter 1

CONSTITUTIONAL FRAMEWORK OF BANKING LAWS IN NIGERIA

OUTLINE

a). Learned Authors
b). Statutory Definitions
c). Views Expressed by the Court
d) Who is a Banker?
e) Supervisory Role of the Central Bank of Nigeria (CBN) over other Banks and Financial Institutions.

Specific Learning Objectives

1.1 Discuss the constitutional frame work of banking law in Nigeria
1.2 Define Bank and Banking
1.3 Identify who a Banker is
1.4 Analyse the supervisory role of Central Bank of Nigeria (CBN) over other banks and financial institutions.

INTRODUCTION

Banking law and regulations refer to all laws made by the National Assembly to guide and regulate banking operations in Nigeria. They also include regulations made from time to time by the Executive Arm of the Government directly or through the Central Bank of Nigeria (CBN) for effective supervision and regulation of the banking industry in Nigeria.

CONSTITUTIONAL FRAMEWORK OF BANKING LAWS IN NIGERIA

The power to make laws in respect of the banking industry in Nigeria derives from the 1990 Constitution of the Federal Republic of Nigeria Section 4 CFRN provides as follows:

(1) The legislative powers of the Federal Republic of Nigeria shall be bested in the National Assembly of the Federation which shall consist of the Senate and House of Representatives;

(2) The National Assembly shall have powers to make laws for peace order and good governance of the Federation or any part thereof with respect to any matter included in the Exclusive Legislative List set on in part 1 of the Second Schedule to the 1990 Constitution.

These provisions refer to the Second Schedule to the 1999 Constitution in Part 1 which consists of sixty-eight items. The following items in the list refer banking, viz.;

- Item 5: Bankruptcy and Insolvency;
- Item 6: Banks, banking, bills of exchange and promissory notes;
- Item 7: Borrowing of monies within or outside Nigeria for the purpose of the Federation or of any state;
- Item 15: Currency, coinage and legal tender;
- Item 68: IS an omnibus item relating to any matter incidental or supplementary to any matter mentioned elsewhere in the list.

Thus, the combined effect of section 4(1) and 4(2) with the Schedule items mentioned therein makes banking law the exclusive reserve of the Federal Government. To underscore the exclusivity to the Federal Government alone, section 4(3) provides that the power of the National Assembly to make laws for peace, order and good governance of the Federation with respect to any matter included in the Exclusive Legislative List, shall save as otherwise provided in this Constitution shall be to the exclusion of the State House of Assembly. Thus, pursuant to the above constitutional provisions (S.A) I the following laws amongst others were enacted in respect to banks:

a. Central Bank of Nigeria Act No. 7, 2007;
b. Banks and Other Financial Institution Act No. 25 of 1991;
c. Regulatory and Supervisory Guidelines for Micro Finance Banks (MFBs) in Nigeria

These laws would be carefully examined in the light of judicial rulings and other statutory enactments. (See also section 16 of the CFRN).

In order to ensure a healthy banking sector aimed at achieving international best practices in our banks and to stop corruption, money laundering, insider dealings, advanced fee fraud and issuing of dishonoured cheques (bounced cheques), some laws were enacted to criminalize practices connected with the banking sector.

Some of these laws include;

a. Economic and Financial Commission Act, No. 1 of 2004;
b. Advanced Fee Fraud and Other Fraud Related Offences Act No. 26 of 2005;
c. Money Laundering Act No. 7 of 2003;
d. Dishonoured Cheques (Offences) Act No. 44 of 1997;
e. Corrupt Practice and Other Related Offences Act No. 6 of 2003

1.1 DEFINITION OF BANKS AND BANKING

It would be difficult or at least cumbersome, to formulate a definition of banking which would be wide enough to embrace the diverse activities carried out by all kinds of banks, and thus the complex activities of the Merchant Banks have little in common with the services of the Microfinance Banks (MFBs) or of the former Community Banks.

In order to accommodate diverse views of definition of Banks or Banker under three headings:

(a) definitions by learned legal writers/authors;
(b) statutory definitions; and
(c) the views expressed by the courts.

A. Learned Authors

B. A. Ganer defines a bank as a financial establishment for the deposit, loans exchange or issue of money and for transmission of funds. It has also been described as the office which such an establishment conducts transactions (B. A. Garner's *Black Law Dictionary* 8th Edition P. 154).

L. A. Miche define a bank as "a quasi-public institution for the custody and loan of money, the exchange and transmission of same by means of bills and drafts, and the issuance of its own promissory notes, payable to the bearer as currency or for the exercise of one or more of these functions."

A bank, he further states, "is wholly a creation of statutes doing business by legislative grace and the right to carry out banking business through the agency of a corporation in a franchise which is dependent on corporate powers by State." (See LA. Miche on *Banks and Banking* (1993) 2nd Edition at P. 5-6). In his book, *Law of Banking*. Dr. Herbert Hart, A Briton, defines a bank as:

> A person or company carrying on business of receiving monies and collecting drafts for customers subject to the obligation of honouring cheques drawn upon them from time to time by customers to the extent of the amount available on their current account.

This invariably is an exposition of the deposit collection covering services commercial banks. Sir John Paget's definition of a bank in his book, Law Banking, see a bank as "*a corporation of person (s), which accepts money on current account and collects cheques from customers.*

B. Statutory Definitions

Bank, according to the Central Bank Act, 2007 No. 7 Section 66 means a bank licensed under the Bank and Other Financial Institutions Act 1999, or under the regulated Banking Act or any other prior legislation.

"Banking business" according to section 66 of the Banks and other Financial Institutions Act means the business of receiving deposit on current accounts, savings accounts and other similar accounts, paying or collecting cheques drawn by or in part by customers, provisions of finance or such other business and the Government may be order publish in the Federal Gazette designated as banking business.

C. View Expressed by the Courts

The opinions expressed by judges concerning essential characteristics of banking have changed over the years. The traditional view is that no one may be considered a banker unless he pays cheques drawn on himself (see *Sinclair* v. *Brougham* (1914) AC at 398, *Halifa Union* v. *Wheelwright* (1875) From time to time, however, this view has been rejected; for example Lord Goddard rejected it when delivering judgment in a case in 1954. *R.* v. *Industrial Dispute Tribunal*. The point at issue was whether the

Industrial Dispute Tribunal had power to determine a dispute between a trustee savings bank and members of National Union of Bank Employee who were in the employment of the bank. The bank applied to the court for an order of prohibition on the ground *inter alia* that the tribunal had no jurisdiction. This contention failed, and in the course of his judgment, Lord Goddard said that although a trustee saving bank did more than post office savings banks, it did not carry out the business of banking in the same way as the big five banks in the sense of issuing cheque books to its customers and performing various services for the customers, it nevertheless carried out the business of banking.

The traditional view, namely that no one may be considered a banker unless he pays cheques drawn on himself, as reaffirmed by Mocatta J. and by the Court of Appeal in *United Dominion Trust Ltd* v. *Kirkwood (1954).* The decision of the court was a majority but all three members of the court shared the view that the usual characteristics of banking at the present are:

(i) the acceptance of money from and collection of cheques for customers and the paying of them to the customer's credit;

(ii) the honouring of cheques or orders drawn in the bank by the customers when presented for payment; and

(iii) the keeping of some of current and running account in their books in which the credits and debits are entered. In addition to theses, there is the lending of money.

Until recently, disputes have risen as to whether an enterprise is a bank or merely a money lender and this has led to several tests being applied. In *Chief Abdul Yekinni Ojikutu* v. *Agbonmagbe Bank and 2 others (1966)* for example, the rate of interest chargeable by bank was applied and it was held that it would not be proper to apply the Money Lenders Act to a licensed bank whose interest rates are normally rates are normally prescribed by the Central Bank.

The above case decided at the Lagos High Court in number, 1966, was confirmed by the Supreme Court in February, 1968. The facts of the case were that Chief Ojikutu raised an overdraft from Agbonmagbe Bank supported by a charge over three of his properties and interest rate was agreed at 15 per cent. As at June, 1965, debt had built up to the sum of £6, 624.9 (pound sterling was then in use in Nigeria), and he promised to settle same between September, 1965, and March, 1966, if the bank could stop charging interest. If he failed, the bank could realise its security. The plaintiff defaulted and the bank sold one of the houses without further notice to him. He then brought an action claiming among other things, that the interest was excessive as it contravened section 13 of the Money Lenders Act. Alexander J. held that a bank is not subject to the provisions of the Money Lender Act.

The overriding interest in this case with regards to the definition of a bank is that as much as a body is legally recognized as a bank, it is not subject to the provisions of the Money Lenders Act. It can also be inferred from the decision that although lending money and charging interest are clearly banking activities, they do not necessarily make one a baker because money lending do undertake these activities and they are not bankers. An institution has to be duly licensed as a bank before it can be subjected to the privileges and obligations of the banks.

Another test that was applied at one time, 'that for a business to be seen as banking' banking has to form "a substantial part" of the business. However, what constitutes "a substantial part" will depend upon the merit of each case. In *Stafford* v. *Henry (1950)*. It was decided that the business of someone who engaged in stock broking and some banking activities was not banking business because banking was not the core of his business. There is also a significant difference between a bank and daily collector or savings organization. In the criminal case of *Attorney General of the Federation* v. *Umoh Ekpa (176)*, the Federal Revenue Court sitting in Port Harcourt, decided that collecting money from market women and paying same into bank (as daily collectors do) does not constitute banking business.

The substance of the case was that Umoh Ekpa operated a business named Global Savings Syndicate which engaged in daily collection of money from market women and others using agents and employees. Money collected was deposited with a bank and the syndicate was paid an agreed commission. The accused issued out advertisements in form of handbills and radio announcements and was consequently charged with transacting business without valid licence, but was discharged and acquitted, as according to the court, his business was not the sort contemplated by the Banking Act and the institutions like commercial banks, discount houses etc., (where normal banking may be transacted) without holding valid licence to do so.

In *State Savings Bank of Victoria Commissioners* v. *Fermewan Wright & Co. Limited (1915).* THE High Court of Australia held that the essential characteristics of the business of banking may be described as the collection of money by receiving deposits on loan payable as and when agreed upon, while the Privy Council of England in *Bank of Chettincal Ltd of Colombo v. Income Tax Commissioner (1948) AC 398* described banking company as a company which carries out as its principal business, the acceptance of deposits of money on current accounts or otherwise subject to withdrawal by cheque, draft or order. Also in *United Dominion Limited* v. *Kirkwood (1966),* the British Court of Appeal decided that a firm cannot be a banking business unless it accepts deposits, withdrawable by cheques and acts as agent in collecting cheques and other payments.

The Nigerian Banking Act of 1990 (hereinafter referred to in this chapter as "the Act") adopted the same approach when in section 53, the Act defines a bank as "any person who carries out banking business and includes a commercial bank, acceptance house, discount house, financial institutions and merchant bank." The same section of the Act goes further to define banking as:

> The business of receiving monies from outside sources as deposits irrespective of the payment of interests or the granting of money loans, and acceptance of credits or the purchase of bills and cheques or the purchase and sale of securities for other or the incurring of the obligation to acquire claims in respect of loans prior or their maturity or the assumption of guarantee and other warranties for other or the effecting of transfer and clearing the such other transactions as the Minister may on the recommendation of the Central Bank, by order published in the Gazette designated as banking business.

From the above statutory definitions, it becomes clear that a bank is any person whose business consists of mainly of accepting deposits, granting of loans acceptance, etc. This, in fact, is in accord with the traditional pursuits of banks and it is perhaps based on the main activities of practicing bankers as at the time the Act was passed with provision for inclusion of other activities that may be seen as banking business in future.

1.2 WHO IS A BANKER?

Although in normal usage, people see anybody working in a bank as "banker". The Supreme Court of Nigeria held in *Akwule and 10 others* v. *Reginum (1963),* the word "banker" refers to the company carrying out the business and not the individual employees. In the above case, Akwule was branch manager of the Bank of West Africa and he had a lending power of £200 pounds. He granted overdraft in excess of this amount to the other defendant some of whom were bad debtors of the bank and had, for that reason, been black-listed for credits and the facts were known to Akwule. He did not declare these lending to his control office, but the returns were made to balance the books. Akwule was charged and convicted for criminal breach of trust and others for aiding and abetting him. They appeal to the Supreme Court and deciding the criminal Appeal, a questions to be decided was whether Akwule was in fact a "Banker". The Court decided that he was not and the words of the Chief Justice of the Federation, Sir. Adetokunbo Ademola are worthy note:

> The word "Banker" does not, in our view, include a person who is a mere employee of the bank. The relationship between a banker and a customer is that of a debtor and a a creditor in respect of the money deposited with the banker by the customer. This position becomes clearer when a customer asks for his money. If the money is not paid, the customer can sue the bank. The action will lie against the bank, not the bank manager: It is therefore not possible to agree with the view that the first appellant in this case was a banker: If the bank defaults, the bank will be sued. The cheques were drawn on the Bank of West Africa Limited and Customer's account with the Bank of West Africa. The first appellant is not

more than an official of the bank's instruction as to the method its business should be carried out.

It thus becomes judicially established that the word "Banker" refers to a company licensed to carry out banking business and not to an employee or director or shareholder and this is in line with the literal usage. The question, "Who are your bankers?" for example, means "Which bank do you use?" and does not in any way refer to the bank officials, directors or shareholders. Despite this position, however, the word will be used in many cases in this book it is colloquial or informal sense, to refer to any person who is taking part in the control of the operation of a bank. A bank is only one entity, despite any number of branches it may have. A single bank is therefore only one "person" in law. In *Bank of Ireland* v. *Huseey 1965),* it was held that no matter how many branches it has, a banking company has only one legal existence. The branches as agents have no right of their own and are always under the control and direction of the headquarters.

1.3 SUPERVISORY FUNCTIONS OF THE CBN OVER OTHER BANKS AND FINANCIAL INSTITUTIONS

As noted earlier the CBN is the apex Bank in Nigeria. In addition to this position, the various legislations on banking confer on the CBN supervisory roles over all other banks and financial institutions in Nigeria. These powers are exercised either directly by the bank or indirectly by way of recommendation to the Minister of Finance. The following are the functions of the CBN:

i. Grant of Licence to Operate

By far one of the most important ties or relationship between the CBN and other banks can be traced to the fact that a bank comes into existence with the blessing of CBN, Section 3 of BOFIA Cap 25 of 1991, provides that any person who wants to undertake a banking business in Nigeria shall apply in writing to the Governor of the CBN for a grant of licence and shall accompany the application with the following five requirements:

a. a feasibility report of the proposed bank;

b. a draft copy of the articles of association;
c. a list of shareholders, directors and principal officers of the bank;
d. such other information, documents and reports as the CBN may prescribe.

It is also required that the applicant, in addition to the above items, deposit with the bank a sum equal to the paid up capital, (S. 3[2]). Upon satisfying the requirements in S. 3(1) & (2), the Governor of CBN may issue a licence with or without condition or refuse to issue a licence. The Governor upon refusal is not expected to give reason why he has refused, (S. 3[3]). If the licence is granted, the CBN shall give written notice of that fact to the applicants and the licence fee shall be paid. It should be noted that though all applications for licence are forwarded to the Governor of the CBN, prior approval of the Minister of Finance is required. These requirements are in line with those in the Banking Act 1990, S. 2.

ii. Banking Examiner

The (BOFIA) law provides for the appointment and powers of examiner under which there shall be a Chief Bank Examiner (Director of Banking Supervision) who: shall be an officer of the CBN appointed by the bank with power to examine periodically, under condition of confidentiality, the books and affair of each licensed bank. He shall have access, at all time, to the books, account and vouchers of the bank. He has the power to demand from the officers and directors of banks, such information and explanations as he thinks necessary for the performance of his duties. Consequently, he shall have access to any account, returns or information regarding banks that are in the; possession of Federal Ministry of Finance. In examining the affairs of a bank, the examiner shall at all times avoid unreasonable hindrance to the daily business of that bank and shall confine the investigations to matter strictly relevant to the examination.

iii. Minimum Ratio

Section 6 of the Banking Act gives the CBN specific powers of supervision of institutions to which the Act applies to under section 6(2) of the Act; for instance, the CBN may after consultation with the Minister of Finance, specify the minimum ratio which licensed banks shall maintain, their minimum paid up capital, and all retained earnings on the other hand, and their loans and advances, on the other. In respect of Merchant Banks, the CBN shall from time to time specify the ratio of:

a. deposits and call money held for other banks to be maintained in liquid assets;
b. loans and advances to the bank's total assets; and
c. total loans and advances that may be repayable within one year.

In the case of *Effiwat* v. *Barcalys Bank Nigeria and Central Bank of Nigeria 1970*, the plaintiff as challenging the authority of the CBN for partly freezing his account under the Currency Conversion Promulgation Decree 1968, claimed that the CBN has no power to freeze account, but only to close banks. Justice J. I. C. Taylor at the Lagos High Court affirmed that the powers to freeze the account under the circumstance was within the general powers conferred on the CBN.

iv. Revocation of Licence

The Central Bank of Nigeria recommends to the Minister of Finance who will obtain approval from the Federal Executive Council, and by order published in the *Federal Gazette* revokes any licence if:

a. the holder thereof ceases to carry on in Nigeria the type of banking business for which he was licensed, or goes into liquidation or is wound up or otherwise dissolve;
b. the holder thereof fails to fulfil the prescribed conditions and regulations; or
c. in the circumstances and in the manner where under this Act, failure to comply with the provision thereof is a ground for revocation of licence.

This power is vested in the Minister upon the recommendation of the CBN, therefore the courts would hardly interfere with these powers unless it is not judiciously exercised. Neither are the courts bestowed with the powers to revoke the licence as was argued in the case of *Merchant Bank Limited* v. *Federal Ministry of Finance (1961).* The plaintiff was a licensed bank; the Minister of Finance by an order dated 23rd September, 1960, revoked the licence ordering the winding up of the banking business. Counsel to the Minister contended that the bank did not possess a civil right in this matter and that all they had was a privilege to carry out banking business which was granted within their provisions of the Ordinance and can be revoked in the manner provided for by the Ordinance. The court agreed.

v. Special Examination

In addition to the routine examination, the Minister may at any time, require the Governor of the CBN to require the Banking Examiner or other qualified persons appointed by the Governor, to make a special examination under condition of secrecy of the books and affairs of any licensed bank in any of these three circumstances;

a. Where after consultation with the CBN, the Minister has reasons to believe that a licensed bank:
   (i) May be carrying on its business in a manner detrimental to the interest of its depositors and other creditors
   (ii) May have insufficient assets to cover its liabilities to the public, or
   (iii) May be contravening the provisions of the Act.
b. Where application is made by:
   (i) Shareholders holding not less than one-third of the total shares for the time being issued and paid-up
   (ii) By depositors holding not less than one third of the gross amount of the deposit of the bank.
c. Where the licensed bank suspends payment or informs the Minister or Governor of CBN of its intention to do so. (See sections 30, 31, 32, and 33 Banks and Other Financial Institutions Act.

vi. Tenure of Banks Managing Directors

The CBN fixes the term tenure of the Managing Directors of Banks. The current term for MD/CEOs of banks is 10 years tenure. It is pertinent to note that such appointment must be confirmed by the CBN.

vii. Minimum Capital Base for Banks

The CBN fixes the amount as capital base for banks. The current amount fixed is ₦25,000,000,000.00 (Twenty-five billion naira) for commercial banks.

1.4 RELATIONSHIP BETWEEN THE CBN WITH SPECIALISED BANKS AND FINANCIAL HOUSES

The CBN exercises some control over specialised banks and finance houses in that the Governor has power to examine from time to time the accounts and books of the Nigerian Industrial Development Bank, the Nigerian Agricultural Books Credit and Rural Development Bank. The Urban Development Bank, all mortgage institutions, examine the accounts of Bureau De Change, discount Houses and such other financial institutions and in that regard has power to issue reports from time to time regarding the amounts of such financial institutions.

Chapter 2

LEGAL REQUIREMENTS FOR ESTABLISHING A BANK IN NIGERIA

OUTLINE

- Distinction between a Bank and a Money Lender
- The Structure of Banking in Nigeria
- Central Bank of Nigeria
- Bank Customers

Specific Learning Objectives

2.1 Discuss legal requirement for establishing Banks in Nigeria.
2.2 Make a distinction between a bank and a money lender.
2.3 Discuss the structure of banking in Nigeria.
2.4 List the bank customers of Central Bank of Nigeria.

INTRODUCTION

Section 2(1) of the Banks and Other Financial Institutions Decree (BOFID) provides *inter alia* that no person shall carry out banking business in Nigeria except a duly incorporated company in Nigeria holding a valid banking licence, Violation of this provision attracts on conviction, a penalty of up to ten (10) years imprisonment or a fine of ₦2,000,000 or both. See BOFID (amendment) Decree 38 of 1998. Also section 44, Investment and Securities Decree No. 45 1999 provides:

> No persons shall make any invitation to the public to deposit money with anybody corporate for a fixed period or payable to call whether bearing or not bearing interest unless the body corporate concerned is a body corporate licensed under the Banks and Other Financial Institution Decree No. 25 1999, to carry on banking business.

Contravention of this provision attracts ₦100,000 in the case of a body corporate and in other case 2 years of imprisonment or a fine of ₦100,000 or both. This requirement is not in any way compromised by the liberal provisions of the Nigeria Investment Promotion Commission Decree 16, 1995 (See S. 6[3] BOFID 38 of 1998).

Furthermore, no foreign bank shall operate branch offices or representative offices in Nigeria without approval of the CBN. The consent of the Government must be obtained before any bank can embark on any restructuring, re-organisation, mergers and disposal by the banks. No branch shall be opened or closed within or outside Nigeria except with the prior approval of the CBN in writing. The CBN may also grant approval for offshore banking from Nigeria. Any person desiring to undertake banking in Nigeria shall apply in writing to the Governor of the CBN for the grant of banking licence. The application shall be accompanied with the following:

(a) A feasibility report of the proposed bank;
(b) a draft copy of the memorandum and articles of association of the proposed bank;
(c) a list of the shareholders, directors and principal officers of the proposed bank and their particulars;
(d) the prescribed application fee; and
(e) such other information, documents and reports as the bank may from time to time specify.

The shareholders of the proposed bank shall deposit with CBN a sum equal to the minimum paid up share capital. The Governor may issue a licence conditionally or unconditionally or may refuse to grant the licence and need not give any reason for refusal. If the application is granted, a written notice of the approval shall be made to the applicant and thereon the licence fee shall be paid. The bank is also authorised to vary the conditions subject to which a licence is granted or may impose fresh conditions (See Sec. 3 BOFID 38 of 1998).

The president of the Federal Republic of Nigeria, on the recommendation of the CBN shall from time to time determine as he may deem appropriate, the minimum paid up share capital each category of banks. Acting under this provision, the president in 1997 raised the minimum paid up capital of banks to ₦500,000,000. However, section 7 of BOFID requires the banks to maintain Reserve Funds with the CBN (S. 16), keep proper books of account (S. 24), deliver return to the CBN not later than 28 days after the last day of each month or such period as the CBN may specify.

The bank must publish its profit and loss account and balance sheet in the daily newspapers not later than four months after the end of any financial year.

2.1 DISTINCTION BETWEEN A BANKER AND MONEYLENDER

While they both deal in money and lend credit to their customers, there are major differences between the two. While a banker generally remains a debtor to its customers to the extent of monies received from its customers, a moneylender on the other hand is always a creditor to the extent of monies advanced to his customers. While the banker's main source of funds is deposits received from its customers, the moneylender on the other hand, is free to seek fund from any source. While a banker is protected by the Bills of Exchange Act 1990 when they pay or collect cheque in good faith and in the ordinary course of business or without negligence, no such protection is available to the moneylender.

The two are regulated by difference laws; the banker is not governed by the Money Lenders Law, i.e. Money Lenders law, Cap. 74, Laws of Northern Nigeria, 1963. In *Ojikutu* v. *Agbonmagbe Bank (1966) 2 ALL NLR 279* the plaintiff was required to pay interest at 15% for a loan received from the defendant bank. When the plaintiff's property pledged as security for the loan was sold, he sought to set aside the transaction on the ground that the interest charged was contrary to section 13 of the Money Lender Law.

HELD: That THE Defendant was not a money lender but banker and the transaction was a banking business not covered by the provision of the Money Lenders Law. (See also *UDT* v. *Kirkwood* (1966) 2 QB 431).

2.2 THE STRUCTURE OF BANKING IN NIGERIA

As a result of the umbilical tie between financial services and technological advancement, especially in this age of information technology, responsive financial specialisation and services are necessary engine house for real economic development of any country.

The structure of banking regulation in Nigeria is monolithic. It is the sole prerogative of the Federal Government of licence and supervise banks in Nigeria and to legislate in that respect. It is thus a matter on the Exclusive Legislative List. (Section 4[2] item 6, Part 1 Schedule 2, 1999 Constitution).

A structural feature of banking in Nigeria is the branch system. A single bank can have branches all over the Federation. Banks are also categorized into commercial and merchant banks. While the former is into retail, the latter is more concerned with whole sale and investment banking. As yet universal banking is still prohibited.

2.3 TYPE OF BANKS

The following are the types of banks:

(a) Regular Banks;
(b) Commercial Banks;
(c) Profit and Loss Banks;
(d) Merchant Banks;
(e) Community Banks. (Section 9 and 61 of BOFID), now Micro Finance Banks;
(f) Nigerian Agricultural Credit and Rural Development Bank (NACRDB);
(g) Nigerian Bank for Commerce and Industry (NBCI);
(h) Bank of Industry (BOI);
(i) Federal Mortgage Bank of Nigeria (FMBN);
(j) Nigerian Export/Import Bank (NEIB);
(k) Urban Development Bank (UDB) Plc.

These banks are set up by enabling laws for specific developmental purpose.

2.4 THE CENTRAL BANK OF NIGERIA

The Central Bank of Nigeria (CBN) is the apex bank of Nigeria and the banker's bank. As such, it is the custodian of the nation's finance. It issues and manages the currency, advising the government on the direction of policy likely to affect its value. The bank acts as a banker to the other banks in Nigeria as earlier mentioned and to the government. As agent for the government, it arranges for the issue, servicing the redemption of government securities and assists the government by raising the finance to meet any day-to-day financial transactions. It operates in the security and short term money markets, buying and selling government debts so as to stabilise from time to time, the level of interest rates.

In all these operations, the bank keep closely in touch with government on the one hand and with other financial institutions on the other.

Section 1 of the Central Bank of Nigeria Act 2007, provides as follows:

(1.1) There is established for Nigeria, a body known as the Central Bank of Nigeria;

(1.2) The Bank shall be body corporate with perpetual succession and a common seal and may sue and be sued in its corporate name;

(1.3) In order to facilitate the attainment of the objectives under this Act and the Banks and Other Financial Institutions Act and in line with the objective of promoting stability and continuity in economic management, the Bank shall be independent body in the discharge of the functions;

Section 3 of the Act provides for the principal objectives of the bank which includes, to

(a) Ensure monetary and price stability;
(b) Issue legal tender currency in Nigeria
(c) Maintain external reserves to safeguard the international value of the legal currency;
(d) Promote a sound financial system in Nigeria; and
(e) Act as a banker and provide economic and financial advice to the Federal Government.

Section 6 provides for the Board of Directors which shall be chaired by the Governor of the Central Bank of Nigeria.

2.5 BANK CUSTOMERS

The entire law of banking is mainly concerned with the relationship between a banker and a customer. The protection afforded a paying or collecting bank is only assertable when the bank purportedly acts on behalf of bank customers.

This makes an understanding of who a customer is imperative.

No Nigerian statute has adequately defined 'customer'. Academic writers prefer to avoid the semantics of definition and the general attitude is to look at how the courts have grappled with determining in an instant case who a customer is. In an ordinary usage, a customer can be said to be one who has a repeated patronage of some goods and services. According to *Black Law Dictionary*, 6th Edition, a customer is one who regularly makes purchase of or has business dealings with a trade man or business man. A long this line, it is thought that once a person had persistent relationship in the course of business over a span of time, he is said to be a customer of the other.

In *Lacave* v. *Credit Lyonnais (1897) 1 QB. 148* the defendant bank carried out business in London and had a branch in Paris. A cheque was drawn on the bank's London office in favour of the plaintiff who generally crossed the cheque to a company in London and posted the same to the company. The cheque was intercepted and with forged endorsement presented at the Paris branch. The presenter had no account with the bank, nonetheless, the Paris branch collected the proceeds of the cheque from the London branch and paid the thief. The original owners of the cheque sued the bank for conversion. (Robert Reld Esq.) counsel tot eh defendant, argued that the word "customer" be given a wide meaning and no difference ought to be seen between a person who keeps and account and a person who comes with a cheque to be turned to cash. Collins J. rejecting this argument held that:

> The person who obtained the payment was not a customer of the bank, therefore the protection under section 82 of the Bills of Exchange Act 1882, did not avail the bank. Payment was not made in the course of business in good faith and without negligence. The bank was liable for conversion.

In *Ladbroke & Co.* v. *Todd (1914) 30 TLR 433*, the plaintiff drew a cheque and sent it by post to the payee. The latter was stolen in transit, and the cheque used to open an account with the payee's endorsement forged. The proceeds of the cheque was subsequently cleared from the account. The plaintiff sued the bank for conversion. The question was whether the account having been opened for payment of the cheque to be collected, the bank could properly be regarded as having received payment for the customer.

HELD: As the account was already opened when the cheque was collected, payment had been received for a customer even though the thief had not engaged in repeated patronage. In *Merchant Bank* v. *Onigbanjo 1969) NCLRT*, the plaintiff bank brought an action to recover the balance of overdraft owed by the defendant. The defendant denied being the customer of the bank on the ground that he merely acted as agent for somebody else.

HELD: Since it was the defendant and nobody else who opened the account and drew the cheques on the bank and it was he who obtained the overdraft, the defendant was liable there on as customer of the bank.

In conclusion, whether a person is a customer or not will depend on the particular circumstances of every case, but the enjoyment of the facilities for depositing monies, the convenience of the cheque book and the beneficial use of the money deposited is at the root of conception of customer.

One bank will itself be a customer of another bank if the first bank has an account with the second and sends its cheque for collection.

Chapter 3

THE LEGAL NATURE OF BANKER-CUSTOMER RELATIONSHIP

OUTLINE

Principal and Agent
Trustee and Beneficiary (Debtor - Creditor

Specific Learning Objectives

3.1 Discuss legal nature of banker-customer relationship
3.2 Discuss the Principal and Agent relationship
3.3 Analyse the Debtor - Creditor relationship between the Banker and Customer

INTRODUCTION

The relationship of banker and customer creates contractual obligations and right on both parties. For these rights and duties to be enforceable, the relationship of banker and customer must exist in the first place. The nature of relationship must be discerned to know what rights and to enforce any accruing rights and obligations. This makes it necessary to examine the nature of the relationship first place. The following views have been advanced.

3.1 PRINCIPAL AND AGENT

The relationship of principal and agent arises where on party, the principal consents to act on his behalf and the agent also consents to the act. In each case, the consent of the parties may be implied. *Nsirim* v. *Omuna Const. Co Ltd (1994) 1 NWLR,* it was held that the relationship can be explained on the basis of the principal and agent, Customer being the *principal* and *agent* being the Bank. This may be true to a limited extent, especially when the bank is specially engaged to undertake business of stock-dealing, payment of bills on behalf of the customer or undertaking duty of collection for customers. To a larger extent, the principal and agent position does not fully explain the basis of the legal relationship between the banker and the customers especially from these angles:

(i) accountability;
(ii) remuneration;
(iii) liability.

The agent is accountable to his principal in respect of his contractual assignment he is correspondingly, entitled to be remunerated. The principal is vicariously liable for his agent's act if the latter acts within his authority. However in the banker-customer relationship, the banker owes no obligation of accountability to the customer of how the customer's deposit is profitably employed. The banker's obligation is to pay on demand.

3.2 TRUSTEE AND BENEFICIARY

Generally a trustee is one vested with the property to hold for the benefit of another, the beneficiary. The trustee must always act for the interest of the beneficiary, render account to the beneficiary and must not take risk with the trust property, These requirement are inflexible.

The banker may however be constituted into a trustee by a special arrangement, i.e. trustee of a will. In this sense, trustee are usually legal owners of properties vested in them, the same way the banker is the legal owner of the funds deposited with it. On the other hand, bankers are not obliged to render accounts of how depositors' funds are utilised, neither are they under any obligation to act for any perceived ultimate or best interests of customers. The banker may venture with the depositor's funds by lending same out as loans. *Nsirim* v. *Omuno Const Ltd (1994) NWLRPT 318, 1, 23,* the court opined that no account can be obtained by a customer against his banker, for the relationship between them is not that of fiduciary, and is merely that of debtor and creditor. The trustee/beneficiary concept does not adequately capture the nature of the banker-customer relationship.

3.3 DEBTOR AND CREDITOR

The debtor-creditor relationship has been advanced as providing a fuller understanding of the basis of the legal relationship between the banker and the customer. Here the banker who deposits his money with the banker is the creditor, while the customer who accepts the customer funds is the debtor. In *Foley* v. *Hill* (1848), the appellant opened an account with the respondent in 1829, and it was agreed that interest at 3% per annum shall be allowed on this account. Certain credits were made to account and interest charged therein up till 1831, but not afterwards. In 1834, the account was closed. In 1938, the appellant brought this proceeding seeking to recover all sums owed him with interest.

The appellant argued that it was the bank's duty to keep the account clear and intelligible, to calculate interest on the balance and to make proper entries of the same and to preserve other evidence of their transaction with them. The appellant in addition contended that the duties and transaction constituted a relation more complex than that of mere debtor and creditor.

The House of Lord rejected this argument and held that the relationship between the banker and his customer who pays money into the bank is the ordinary relationship of debtor and creditor, with a super-added obligation arising out of the customer of bankers to honour the customer's cheques. When a customer pays money into his account at a bank, it ceases to be his money, it become the banker's money and he can deal with it as his own. He is not vis-à-vis the customer in the fiduciary position of a trustee or quasi-trustee holding the money for the customer as for a *cest-ce qui* trust.

To Lord Cottenham LC:

> The money placed in the custody of a banker is to all intent and purposes the money of the banker, to do with it as he pleases. He is guilty of no breach of trust in employing it; he is not answerable to the customer if he put it into jeopardy, if he engages in a hazardous speculation; he is not bound to keep it or deal with it as the

> property of the customer; but he is contracted having received that the sum equivalent to that paid into his hand. That has been established to be the relative situation of banker and customer. The bank is not an agent or factor but he is a debtor.

To Lord Broughan:

> It is a totally different thing if we take into consideration certain acts which are often performed by a banker and put him in a totally, different capacity. He may in addition to his position as a banker make himself an agent or trustee towards a *cest-ce-qui*, but he does that incidentally to his trade of a banker.

To Lord Campbell:

> It has been said that the banker is liable to do something more, merely to repay the money. He is bound more to honour cheques and perhaps to accept bills of exchange of drawn upon him, he having assets in his hands, but these purely are matter of legal contracts.

Chapter 4

CONTRACTUAL OBLIGATIONS OF CUSTOMER

OUTLINE

- Relationship between Banker and Customer
- Interest on Overdraft
- Payment of Overdraft

Specific Learning Objectives

4.1 Analyse the Contractual Obligations of Customers of a bank.
4.2 Analyse the relationship of banker and customers.
4.3 Discuss interest on overdraft.
4.4 Enumerate the terms of repayment of overdraft.
4.5 List the special incidences.

INTRODUCTION

Rights and Duties Arising from a Banker-Customers Relationship

Banker-Customer relationship comes into existence like any other contracts See *Barclays Bank* v. *Okenarhe (1966) 2 I LLOYDS REP. 94.*

The contractual relationship between a banker and its customers gives rise several duties and obligations a remarkable feature of this contract is that terms are not wholly embodied in any written agreement executed by parties. No attempt is usually made to prepare a comprehensive list of respective rights and duties of the banker and customers.

The contractual relationship between the two is a complex one founded originally upon the customs and usages of the bankers. Many of those customs and usages have been recognised by the courts and to the extent that they have been so recognised and not expressly stated; they must be regarded as implied terms of the contract. It follows therefore that this is a branch of law where implied terms are of vital importance. Little does a customer realise, when with a minimum of formality, he opens a bank account that he is entering into contract. The implied terms of which if reduced to writing run into several pages.

CONTRACTUAL OBLIGATIONS OF A BANKER

(i) Duty to Honour the Customer's Cheque

The legal relationship of debtor and creditor arising out of banker-customer relationship is coupled with a superadded obligation arising out of the custom of bankers to honour the customers' cheques. Since it is incumbent on the customer to make a demand for his money, he makes this demand usually writing by the instrumentality of a cheque.

This is the most sacred of the banker's duty to customer. The banker is duty bound to honour the customer's cheque to the extent of the credit in the account or limit of agreed overdraft or to the limit of granted loan. As far back as 1903 Lord Lindley in *Capital & Countess Bank* v. *Gordon (1903) A.C. 240*. "It must never be forgotten that the moment the bank places money to its customer's credit, the customer is entitled to draw upon it." In *National Bank* v. *Fasoro (1977),* the bank granted the facilities to assist the latter organize his business. Shortly afterwards, the bank withdrew the facilities and dishonoured the plaintiffs cheque drawn on the facility. The court held the action of the bank wrongful.

(ii) Duty Not Cease to do Business with Customer Except Upon Reasonable Notice

The bank is not at liberty to unilaterally close the customer's account or to cease to perform its contractual duties to the customer unless upon the customer's request or upon reasonable notice from the bank of intention to cease to do business with the customer. In *Prosperity Limited* v. *Lloyd Bank (1923) TLR 342,* a company originated a "show ball" scheme of insurance to which the bank agreed to receive application form from subscribers. The scheme gained wide publicity but subsequently, the bank gave the company one month notice of intention to discontinue with the

scheme on the ground that the bank ought not to have been associated with the scheme in the first place.
HELD: The one month notice was insufficient and thus unreasonable.

(iii) Duty to Accept Cash Deposits, Cheques (Proceeds) or Bills of Exchange on Behalf of the Customers

In *Ide Chemist* v. *National Bank of Nigeria (1976) NWRL, 145,* the plaintiff paid a number of cheques into his account which were not credited with the proceeds until 21 months after. Cheques issued by the plaintiff were dishonoured and marked "Represent". The court per Okagbue J. held that the bank was liable for the worst type of negligence and since the plaintiff was a businessman, ₦30,000.00 was awarded as damages.

(iv) Duty to Pay Only According to Customer's Mandate

The obligation on the bank to honour the customer's cheque is only so according to the contractual mandate. Where there are two signatories, the bank must strictly pay upon that authority where there is a valid counter-man, *Cyrus Banking Corporation London Limited 1831 ALR 809,* the husband and wife had a joint account operating on their joint signature. The bank permitted the husband to make certain withdrawals from the account on his signature.

The court held that this was a breach of banker's duty to pay according to the customers mandate and accordingly held the bank liable to the wife in damages.

In *Union Bank of Nigeria Limited* v. *Adediran (1987) I NWLR PT. 147,* a church had changed its signature for its accounts with Union Bank and given notice of the change to the bank. Nonetheless, the bank honoured a cheque the bank was in breach of duty to pay according to customer mandate.

(v) Duty to Keep Customer Account Accurate:

The bank must keep proper account of the customers' deposits and withdrawals. If the customer maintains two or more different accounts, it is an implied term between the banker and the customer that the banker will keep the accounts separately. In addition, if the customer makes payment to credit, he has the right to appropriate the funds to whichever account he chooses. Where deposits are not accurately recorded and that customer's cheque is unjustifiably dishonoured, an action for defamation and wrongful dishonour may lie against the bank. Where the bank places funds in the customer's account to which the latter is entitled, the doctrine of estoppels may operate to stop the bank from retrieving such funds. In *Holland* v. *Manchester and Liverpool Banking Co. (1999) 25 TLR 386,* the customer's passbook showed a credit balance of 70 pounds. Instead of the true situation of 60.95 pounds. The customer then issued a cheque for £65 pounds which was dishonoured.

HELD: The bank was liable for wrongful dishonour.

In *Sky Ring* v. *Green Wood and Cox (1825) 4 B & E 281,* a banker Continued to credit the account of a military officer with certain sum of money which he was thought to be entitled to. This mistake was brought to the bank's attention, but the credit continues for about five years and the customer was so advised in his statement of account. Thereafter, the bank sought to reverse the entries by monies in the customer's account. The Court held that the bank could not do so. Where the customer is aware of the error such that it will be inequitable to claim advantages, he too may be stopped from claiming the benefit of the error.

(vi) Duty to Make Demand on the Customer to Repay any Overdraft Granted and to Allow Reasonable Time for Payment

In *Johnson* v. *Sobaki (1968) 3 ALR COM 24,* a bank granted overdraft facilities to the defendant between 1959 and 1960. In 1962, it demanded the repayment and the defendant failed, hence the suit. The defendant claimed that the action was statute barred in 1966. The court held that the limitation period would start to run from the date of the demand and not from the date of grant of facility. Adopting the reasoning of Dickson J. In *Official Receiver and Liquidator* v. *Moore* stated:

> In view of the decision in Joachimson's case. I would be inclined to take the view that it would be unreasonable for the bank, having after granted an overdraft to immediately proceed to sue for it, without making a demand and giving the customer reasonable time to pay. I can hardly think that it would be within the contemplation

> of a customer to whom an overdraft was given that the bank would without warning issue a writ. If banks were at liberty to act that way, commerce and industry would be greatly handicapped.

The court held that the defence must fail.

4.1 SPECIAL INCIDENCES

i. Duty of Secrecy

Banks are expected to keep secret and confidential information regarding the business and account of the customer. It was initially thought that the duty of secrecy was merely a moral duty and not a legal one. In *Hardly* v. *Veasey (1868) 17 REP 607,* the plaintiff kept on account with the overdrawn. The plaintiff pleaded with the defendant not to dishonour cheques issued by him and promised to pay in certain money during the day. No sum having been paid, the defendant called a money-lender in the neighbourhood, told him how matters stood and asked if he could assist, the plaintiff refused the assistance and sued the defendant of breach of contract. The jury held for the defendant Kelly, C. B. stated:

> There can be no doubt that there is a normal obligation on the banker not to want only or unnecessarily to disclose the state of the customer's account, and more especially if injury may be caused to the customer thereby unless upon some special occasion on which a conflicting duty may arise; but still looking at numerous authorities and dicta, I should pause long before holding that such duty exists in point of law.

Subsequently, it graduated from moral persuasion to a legal duty.

In *Tournier* v. *National Provincial Bank of England (1924)* the plaintiff's account with the bank was overdrawn and the plaintiff agreed to pay the overdraft by a weekly instalment of £1 Pound. He failed to make the weekly payment and the manager of the bank phoned his employer to ask for his private address. In course of their discussion, the manager informed the employer that the plaintiff as he had promised, and that he was suspected of betting as cheque drawn by him were paid to book-makers. As a result, the plaintiff got into difficulties with his employers who refused to renew his employment and he the employee sued the defendant for damages.

HELD: the defendant was liable as he had failed in his duty to the defendant to treat the plaintiff's account and affairs confidential.

This did not cease, the account remained confidential. The confidence is not confined to the actual state of the customer's account only it extends to information derived from the account itself.

The nature and scope of the duty of confidentiality was spelt out by Bankes LJ in the Tournier's case thus:

> In my opinion, it is necessary in a case like the present to direct the jury on what are the limits and what are the qualifications of the contractual duty of secrecy applied in relation between banker and customer. There appear to be no authority on the point. On principle, I think that the qualifications disclosure is under compulsion of law; where there is duty to the public to disclose; where the interest of the bank requires disclosure; where the disclosure is made by the express or implied consent of the customer.

These four constitute exception to the duty of secrecy.

a. Under Compulsion of Law

The law provides in certain situations a duty on the banker to divulge information on the customer's account. Where the law so compels, the duty of secrecy cannot hold.

Section 10(1) Money Laundering Decree No.3, 1995, compels financial institutions to disclose to NDLEA any single transaction, lodgement or transfer of funds in excess of ₦500,000.00 in the case of an individual and ₦2,000,00.00 in the case of body corporate. S. 12(2) expressly excludes the defence of secrecy.

Also, by S. 145 (1) Investment and Securities Decree 45, 1999, the Securities and Exchange Commission may appoint one or more competent inspectors to Section (7), nothing in the section shall require a person carrying out the business of banking to disclose any information or produce any document relating to the affairs of a customer unless:

The customer is a person who the inspectors have reason to believe may be able to give information relevant to the investigation; the commission is satisfied that the disclosure or production is necessary for the purpose of the investigation.

Section 97(1)(h)(2)(e) Evidence Act, Cap. 112, LFN 1990, the limit if this exception was candidly stated by Diplock LJ. In *Parry Jones* v. *Law Society* (1968) All ER 117, 180, thus:

> Such a duty of confidence is subject to and overridden by the duty of any party to that contract to comply with the law of the land. If it is the duty of such party to contract whether at common law or under statute to disclose in defined circumstances, confidential information then he must do and, any expressed contract would be illegal and void. For example, in the case of banker and a customer, the duty of confidence is subject to the overriding duty of the banker at common law to disclose and answer questions as to his Customer's affairs when he is asked to give evidence on them in the witness box in the court of law. Beautiful exposition it must be admitted but it is necessary to observe that "compulsion in law" can only mean and indeed must be confined to the regular exercise by the appropriate officer, of actual power to compel the banker's disclosure. Certainly it cannot be said that every inquiry made by a public official comes within the ambit of this exception.

b. Public Interest

Public interest may demand that a banker discloses certain information about a customer's account or business. An example of this would be when during time of war the customer is dealing with an enemy. In such a situation is the duty to the public to disclose. In *Weld Blundedere Stephens (1920) AC. 966*, it was suggested that the giving of information to the police in respect of a customer suspected of crime would be prohibited.

c. Banker's Interest

The interest of the bank may require disclosure of information concerning the customer's account. Where for instance, the bank makes a demand in writing for payment of a loan or of an overdraft, issues a writ claiming payment of a loan or draft or where debt due to the bank is issue. In *Sutherland* v. *Barclays Bank Ltd (1938)*, Mrs. Sutherland had an account with the bank; she drew a cheque in favour of her dress maker which was dishonoured for lack of sufficient funds. She informed her husband who took up the matter with the bank. In the course of the discussion, the bank informed the husband that many of cheques drawn by his wife were to book makers. The wife sue for breach of duty of secrecy.

d. Authorised Disclosure

There can be no breach of duty where the party to whom the duty is owed has consented to the breach, therefore in circumstances where the customer authorise a reference to his banker to give information concerning his credit worthiness and this done, he could not successfully bring an action for breach of duty of secrecy.

(vii) Duty to Give Reference on Customers

Situation may arise where the bank may be required to give a reference on the credit standing or credit worthiness of a customer of a bank. Where the bank obliges, it becomes of a legal interest when such references turn out to be false and the recipient suffers loss in consequence of relying on the false reference.

This has become part of the everyday business of bankers in the word of Devlin J. in *Midland Bank Limited* v. *Symour (1995) 2I LLOYD'S REP 147*: "It is one of the services which a bank offers to its customers." The bank must take due care not to furnish information which is false or misleading. If as a result of the breach of this duty, the customer suffers damage, the bank will have to compensate him, as regards an enquirer who is not a customer of the bank. It was initially thought that the banker's duty in this respect is that of common honesty and no more. Since the enquirer is not a customer of the bank, there is neither privacy nor contractual relationship between the bank and the enquirer and thus no duty arises. Per Lord in Haldane in *Bulbury* v. *Bank of Montreal* (1981) AC. 626. This view was later changed and in the post-war period, the opinion became widely held that when a businessman gives information or advice in respect of matters on which he has or should have competent knowledge to another person whom he knows is likely to act upon it, he ought to be held responsible for the exercise of due care in the matter. In

Hedley Bryne & Co. Ltd (1964) AC 465, the plaintiffs, who were advertising agents, inquired through their own bankers as to the creditworthiness of a client of theirs, who banked with the defendants. The inquiry was put through to the defendants who gave satisfactory answers but id not "without responsibility on the part of the bank or its officials." The plaintiffs, relying upon the answers placed large orders of advertising space for which they did not receive payment and on the subsequent liquidation of East Power Ltd (their client), they lost more than £17,000 pounds which they could not be liable, as they have expressly answered to inquiries without responsibility'. The trial judge held that the defendant had in fact been negligent, but on the atrocities, there was no duty of care and dismissed the claim. The court of appeal affirmed the decision. The House of Lords on appeal held that:

> A banker who receives a request for information in circumstances which shows that his skills and judgment are ' being relied upon accepts a legal duty to exercise proper care in replying, even though he is under no contractual or fiduciary obligation to the enquirer. The banker is however entitled to insist that he will give the information on the basis that he does not accept such duty. The word "without responsibility" used by the defendants made it clear that they had taken up that position in the case. In the circumstances, therefore, the bank was not liable. From the foregoing unless a disclaimer is inserted as in the Hedley Bryne's case, a position duty win arise only in two situations. In *Mutual Life and Citizens Assurance* v. *Evatte (1971) AC 793,* the Privy Council stated that this duty will arise where:
>
> > The statement was made in the ordinary course of the adviser's business or profession and the adviser knew that he was being relied on by the plaintiff to exercise the skills in giving that advice that would be expected of a member of that business or profession; where the adviser has held himself out as having the skill requisite to a business or profession and had undertaken to use that skill in advising the plaintiff in the Nigerian case *Imersel Chemical* v. *National Bank of Nigeria (1974),* a manager of the defendant bank gave reference on a customer as a good and credit worthy customer which in fact was false. The plaintiff relaying on this suffered loss and sued the bank. It was held that the manager as the head of the bank acted within his actual,

usual or ostensible authority when he gave the reference, the defendant bank was vicariously liable.

(viii) Duty to Advise on Investment

For some time now, bankers have assisted customers in connection with investment. At first, this service concerned with carrying out specific instructions concerning the purchase or sales of stocks, shares or other securities. Since the documents of title were frequently deposited with the bank for safe custody, it was considerably convenient for the banker to undertake this duty but the scope of such business did not extend beyond carrying out the specific instructions of the customer. The question that arises here is whether such duty falls within the scope of banking business as to establish a duty a measure of skills non-exercise of which may constitute negligence. In *Bishop* v. *Countess of Jersey (1854) 2 DREW 1443, 163,* it was held that it is not within the Scope of the business of bankers to seek or make statement generally for their customers. In *Wilson* v. *United Counties Bank Limited (1920) AC 103,* the Plaintiff, a customer of the bank was leaving for war service. It was agreed between him and the general manager that the local manager should supervise the plaintiffs business and reasonable on, particularly the financial side, and take all reasonable steps to maintain his credit and reputation. The bank was negligent in performing these duties and was held liable in damages.

The truth of the matter lies in the consolatory words of Lord Finlay LC in *Banbury* v. *Bank Montreal (918) AC 626*:

> The limits of a banker's business cannot be laid down as a matter of law." If he undertakes to advise, he must exercise reasonable care and skills in giving the advice. He is under no obligation to advice, but if he takes it upon himself to do so, he will incur liability if he does negligently.

(ix) Duty to Take Custody of Valuables

This duty is as old as origin of banking itself. In England, it was out of the practice of the deposit of gold and other valuables with the goldsmith during the troubled times of the parliamentary war that the England system of banking arose" For the convenience of customers, bankers assumed custody, of plates, securities and relationship of bailment crystallized between the banker and the customer. This however does not constitute the banker as an insurer of the goods. A bailment is the delivery of a movable property by one person (the bailor) to another (the bailee) on condition that it shall be in due course be delivered to the bailor or to his order, Liability under a contract of bailment arises under two headings: Negligence and Conversion. If the property is lost, damage or destroyed owing to want of exercise of care by the bailee, an action for negligence may lie against the bailee. Where however, the property is wrongfully disposed off so, as deprive the value of possession, the bailee may be guilty as conversion and liable to pay the value to the owner as compensation. It is immaterial that the wrongful conversion was made bona fide and without negligence.

Liability under this heading will also depend on whether the bailee is a gratuitous or bailee for reward. A gratuitous bailee must do his best with what he has got. He must use all facilities of which he is possessed but he is not bound to do so. He is bound to undertake reasonably as he would in undertaking his own affairs. A bailee for reward on the other hand is expected to provide at his own expense all appliances and save guard procurable to safeguard the bailed properties. Where the bank makes charges for the accommodation, it is acting as bailee for regard, where no extra charge is made, he is said to be acting as gratuitous bailee. As regard the standard of care, *Paget's Law of Banking* 8th Edition, Pages 191-197m, is of the view that notwithstanding the employment of the facilities at the banker's disposal such as safes-rooms and adoption of all precaution and means of ensuring safety known to the contemporary science, suggestive of a care slightly above ordinary care, the banker is nonetheless a gratuitous bailee. Lord Chorley's *Law of Banking*, 6th Edition page 245, seem to be in agreement with Dr. Hart that the banker is now a bailee. However, the distinction between a bailee for reward and a gratuitous bailee as far as the banker is concerned may now be largely academic as the peculiar fact of the case dictate the attitude of the courts. Ormerod LJ in *Houghland* v. *R.R. Low (Luxury Coaches) Ltd (962) 1 QB 694, 698,* on this point said:

> To try and put a bailment for instance, into a water tight compartment-such as gratuitous bailment on one hand and bailment for reward on the other; is to overlook the fact that there might well be an infinite variety of case which might come into one of the other category. The question we have to consider in case of this kind if it is necessary to consider negligence is whether in the circumstances of this particular case, a sufficient standard of care has been observed by the defendants or their servants.

In *Langtry* v. *Union Bank of London (1696) 17 JIB 338,* the plaintiff deposited very valuable Jewelleries for safe keeping. A thief stole her note paper, forged a request safe signature in the name of the plaintiff to the bank to hand over jewels to the bearer. The forgery was executed with such skills that the officials of the bank were deceived and thief obtained the jewellery. The plaintiff sued the bank for the value of the jewellery but the action was compromised on settlement. In *Re United Service Co. (1870) 6 CH. APP. 212,* the owner of a certain share deposited the certificates with his bank when they were kept in safe custody to which the manager had the only key and uncontrolled thereon; they were accordingly bailee for reward. The manager took advantage of the certificate and converted them to his own use. The bank was held liable for negligence.

CONTRACTUAL OBLIGATIONS OF CUSTOMERS

The customer also owes certain reciprocal duties to the banker. These includes:

i. **Duty to make a demand**: The customer many demand part or the whole of his money in the hands of the banker at anytime. The demand must be made at the branch where the customer keeps his account although there is no restriction now with the online banking facility; this demand must be made before a cause for action accrues to the customer.

ii. **The customer if bound to draw up his cheque**: in a manner to prevent the misleading o the bank or facilitating forgery. This is the most important duty owed the bank by the customer. In *Stock Bank Ltd Mcmillan & Arthur (1918) AC 777,* a firm of general merchant clerks whose duty it was to prepare cheque for signature by the employers, drew a cheque payable to the firm or bearer. He filled in the account in figure as £2 pounds but he left a space between the "pounds" and the "2". At that stage, the amounts in words was not filled in at all. He then had the cheque signed by a partner. Next, he fraudulently raised the amount of the cheque. He placed the figure "1" and "0" on either side of the figure "2" thus producing a figure of "£120" pounds. He filled in the amount in word as One Hundred and Twenty Pounds", presented it to the bank on which it was drawn, received payment and absconded with the money. McMillan and Arthur contended that their account ought not to be debited with the amount. The House of Lords deciding in the bank's favour observed:

> It is beyond dispute that the customer is bound to exercise reasonable care in drawing the cheque to prevent the banker being misled. If he draws the cheque in such a manner which facilitates fraud, he is guilty of a breach of duty as between himself and the banker and he will be responsible to the banker for any loss sustained by the banker as a natural and direct consequence of his breach of duty.

a. **A customer is duty bound to handle his deposits with care:** In *Isokwa* v. *UBN (1996) 12 SCNJ 445-447,* the court warned that a customer of a bank who fills a bank teller gives the teller and money to which relates to just any of the bank employee for payment into his account does so at his own risk turns out that the bank employee in question is. If official duty authorised to accept or receive not on payment for and on behalf of the bank, the bank would not be vicariously liable if the employee fraudulently converts the money to his own use.

b. **Duty to disclose forgeries to the bank**: Equal important is the duty on the customer to disclose a known case of forgery to the bank immediately. In *Green Wood* v. *Matins Bank Ltd (932) 1 KB 371* the plaintiff had an account with the bank. His wife kept the bank books and gives him cheque from when he asked for them. The wife forged his signature and made withdrawals from the account which he later discovered and she begged him not to inform the bank about the forgeries, and he agreed not to do so. He later discovered that his wife lied to him as to the purpose for which he had used the money. And he threatened to report the forgery to the bank. The wife shot herself. A few months later he brought an action against the bank to recover the amount paid out on the forged cheque. At the trail court, it was held that the plaintiff was entitled to succeed. The Court of Appeal reversed the judgment holding that there was a duty on the plaintiff to disclose the forgeries to the bank and the failure to do so gave rise to an estoppel.

c. **The customer is bound to pay all lawful charges in respect to banking transaction which the bank is entitled to for all services which the bank renders where these are chargeable**: Pay on due dates or on demand all overdraft or loan facilities granted by the bank in accordance with the agreement regulating the grant. The obligation on the banker and customer are no doubt multi-faced out of the contractual relationship between the two. These rights and obligations are hardly ever spelt out but are largely implied by law and the courts are always willing to enforce them.

4.2 RELATIONSHIP OF BANKER AND CUSTOMER OVERDRAFTS

This is a privilege which the banker allows the customer by permitting the letter to issue a cheque over and above his credit standing in his current account. It represents the excess of credit balance of a customer which he is allowed to draw upon. Technically, this is money lent by the banker to the customer. A banker is not obliged to let the customer overdraw his account but where overdraft facilities have been granted, the bank cannot unilaterally withdraw same.

Overdrafts can be *expressed* or *implied*:

Expressed Overdraft arises from the agreement between the customer and the banker when upon the former is allowed to draw over and above his credit balance sequel negotiation and previous agreement between the parties. Here, the limit and terms of the facility are agreed upon the documented and as it is often the case collaterised.

Implied Overdraft_on the other hand arises where in absence of any previous or expressed agreement, the customer is permitted to draw above the credit in his account. A customer who draws a cheque in excess of his credit account is said to be making an implied overdraft. In *Cuthbert* v. *Robarts, Lubbock & Co. (090) 2 CH, 226,*

Lord Cozen Hardy said respect:

> If a Customer draws a cheque for sum in excess of the amount standing to the credit of his account, it is really a request for loan and if the cheque is honoured, the customer has borrowed the money.

In the case of implied overdraft, the customer is taken the facility on current prevailing terms and said to absence of fixed time for repayment, shall repay at a reasonable time. In *African Continental Bank* v. *Eke (1969) NCLR 292: 1 ALR COMM. 174,* the defendant customer of the plaintiff drew a cheque on another bank and lodged it with the plaintiff for clearance. The plaintiff credited the defendant's account and sent the cheque for clearance. Subsequently, the bank debited the account with the amount of the cheque as having dishonoured. The defendant drew cheques on the account into debit. After about a year, the plaintiff instituted the present proceeding, claiming the debit balance and the interest thereon as debt on overdraft. The defendant contended that he had never requested for an overdraft neither was there any agreement for any loan. It was held that the defendant cannot escape liability for securing an overdraft provided the cheques were genuinely drawn by him and forwarded for clearing. In *African Continental Bank* v. *Babayemi (1969) 363,* the defendants carried on business as building the civil engineering contactors under the name of "Mercury Builders" and maintained an account with the plaintiff, the first defendant, alone operated the account and obtained overdraft facilities thereon. Following a newspaper report of the firm's cessation of business, the plaintiff brought an action to recover the amount overdrawn and accrued interest on the same. Holding the first defendants not liable for overdraft, Dosunmu J. found that there was an implied overdraft contract between the bank and the first defendant and also that:

> It has been held in number of authorities that overdrawing a banking account is borrowing money.

Overdraft facility is available on current account though no law prescribe this but crystallised from practice of bankers.

4.3 INTEREST ON OVERDRAFT

There is no common law right o charge interest on overdraft granted. Where the overdraft is an expressed one, the item of interest is usually discussed an agreed upon and subject to any limitation provided by the apex bank or status binding upon the parties. However, where the overdraft is an implied one, the right to charge simple interest accrue to the banker on two grounds viz.: the universal chargeable shall be at preventing market rate. In *Mahmud* v. *Barclays Bank* (1877) *NCLR* 115, the plaintiff, a pilgrim agent operated current account in his own name with the defendant bank for the sole purpose of obtaining foreign exchange draft for pilgrims intending to travel to Mecca for Hajj. The defendant orally agree with the plaintiff bank that the latter would issue the bankers draft only upon money actually paid in by the defendant. Neither parties intended the account to go into debit, but owing to exigencies of the period, the bank against the signature of the defendant issue bankers draft even when there was no money paid by the defendant to cover the drafts. The account therefore went into debit. The bank claimed for the resultant plus interest. The defendant resisted on the ground that instructions had been negligent, having acted contrary to his instruction should be responsible for its act. The bank argued that the defendant's drawing of the cheque which amounted to a request for overdraft in the circumstances.

Jones SP found for the bank on the ground that there was an implied agreement between the parties for the overdraft. The penumbral issue in this area is the right of the banker to charge interest on overdrafts granted by the banker. It was initially thought that the universal custom of banker which entitles the bank to charge simple interest which established as a fact before a bank resorts to it as an authority to charge simple interest. In *Enahoro & Enahoro* v. *Bank of West Africa (1971) ALR. COMM 180*, the bank that universal custom of bankers gave the banker the right to charged simple interests at a reasonable rate on all overdraft referring to Halsbury *Law of England*, third edition paragraph 427 and citing *Crosskill* v. *Bower*. The Supreme Court held in respect that since there was no evidence of any agreement to pay any interest and no evidence or Nigerian case was cited to show that what Halsbury Law called universal custom in fact applies in Nigeria, but it is a matter of proof whether its in fact does no, but no such was proved. The banking custom in the Gold Coast in 1933 decided in *Pappoe* v. *Bank of British West Africa* could not be held to prove that such a banking custom existed in Nigeria today without further independent proof. Also in *Missiri* v. *Bank of West Africa (1967) ALR COMM 427*, the Supreme Court opined:

> We consider that quite independent evidence of such banking custom in Nigeria today would need to be called before the custom could be held to apply here and this was not done.

Judicial attitude on this point later changed in recognition of the banker's right to charge interest on implied overdraft based on the universal custom of bankers. In *Continental* v. *Animashaun (1976) 3 CCHCJ 538*, even though the overdraft in this case was an expressed one the judge held that even in the absence of expressed provisions, it was the universal custom of bankers to charge interest on an overdraft. The emerging deviation in Animashaun's case was consummated in *Barclays Bank* v. *Abubakar (1977) 10 SC 13, 23* where Obaseki JSC (as he then was observed:

> Where there is no expressed agreement it is settled law that the bank is entitled to charge compound interest on the basis that there is a custom to that effect or that the customer has implied consented where without protest allows his account to be debited. As banking is of comparatively recent origin in this country, the origin of the custom of bankers to charge interest on overdraft has to be traced to England from where our legal system derived a lot inspiration and guidance.

In *NDIC* v. *Manu & Co (1997) 2 FBTLR 270. 284*, the Court stated that:

> It has been that in normal banking practices and in consonance with the universal custom of banking, it is an implied term of overdraft or loan agreement between the bank and the customer, a reasonable interest will be charged on such loan and overdraft where no rate of interest is expressly agreed upon.

In Nigerian case of *Ricketh* v. *Bank of West Africa (1960) 5 FSC 112*, the Federal Supreme Court held that compound interest on (implied) overdraft is chargeable where the customer has agreed to it or where he is shown or on must been taking to have acquiesced in the account being kept on that basis. See also Halsbury *Law of England*, Third edition; page 229 distilling from the case law are the following:

> On expressed overdraft, the parties may agree on the rate of interest and whether interest shall be chargeable on compound basis or not. On implied overdraft, simple interest is chargeable arising from the universal custom of bankers. Unless the customer consents to compound interest being charged or have acquiesced on compound interest being charged compound interest is not charged on implied overdraft.

4.4 PAYMENT OF OVERDRAFT

Where the overdraft is an expressed one, the obligation to pay will arise at the contractually agreed date. Where it is implied, the banker must make demand on the customer and allow reasonable time for the customer to pay the overdraft, in *Odumosu* v. *African Continental Bank (1976) NCLR 53*, the appellant obtained overdraft from the respondent payable at the financial year ended on 31st December, 1971. Come this time, the appellant's account was still overdrawn; the appellant was notified. In July 1972, the respondent commenced action to recover the overdraft. The Supreme Court found for the appellant that the action was premature and allowed the appeal. In *Official Receiver & Liquidator* v. *Oladipo More (1959) LLR 46, 50*,_Dickson J. summed up the law on this point and the reasoning behind are the rule thus:

> In view of the decision in Joachimson's case, I would be inclined to take the view that it would be unreasonable for a bank having granted on overdraft to immediately proceed to sue for it, without making a demand and giving the customer a reasonable time to pay. I can hardly think that it would be in the contemplation of a customer to whom an overdraft was given that the bank would without warning issue a writ, if banks were at liberty to act that way, commerce and industry would be greatly handicapped.

Deeley v. *Lloyds Bank (1912) AC 756* in 1893, G secured an overdraft for 2,500 pounds on his account and mortgaged his property as a security for the advances. In 1985, G raised a loan from the plaintiff and mortgaged the same property, of which the defendant has notice. G made various payments to his account which by 1986 amounted to 2,500 pounds over the same period made withdrawals on his account so that his account again fell into debit. The bank afterwards realised the security and G became bankrupt. The plaintiff claimed entitlement to the proceeds of the security. It was held that by the application of the rule in Clayton's case, the original loan has been extinguished in 1896, and the subsequent advances must rank after the plaintiff's second mortgage, Lord Shaw of Dunfermline adopting the statement of Eve J. at first instance succinctly stated the rule thus:

> According to the law of England (Nigeria as well) the person paying the money has the primary right to say what account it shall be appropriated, the creditor, if the debtor makes no appropriation, has the right to appropriation, one can look at the matter as a matter of account and see how in fact he appropriated it. And if there is nothing more than a current account kept by the creditor, or a particular account, then, the court concludes that the appropriation has been made, and, having been made, it is made once and for all and it does not lie in the mouth of the creditor afterwards to seek to vary that appropriation.

For this rule to apply, the account must be running, one kept in a chronological order and not a broken one. The bank prevent the application of this rule on the grand of facility or on the provision of security by halting further transaction in terms of payments into the account and withdrawals from the particular customer's account, passing all future transaction through a new account. The bank can also prevent the application of this rule to set free a security by expressly stipulating that security advanced for any facility shall be on continuing basis for all advances. In *Westminster Bank* v. *COND (1940) 46 COMM CASS 60*, the custom given a guarantee as a continuing security for the bank's advances. The customer claimed the benefit of the rule in Clayton's case to extinguish the said guarantee. The court held that the effect of the continuing guarantee effectively prevented the application of the Clayton's rule.

Chapter 5

SECURITIES FOR BANKERS' ADVANCES

OUTLINE

- Legal Principles of Lending in Banks
- Types of Securities
- Discharge of Mortgagee
- Enforcing the Security

Specific Learning Objectives

5.1 Discount securities for bankers' advances.
5.2 Enumerate the legal principles of lending in Banks.
5.3 List Specific types of securities.
5.4 Discuss discharge of mortgagee.
5.5 List steps in enforcing security.

INTRODUCTION

Banks grant facilities to their customers by way of advances, loans and overdraft. This is referred to as loans which mean the aggregate principal amount borrowed and from time to time outstanding under the loan facility. Other facilities include the overdraft and loan.

Banks borrow in order to lend for gain. Every lender of money must have regard to the change of payment, and the obligation to repay hardly satisfies this. Unless buttressed by security, the business of lending is very speculative. Security in the law of banking refers to any form of assurance customers. In other words, due from his defaulting in the event of the latter's inability to repay or meet his obligation, Bank securities take the legal forms of mortgage, charges, liens, pledges and hypothecation.

5.1 LEGAL PRINCIPLES OF LENDING IN BANKS

The most important factor to be taken into consideration when assessing the safety of an advance is the borrower's capacity to repay the loan in accordance with his promise. It follows therefore that a banker always requires to know the purpose for which an advance is required and the source which repayment is expected. Regard must also be given to the amount involved vis-à-vis the borrower, the duration, the profitability of the transaction, security offered and prevailing regulations.

Section 18(1)(b) BOFID 1991 provides that no manager or any officer of a bank shall grant any advance, loan or facility to a customer unless it is authorised in accordance with the rules and regulations of the bank; and where adequate obtained prior to granting the advance, loan of credit facilities and shall be deposited with the bank.

5.2 SPECIFIC TYPES OF SECURITIES

1. Land

Land is a universally acknowledge security for various forms of lending. Land as security is more often available in the legal form of mortgages. Mortgage is conveyance of interest in a property as security for the payment of debt or for the discharge of some other obligation. The borrower is called {mortgage and the lender "mortgagee". A mortgage may be legal or equitable. A legal mortgage is the conveyance of an interest in land, contained in an instrument, equitable mortgage on the other hand, is that which falls short of a legal mortgage, but evidence abound of parties' intention to create a legal mortgage.

The deposits of title documents to land evidenced in a memorandum of deposit constitutes an equitable mortgage. Before accepting the mortgage of land as security, it potential worth as security must be ascertained, where the land is indeed as expense with developments thereon the services of professional estate valuers may be enlisted to advice thereon. The current market value of the land will generally assist the lender in placing the worth of the security. Once the value is found satisfactory, the banker must then establish that the customer has good title to the property. For this purpose, the banker searches conducted at the land registry will in addition reveal whether the property is encumbered or not.

If the banker is satisfied, then he may take from the customer's legal or equitable mortgage on the property. If he takes a legal mortgage upon default for repayment if he realise the property and proceed to sell. However if may mortgage is an equitable one, he would need the leave of court to sell. The bank must take custody of its documents of the title to safeguard its interest as persons who find the owner of property in possession of its title documents can reasonably assume that the property is unencumbered. The second mortgage be taken of landed property where the worth of the property is enough to rank after the debt of the first mortgage has been extinguished. A banker taking second mortgage will cautiously take not of the following;

(a) he must ensure that there is an ample margin between the value or the property and the debt secured by the first mortgage;
(b) the mortgagee's title must be investigated;
(c) the second mortgage will be executed in form similar to the first mortgage and refer specifically the first mortgage to which the title document will protect itself by registering its mortgage as a land charge;
(d) the bank will send formal written notice of the second mortgage to the first mortgagee, who will be asked to confirm that his mortgage does not impose upon him any obligation to make further advances;

This notice serves two purpose:

(I) it prevents the first mortgage from making further advances which will run in priority to the bank (except where the first mortgage obligation to make further advances); and
(II) the first mortgagee is thereby obliged when his own mortgage is discharged to hand over the title documents to the second mortgagee.

5.3 DISCHARGE OF MORTGAGEE

Where the mortgagor has repaid the advances, the mortgagee is discharged and the property is set free from the mortgage. If the mortgage is legal, a receipt for the repayment is then endorsed on the instrument creating the mortgage and then handed over to the mortgagor, destroyed or cancelled. Where the mortgage is an equitable one, a receipt is endorse on the memorandum of deposit and together with the title documents handed over to the mortgagor. In all the cases, the repayment of the advances discharges the mortgage.

5.4 ENFORCING THE SECURITY

Where the mortgagor has defaulted in repayment, the banker may enforce the security by realising the property mortgaged. He may:

i. Sell the Property

Where the banker takes the property, a legal mortgage with the usual clause authorising the sale by the mortgagee in the event of the mortgagor's default in repayment, the banker may proceed to enforce the security by proceeding to sell, once the power of sales accrues. This is further subject to the governor's consent under the Land Use Act 1978. See section 22 Land Use Act 1978.

ii. Appoint a Receiver

Where the power of sale has crystallised but because of the existence of some other interests on the property (i.e. a tenant) the mortgagee may instead appoint a receiver to collect rents and profits on the mortgaged property which will be applied to reduce the debt secured by the property. The equitable mortgagee can only appoint a receiver by an order of the court.

iii. Foreclosure Order

The mortgagee may also apply to court for a foreclosure order against the mortgagor to prevent the mortgagee from exercising rights of redemption of the mortgage. This is a ready remedy for an equitable mortgagee. The court may however order a sale of property, this is especially so where the worth of the mortgaged property is more than the debt secured by the mortgaged transaction.

iv. Possession

The legal mortgagee may enforce his security by taking possession of the property peacefully if he can or means of an action for recovery of the land against the mortgagor, who may even be evicted by court order. If the property is already let to tenants, the mortgagee may take constructive possession by directing he tenants to pay rent to him instead of the mortgagor. Such rents being applied in reduction the mortgage debt.

v. Sue

The mortgage equitable or legal can sue the mortgagor for the debt. In the enforcement of security for advances, the legal mortgagee stands in a surer grounds as the two principal remedies of sale and appointment of receiver can be exercise at any time once they accrue without the necessary to resort to court as the equitable mortgagee will need to.

2. Guarantee

One of the commonest methods by which bankers protect themselves against loss on advances is by taking a guarantee. The person who gives the promise is the guarantor or surety and the person on whose behalf the promise is giving is called the principal debtor. Through a contract may be oral or in writing, a guarantee contract is one which is required by law to be evidenced in writing. The absence of such memorandum in writing may deny it of any enforcement at law. Banks normally have form the subject their printed guarantee forms which the customer is often required to fill.

3. Ships

Ships sometime form the subject of the mortgage to a bank as security for advances. It is however usual to request the customer to sign a memorandum on which he agree that the advance shall be payable on demand and that the security shall be enforceable in the event of default.

4. Life Assurance Policies

Theoretically, a banker has an insurable interest in life of a person who is indebted to him, and could take out a policy thereof. It is more usual however for the debtor to utilize as security that which he has taken out himself. Life assurance as a form of security has the advantage of relative ease to charge and to deal with increasing value so long as the premium is fully paid. The mere deposits of the policy constitutes an equitable mortgage and it gives the banker the right of an equitable mortgagee.

To constitute a complete charge, notice of the banker's interest in the policy must be conveyed to the insurer premiums to be paid as and when due. The banker must take steps to investigate the existence of any charge on the insurance and the worth of the policy. Bankers are generally advised not to lend in excess of the surrender value of the policy for the time being.

5. Stocks, Shares and Debentures (Securities Companies)

Stocks and shares or debentures in trading companies are frequently accepted by bankers as security for advance to private individuals and other customers. Stocks and shares denotes the member's interest in the company and so regulate the amount of the company's profit to which he will be entitled by way of dividend. Debentures refers to the document in which the company acknowledges debt and charges some of its assets in favour of the lender. A legal and equitable mortgage can also be created on company securities. In this aspect bankers always prefer securities of quoted companies for ease of assessment of the securities worth the exchanges, easy transferability of securities and ability to monitor the performance of the company concerned. If the advances are repaid, the securities are returned. While in default, the banker may take steps to realize the share and sell same to recover their advances.

Chapter 6

MONEY TRANSMISSION MECHANISMS OR NEGOTIABLE INSTRUMENTS

OUTLINE

- Definitions
- History of Negotiable Instruments and Evolution of Cheque
- Types of Negotiable Instruments
- Characteristics of Negotiable Instruments
- Benefits of Negotiability
- Exceptions
- Requirements for Negotiability
- Bills of Exchange
- Discharge of a Bills of Exchange
- Rights of a Holder of Bill of Exchanges
- Difference between Bills of Exchange and Cheque

Specific Learning Objectives

6.1 Define Negotiable Instruments.

6.2Trace the History of Negotiable Instruments and Evolution of Cheque.

6.3 List types of Negotiable Instruments.

6.4 Enumerate the Characteristics of Negotiable Instruments.

6.5 List the Benefits of Negotiability.

6.6 Enumerate the requirement for Negotiability.

6.7 Discuss Bills of Exchange.

6.8 List the Rights of a holder of Bills of Exchange.

6.9 Differential between Bills of Exchange and Cheque.

INTRODUCTION

The collection, discounting and payment of negotiable instruments form a substantial part of the work of a bank. In this chapter we shall deal with the principal types of negotiable instruments and their characteristics.

6.1 DEFINITIONS

A negotiable instrument is a financial instrument, the full legal title to which is transferrable by mere delivery (in the case of bearer instrument) or by endorsement and delivery (for order instrument) with the effect that its complete ownership and legal interest pass to the transferee who shall be capable of having superior to the title of the transfer provided he takes the instrument complete and regular on the face of it, before it is overdue in good faith and value.

6.2 HISTORY OF NEGOTIABLE INSTRUMENT

Long ago, the British merchants were in the habit of accepting payment instruments endorsed to the settlement of trade debts. These instruments are "*choses* in action" a legal jargon having the characterisation that notice of assignment needed to be given to the person liable to pay on them and the transfer of title was subject to equity. These merchants however found out that the process of given notice was cumbersome, causing delays in trade and settlements. They therefore agreed among themselves that such purely financial like Bill of Exchange, promissory notes and cheques would be transferred to another beneficiary through physical delivery (and endorsement is required) and that notice would no longer be given to the person liable to pay for them. At that initial period of the instruments were still to be transferred subject to equity which makes it impossible for a holder to transfer better title to anyone else, even if the person to whom it was transferred acted in good faith and without any knowledge of the defect in the title of the person who transferred it to him.

It was found also to be so detrimental to trade and commerce, that title of the transfers were challenged, after instrument had been accepted as good for payment for the personal liable to pay for the goods delivered, on flimsy excuses regarding quality of the goods delivered, delay in delivery, wrong specification, issues leading to counter claims etc. at the time of such claim the bill may have been transferred to another person who may have taken it for value, in good faith and honesty believing that the transfer had good title that can never be challenged. However, since transfer then was subject to equity, the transferee's title becomes suddenly defective, even though the transferee gave value and was not aware of the defect. It is because of this type of injustice on the part of the transferee and the tendency for the use of bill of exchange be discouraged, that the merchants agreed unless the instrument is specifically marked, "not negotiable" or the negotiability is otherwise destroyed, a transferee who obtains such an instrument after giving value shall be capable of having it free providing their customer with facilities for making payment to third parties.

Evolution of Cheque as Negotiable Instrument

The cheque system originated with the goldsmiths. For various reason which cannot be explained here, merchants began to leave their money in the hands of the goldsmith and to receive interest upon the sums. They appear to have started this practice shortly before the war outbreak of 1942-1949. Moreover, they soon looked to the goldsmiths and assist them in making payment to the parties. This was the origin of cheques system. At first the depositor would address a short letter or request authorising the payment to the creditor of the sum due. The creditor will take this letter to the goldsmith "shop" and there receive the sum specie.

Before long the merchant debtor drew his "bill" or "note" in favour of his creditor "or order" or in favour of him "or bearer", even though it was not presented by the original payee. The account of those merchants, which nowadays would be called 'current account' were usually known as 'running cashes' and they soon became popular. Furthermore, there is a clear evidence that the goldsmiths employed the funds left with them by making loans to other. Thus, they made loans to merchants who were in need of money. In short, the goldsmiths performed the basic functions of modern bankers by accepting sums at interests, by making loans and by providing their customers with facilities for making payments to their parities.

6.3 TYPES OF NEGOTIABLE INSTRUMENTS

The instruments to be treated as negotiable instrument must be the class generally recognized by law and custom. The following instruments are recognized as negotiable instruments: (i) Cheques; (ii) Bonds; (iii) Bills of Exchange, travellers cheques, banks drafts, promissory notes (example of which a bank note) bearer bond, treasury bill, bearer debentures, dividend warrant and share warrants, bill of lading, dock warrants, insurance policy, title deed to house, share certificate, warehouse policy and postal orders. It must be noted that the list of negotiable instrument is not a closed one. It is true that no tradition has been made to the list in recent years. But this is probably because most instruments which could conceivably be regarded as negotiable had been considered by the courts before the end of the nineteenth century. It is however always possible that new types of instruments may come into use and it would be competent for the courts to decide whether or not they are negotiable.

Example of Some Negotiable Instruments
Some examples of negotiable instruments are:

Example of Cheque

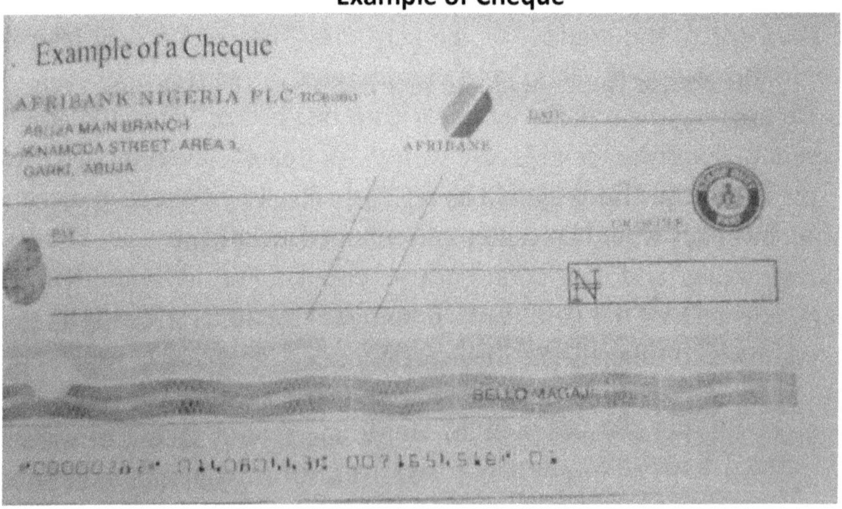

- cheques;
- dividend warrants;
- share certificates; and
- bank drafts.

In the above example of a cheque the following information are evident:

a. Name of the bank in this case of Afribank Nigeria Plc with its registered corporate number as RC 6260, the branch name is also included i.e. Abuja Main Branch Area 3, Garki Abuja;
b. Column for date, Cheques could be post-dated but never backdated;
c. Colum for the person in whose favour the cheque is drawn or his order;
d. The amount column immediately after the payee's name which words are words and correspondingly in figures;
e. Signature column follows immediately i.e. the account holder's signature;
f. The full name of the account holder, i.e. Bello Magaji.

It is however noteworthy that cheque are to be treated with care as they are easily susceptible to be fraudulently used. Accordingly, it is a serious financial crime to issue a dud cheque. Penalty for this is 2 years jail time.

In generally the following caution need to be taken with respect to cheque in order to prevent forgeries and frauds, namely:

a. the Cheque Book should be kept in a place of safety, under lock and key;
b. the Cheque Book should be regularly checked for completeness and missing cheque leaves promptly reported to the bank;
c. cheques should be written in in. not typed, and should be drawn only on forms supplied by the bank;
d. in drawing cheques both the words and figures should be written ruled in such a way as to leave no space for any subsequent address or insertions on either side of them;
e. material alterations must be confirmed b the signature of the drawer;
f. as Cheque Book are specifically prepared for use on specific account, do not allow other persons to use leaves of the cheque. Banks do not

accept liability for cash or cheques given to their staff outside banking hours or not in the bank premises.

Example of Dividend Warrant

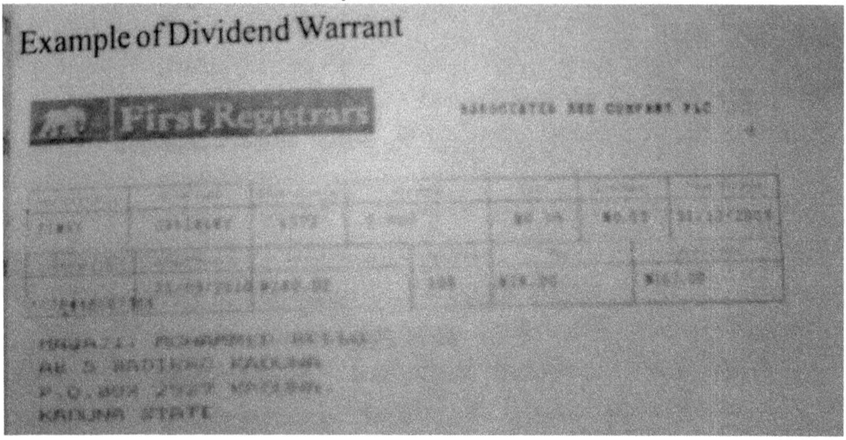

Example of Dividend Warrant

First Registrars

Above is an example of a dividend warrant No. 117044007304 as negotiable instrument in favour of Magaji, Mohammed Bello of AB 5 Badikko, Kaduna.

Example of Share Certificate as a negotiable instrument

SHARE CERTIFICATE

Presented From ______

Presented To ______

No. of Allocated Shares ______

Write here details of share certificate write here details of share certificate write here details of share certificate write here details of share certificate

Example of Bank Draft as a negotiable instrument

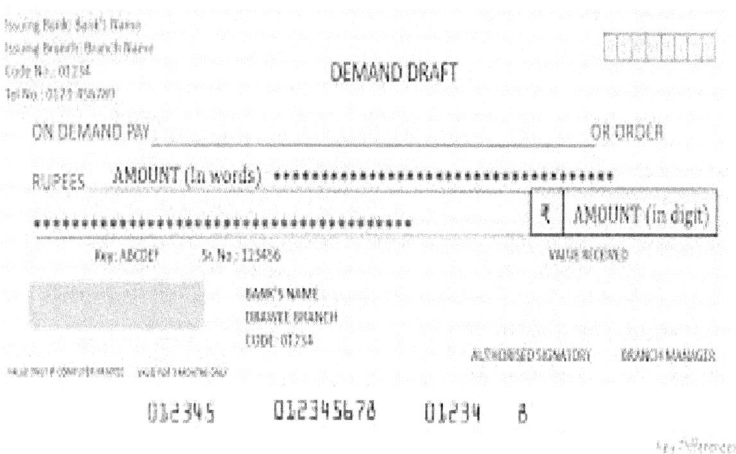

6.4 CHARACTERISTICS OF NEGOTIABLE INSTRUMENTS

The following are the general characteristics of negotiable instruments:

1. The title in a negotiable instrument may be transferred by mere delivery. This characteristic is described as negotiability (the requirement of negotiability are discussed further). The only exception to this rule is a Bill of Exchange payable to order which in addition to delivery, requires endorsement.
2. No notice to the debtor is necessary before a valid transfer can be made. In other words transfer without notice can be made.
3. A *bona fide* transferee requires it free from any defects in the transferor's title provided that he has given valuable consideration for it. (See *Crouch* v. *Credit Funcier of England (1873) LR 8 Q.B. 374 at P. 381).*

6.5 BENEFITS OF NEGOTIABILITY

The benefits of negotiability are numerous amongst which are the following;

(i) It allows a transferee who has met all the condition of negotiability to have a title superior to the title of the transferor;
(ii) The transferee can sue, in his own name, any person liable on the bill, i.e. any person whose signature appears on it and this is known as right of recourse;
(iii) Notice needs to be given to the person liable to the bill in order to register the holder's title;
(iv) Ease of the transfer of title. Mere delivery or endorsement and delivery transfers all the legal title and property in the instruments to the transferee. There is no need to prepare a deed of assignment as would have been done if title in an insurance policy, for example, is assigned.

6.6 EXCEPTIONS

(i) Infants cannot be sued on a negotiable instrument unless where the transaction is based on supply of necessaries for which the infants will normally be liable in law for payments.
(ii) A bankrupt cannot be sued personally, but claimed may be submitted to his trustee in bankruptcy. Also company under liquidation.
(iii) A person who adds "sans recourse" or "without liability" to his signature may subject it to some exceptions to avoid liability.
(iv) A person whose signature is forged on a bill cannot be sued on the bill since he in fact has not signed the instrument.

6.7 REQUIREMENT FOR NEGOTIABILITY

For an instrument to be negotiable these requirements must be fulfilled:

(a) **The transfer must be for value**: That is the older must have given consideration. Consideration here is more embracing than in ordinary commercial usage. Section 27 of the Bill of Exchange Act 1990 allows that valuable consideration may be constituted by a previous debt or liability;

(b) **There must be no evidence on its face to destroy negotiability:** for example, a cheque specifically marked "not negotiable" cannot be a negotiable instrument. Also an instrument whose transferability has been restricted on the face of it, i.e. marked "Account Payee Only" cannot be negotiable instrument as negotiability requires transferability.

(c) **The Bill must be complete and regular on the face of it at the time of transfer**: Before a bill can be negotiable, it must be complete, regular and it deliverable state. It must have all the necessary requirements like name, amount in words etc. if a bill is drawn out but lack any valid requirement, it cannot be a negotiable instrument. As to the fact that the bill must be complete and regular on the face of it. Lord Denning held that "the face of a bill includes the back of it."

(d) **Transfer must before the instruments is overdue**: A bill of exchange is said to be overdue after maturity and in case of a cheque, where it has stayed for too long in circulation usually after six months and in that wise, negotiability will be destroyed.

(e) **Transferee must act in good faith**: Section 92 of the Bill of Exchange Act 1990 stated that the transferee must have acted on that occasion in all honesty without being aware of the defects in the title of transferor.

(f) **Recognised instrument**: The instruments to be treated as negotiable instrument must be of the class generally recognised by law and custom.

6.8 BILLS OF EXCHANGE

It is not one of the objects of this work to provide a detailed exposition of the law relating to bills of exchange, for this reference may be made to the standard textbooks, e.g., Afolabi, L. (2005) *Law and Practice of Banking*.

Legal Principles

The law relating to bills of exchange is to be found in the Bills of Exchange Act 1990. However, the British Bills of Exchange Act 1882 must have a significant influence in the Nigerian Bills of Exchange Act 1990. Thus a bill of exchange is defined in section 1 of the British Bill of Exchange Act 1882 as: "An unconditional order in writing, addressed by one person to another signed by the person giving it, requiring the person to whom it is addressed to pay on demand or at a fixed or determinable future time, a sum certain in money, or to the order of, a specified person or bearer. "The same definition was adopted in section 3(1) the Nigerian Bill of Exchange Act 1990.

Accordingly, an instrument which does comply with these condition or which orders any act to be done in addition to the payment of money, is not a bill of exchange. An order to pay out a particular kind is not an unconditional order for the purpose of the definition of a bill of exchange. The following conditions do not invalid a bill, viz.:

(a) that it is not dated;
(b) that is does not specify the value given or that any value has been given;
(c) that it does not specify the place where it is drawn;
(d) it does not specify where it is payable.

The origin of bill of exchange could be traced to the usage of ancient merchants in Western countries, who when selling goods on credit will draw a bill of exchange on buyer and when accepted by the buyer, enable the seller obtain immediate finance through discounting of such a bill. If Mr. A for example, denies himself of the benefit of making immediate usage from the proceeds of the goods. In the alternative, Mr. A can draw a bill of exchange on Mr. B requiring him to pay at a future time. If Mr. B is convinced that he is financially able enough to pay in such future time, he would accept the bill signing across it with or without the addition of the word "accepted". The importance of the bills as a means of finance in that offer, its acceptance Mr. A the drawer needs not to wait till the due date before raising money. He can discount the bill by making it to his banker how relying on Mr. B's integrity will pay the face value less the discount.

There are three parties to a bill. They are:

(i) The drawer i.e. the person who wrote the order requiring the other person to pay in the above example B. Ummi is the drawer;
(ii) The drawee. This is the party on whom the bill is drawn and he is in fact the person to pay on the maturity of the bill. When he accepts the bill and sign his name across it with or without the word "accepted" he

becomes and "acceptor" and the bill becomes an "acceptance". In the above example Mr. A. Shamsudeen is the drawer;

(iii) The payee. This is the person named on the bill as being entitled receive the proceeds of the bill. Asmau, is the payee in the above example; either the drawee or the drawer may also be the payee.

<u>Specimen Bills of Exchange</u>
Stamp Duty
1st June, 2010

To Mr. A Shamsudeen
2, Magaji Road,
Badikko.

Sixty days after date, pay to Asmau or order
the sum of twenty thousand Naira (₦20,000).
Signed (B. Ummi)

It is pertinent to note that to be valid, the instrument has to fulfil all the essential ingredients on the definitions as follows:

(a) It must be unconditional i.e. the requirement to pay someone after the performance of an act or obligation;
(b) It must be an imperative order, i.e. "Pay".

Date

A bill payable on demand (for example a cheque) or at sigh is due presentation at any time on or after the date of the instrument, it can also drawn payable "after sight" and due date or date payable will start counting after acceptance by the drawee. The data payable may be specified straightforward manner (e.g. pay on 10th June, 2010) or "after date i.e. after the date it was drawn as inserted on the ill. Where a bill was not payable demand, the Bill of Exchange Act made provision for three days 'days of grace' to the time of payment as fixed by the bill and the bill was due payable on the last day of grace.

6.9 RIGHT OF A HOLDER OF BILL OF EXCHANGE

Section 2 of the Nigerian Bill of Exchange Act 1990, defines a holder as "the payee or endorser of a bill or note who is in possession of it or the bearer thereof. He is therefore the person who is in possession of the bill with the intention that the property in it passes to him. The right of such holder are contained-Section 38 of the Bills of Exchange Act as follows:

(1) He may sue on the bill in his own name;
(2) Where he is a holder in due course he holds the bill from any defect of the title of prior parties;
(3) Where his title is defective;
(a) If he negotiates the bill of a holder in due course, the holder obtain a good title;
(b) If he obtains payment of a bill, the person in due course gets a discharge for the bill;
(4) He may enforce payment against all parties liable on the bill;
(5) He may sue anybody who assign the bill prior to him.

Legal duties of a Holder of Bill

These are contained in sections 39-52 of the Act as follows:

(1) Duty of presentation for acceptance;
(2) Obedience to rules in timing for acceptance;
(3) Duties as to qualified acceptance;
(4) Adherence to rules to presentation for payment;
(5) Adherence to rules as to dishonour.

Discharge of a Bill

Sections 59-64 deal with discharge of a bill as follows:

(1) Payment in due course, i.e. payment made by or on behalf of the drawee or acceptance at or after maturity of the bill;
(2) Merger, i.e. acceptance between holder at maturity when the acceptor of a bill is or becomes the holder it at or after its maturity, in his own right, the bill is discharge;

(3) Express Waiver, i.e. when the holder of a bill at or after its maturity absolutely or unconditional renounces his right against it;

(4) Cancellation: where a bill or acceptance is materially altered without consent of the parties liable on it. Material alteration includes alteration of date sum payable, time of payment and place of payment.

6.10 DIFFERENCE BETWEEN BILLS OF EXCHANGE AND CHEQUES

There are many points of similarity between bills and cheques. This is understandable because a cheque is particular type of bill. However, the following points of difference may be noted:

(a) A bill may be drawn upon a person, whereas a cheque must draw upon a banker.

(b) A bill may be payable on demand or at a fixed or determinable future time, whereas a cheque must be payable on demand.

(c) Unless a bill is payable on demand, it is unusually accepted, whereupon the acceptor in the party is primarily liable to the holder. The cheque is not accepted and the drawer is the party primarily liable.

(d) A bill must be presented for payment when due or its drawer will be discharged. The drawer of a cheque is not discharged for six years unless through the delay in presentation he has been injured

(e) Bill takes three days of grace in every case where the bill itself does not provide otherwise. A cheque takes no days of grace.

(f) No provision for bills to be crossed but cheque can be crossed.

Chapter 7

TERMINATION OF BANKER-CUSTOMER RELATIONSHIP

OUTLINE

- Death of a Customer
- Garnishee Order
- Bankruptcy

Specific Learning Objectives

7.1 Discuss death, termination banking relationship
7.2 Discuss Garnishee Order
7.3 Analyse Bankruptcy
7.4 List the stages in bankruptcy

7.1 DEATH OF CUSTOMER

The general principle in law is that a person's right and obligations under a contract pass, on his death, to his personal representative the exception being contracts of service which require the personal skill and aptitude of the deceased. In like manner, when a bank's customer dies, his assets and liabilities with the bank will pass to his personal representatives who can derive their title from either of two sources.

If the deceased leaves a valid will, in which executors are appointed. His bank balances and other assets are vested in the executors but the executors must obtain a grant of probate of the will which is usually granted at the High Court Probate Registry as an official testimony to the genuineness of the will and confirmation of the executor's right in administer the estate.

However, if the customer dies intestate, i.e. without leaving a valid will, or where the will fails to mention any executor (and this is most unlikely) or the executors are unable or unwilling to perform, the property is vested in the Probate registry until administrators are appointed. Some relations like the spouse, children, parent or brothers and sisters of the deceased may apply to the probate registry for appointment as administrators where the estate is insolvent.

Immediately the ban is aware of the customer's death, withdrawals on the account must stop, even if cheque presented have been signed by the customer before his death. Such cheques must be returned marked 'drawer deceased'. Notice of death may be brought by a deceased's relation, but the bank will want to see the death certificate. Publication in reputable newspapers may also be taken as evidence of death whether published as 'Obituary' advertisement or as reported news but care must be taken in using the latter as the news may later prove to be false. In all cases the bank must duly establish the credibility of such information.

As mentioned, the customer's mandate automatically terminates on his death and the executors or administrators will take over as his personal representative. Power of attorney granted to a third party to run the accounts also automatically terminates, even if said to be irrevocable and cheques should not be paid, even if issued by the agent before, but presented after the customer's death. However, although withdrawals cannot be permitted, credits like dividend warrants can continue to be received into the account, but if the bank is aware that the payment represents earning that normally terminate at that, like pension, annuity or salary the party providing the credit must be informed of the death so that payment may cease. If the bank continues to receive the remittance, it may be counted as payment under mistake of fact and the bank may be compelled to refund it if the personal representatives have withdrawn it. All credit balance pass off the personal representatives who have duly obtained probate. However, for small accounts, where there is no parents against presentation of death certificate, sworn affidavit of the relation to be witnessed and confirmed by a reputable solicitor who may also be present witness the withdrawal at the bank.

If the banker has safe custody items, they must be delivered to the personal representatives as the case may be, even if at the time of taking deposit of the item, the customer specifically indicated that the items were to be delivered to a named person. Such mandate is revoked by death. However, where the safe-custody is suspected to be the will and problems arises as to who the executors are, the bank can deliver such safe custody items against the undertaking of a reputable solicitor acting for the estate and who must give undertaking to turn the item to the bank if it is not the will.

The account of the customer does not pass automatically to the personal representatives as they must open their own account as executors or administrators for the purpose of winding up the estate. Where the account is in debit, further drawings by the executors must not be allowed and the bank could prove in the estate immediately. If the account is secured by a charge over the deceased's assets, the bank may still prove the estate and if paid in full by the personal representatives, the bank will have to surrender the security. If not paid, it can realise security. If secured by a third party security, the account has to be broken to be able to maximize recoveries from the third party. Notice that the deceased customer's security is not valid for borrowing by the personal representatives.

7.2 GARNISHEE ORDER

A garnishee order is an order of the Court obtained by a judgment creditor, directed to attach the money of his judgment debtor which is in the hand of a third party, with the effect that the third party is prevented from paying the money so attached to anybody but to hold it as custodian for the Court until the court gives directive as to how the money is to be applied. The third party is called "the garnishee" the garnishee i.e. one commanded' and the money attached will invariably be applied to satisfy the judgment debt.

In application to banking, the bank becomes the third party' the garnishee' or the 'one commanded' if the Court is convinced by the judgment creditor's sworn declaration that the bank is having some money credited to the account of the judgement debtor who is the bank customer. As an example, assuming Mr. Y is indebted to Mr. X, (the debt having been proved in Court and therefore a judgment debt), but the debt is not paid and Mr. X got to know that Mr. Y has some money in AB Bank, Mr. X can apply to the Court for a garnishee order to be served on the bank to prevent it from paying any amount on Y's account so that the amount can in the process be used to pay X. the three parties to a garnishee order therefore are:

The judgment debtor, who is the bank customer and who in the above illustration, is Mr. Y. The judgment creditor, who, following his judgment debtor's failure to satisfy the debt, applies to the Court for the garnishee order to be issued as served on a third party whom he believes to be indebted to his judgment debtor and in the above illustration the judgment creditor is Mr. X the third party on whom the order is served. In the above example, the bank is the third party.

The garnishee proceeding is usually handled in a most confidential manner because if the judgment debtor whose money is to be attached has an advanced notice of the impending attachment, he will withdraw his money from the bank and the purpose of the garnishee order will be defeated.

When an application for issuance of garnishee order is filled, the Court, if satisfied, will as a preliminary step, issue a garnishee order i.e. a temporary injection, under which the bank or the person on whom the order is issued is directed to part with the money attached without the directive of the Court. To be able to obtain a service garnishee order, the judgment creditor must swear to an affidavit mentioning the judgment debtor, the amount outstanding and stating that is far as he is aware, the person to be served is indebted to the judgment debtor. He need not indicate how much the person to be served owes his debtor but the name and address of the person to be served must be given and if it is a bank with more than one branch, the branch where the amount is kept must be mentioned. The Court will then issue the garnishee *nisi ex parte*, that is without hearing the pleas of, or even requiring attendance in Court of, either the debtor or the creditor, as much as the court is satisfied that the applicant stand to be prejudiced if the order is not issued. However, by section 84(1) of the Sheriff and Civil Process Act, where money liable to be attached by the garnishee order is in the custody or control of a public officer in his official capacity, the order *nisi* shall not be made until consent to such attachment is first obtained from the appropriate officer but as bank official cannot be classified as public officer, even if the bank is wholly owned by the government. Such prior consent is not required from the bank before the order *nisi* is made.

The order may be limited or unlimited. It is said to be limited when it specifies the amount to be attached with it such that the bank can know through the order, the amount to be provided for, should the customer's balance exceed the sum of the amount claimed and costs. The order is unlimited if no amount is specified in which case the bank must block the entire balance until the Court gives directives. The bank will, in case of unlimited order, be acting on its own peril if it accepts any pressure from the customer for withdrawal of some money even if the customer is able to provide a proof to the amount of his indebtedness which led to the service of the order. If the customer knows that his credit balance exceeds the debt in question, he should press the court to convert the unlimited order to a limited order. In *Rovers* v. *Whiteley* (1982) decided at the British House of Lords, Lord Watson said:

> The effects of an order attaching 'all debts' owing or accruing due by him to the judgment is to make the garnishee the custodian for the Court of the whole funds attached and he (the garnishee) cannot, except at his own peril, with any of those funds without the sanction of the Court. It is within the points of the Court to restrict its operation to such an amount of the debt owed by the garnishee as will satisfy the judgment debt, but so long as such a restriction is made, and the attachment is unreleased, the garnishee is under no obligation to disregard the attachment and to pay the excess to his creditor.

However, if the order is restricted to a specified amount, i.e. limited and the customer's credit balance exceed that amount, the bank can place the amount of the order in a suspense account pending further directive by the court and allow the customer to withdraw the excess or in fact allow the amount to continue running as before.

After the issuance *ex-parte* of the order *nisi* or temporary order, the Court will hear the pleas of both sides. The judgment debtor will give reasons, if any, why the order should be lifted. He may, for example, be able to prove that he has paid the debt through an agent of the judgment creditor or that he has a right of set-off or that the judgment creditor had in fact agreed to a scheme of instalment payment. The judgment creditor will also give reasons why the order should be confirmed. The order will be lifted if the Court is not satisfied that it should be confirmed (made absolute) and in that wise, the bank is not involved in the proceedings but may apply to the Court if he has a claim to make or stands to be prejudiced by an absolute order One of the reasons why an order *nisi* will not be confirmed was demonstrated in *Barclays Bank D. C. Limited* v. *J. A. Baderinwa (Debtor) Re: Lagos Executive Development Board (Garnishee) (1962)*. Baderinwa was indebted to Barclays Bank and the debt was not satisfied. The Lagos Executive Development Board later acquired a piece of land which gave rise to a debt for compensation in favour of Baderinwa and the bank brought this action to attach the debt so that instead of paying Baderinwa the Board should use the money to satisfy Baderinwa's debt with the bank. A garnishee order *nisi* was issued to restrain the Board from paying Baderinwa and pleadings were ordered during which Baderinwa contended that the land, though bought in his name did not belong to him as he used family money to belonging to him and others to buy it, and as such it would not be equitable for the compensation to be attached. The Court ruled that the order would not be made absolute nor would it be lifted but the enquiry would be ordered about ownership of the land should the bank wish to pursue the matter further. The implication here is that if the bank did not want to pursue the matter further, or when pursued further, it was ascertained that the land did not belong to Baderinwa the order would be lifted. However, if the Court is satisfied that the application has merits, in that the land belongs to Baderinwa in his personal capacity, the order will be confirmed and made absolute and the Board will be informed through the issuance of an absolute order. The absolute order being the final order will be in 'limited' form specifying the amount to be attached and the cost. If the amount in the customer's account, which is attached according to the rules below, it more than the amount specified in the Court Order, the bank will satisfy the Court and leave the balance for the customer who can now continue with the account. If the amount is less, the entire amount should be remitted to the Court. It is not the duty of the bank to make-up for the short-fall.

7.3 BANKRUPTCY

A bankruptcy is a person who, primarily because of his inability to pay his debt as and when due, commits certain acts of bankruptcy as a result of which legal processes are set in motion through which he is adjudged bankruptcy by a competent Court of law.

A person is not necessarily bankrupt simply because his liabilities are greater than his assets or because of insolvency, although all these are preludes to petition filed against him by himself before third party, and undergoes specified legal processes before being adjudged bankruptcy by a competent Court of Law.

If a person has more debts than his assets can repay, there is the tendency that unless there is a legal process through which his assets are equitably distributed, some creditors are likely to suffer because the debtor may dispose his assets in a manner as to jeopardise creditors generally or in the distribution of assets, he may show some preference for some creditors. Also unless there is a way through which such a debtor can start off again, he may never get over from the burden of debt and other members of the public, not knowing the extent of his indebtedness, may continue extending credit, thus allowing him to continue duping the public.

The Bankruptcy Act 1990 provides a set of procedures for dealing with situations whereby a person who is unable to pay his debt can have bankruptcy petition filled against him (or he may file one against himself) so that he can once free himself from the burden of debt. The bankruptcy exercise is therefore aimed at achieving several objectives:

i. to place the debtor's assets in the hands of a third party (the official receiver or trustee in bankruptcy) who will be under legal obligation to ensure judicious distribution of the assets;
ii. to enable such a third party recover assets of the debtor which in the immediate past, have been distributed with the intention of defrauding;
iii. to place the debtor under some legal disabilities and codes of conduct which will prevent him from duping the public and which will guide his future economic transactions;
iv. to give the debtor an opportunity to start all over again, the past debt having been wiped off by the bankruptcy exercises, whether paid in full or not during distribution of the assets of the bankruptcy;
v. to provides an avenue for other people to learn why people go bankruptcy as a guide for general conduct.

7.3 STAGES IN BANKRUPTCY

The following are the stages in bankruptcy proceedings:

(i) ***Acts of Bankruptcy*** - Section 1 of the Act states that a debtor commits an act of bankruptcy if anyone of the following circumstances occurs;

(ii) ***Failure to Comply with Bankruptcy Notice*** -A judgment creditor may serve bankruptcy notice on the judgment debtor and if the debtor fails to pay or fails to set up a set-off, counter-claim or cross demand within 14 days.

(iii) ***Seizure of Goods*** - If the debtor's goods gave been seized through legal process and either been sold or held by the Court bailiff for 21 days

(iv) ***Debtor's Declaration*** - This is when a debtor files a declaration of his inability to pay his debt or presents bankruptcy petition against himself.

If the debtor commits any of the bankruptcy acts stated above, creditor will be entitled to present a bankruptcy petition provide:

- The debt which may accrue to one or more creditors is not less than ₦2000;
- The debt is a liquidated sum payable immediately at certain future time;
- The act of bankruptcy has been committed in three months preceding the petition. If committed more than three months before the petition, the petition will not hold as only acts committed within three months prior to petition are available acts of bankruptcy and it is only on available acts on which petitions may be brought.

The debtor is ordinarily resident in Nigeria at the time of petition or within 12 months previous to the petition or has a dwelling house or business in Nigeria.

If the debt is secured by any asset of the debtor, the petitioning creditor must either state that he is prepared to give up the security or value the security and prove for the difference. Third party securities may be disregarded for this purpose. Under section 98 of the Act, where two or more bankruptcy petitions are presented against the same debtor or against joint debtors, the Court may consolidate the proceedings of any of them on such terms as the Court thinks fit.

Chapter 8

PERSONAL SECURITIES: GUARANTEE AND INDEMNITY

OUTLINE

Introduction: principles underlying guarantee and indemnity between guarantee and indemnity

Specific Learning Objectives

8.1 Enumerate the principles underlying guarantee and indemnity.
8.2 List the differences between guarantee and indemnity.
8.3 Discuss hints on guarantee and indemnity.

8.1 INTRODUCTION: PRINCIPLES UNDERLYING GUARANTEE AND INDEMNITY

The general legal situation is that nobody who borrows money has the obligation to repay it, as much as the debt is legally enforceable. The same situation arises if someone obtains good or services on credit; the responsibility to pay at a later date falls squarely on the debtor and an innocent third party cannot be brought into liability unless he gives consent. Where the debtor dies or loses his legal personality through bankruptcy or mental capability, his personal representative would be liable subject only to availability of assets of the deceased or bankrupt debtor. Even if the debtor has a relation or friend who is wealthy, such person does not automatically acquire a relation or friend who is wealthy, such person does not automatically acquire the responsibility to pay another person's debt.

There are, however, circumstances in which a third party, through his promise or conduct, would be liable on debts that he does not actually incur: if the third party gives a guarantee or an indemnity, and in case of a bank's guarantee, it is usually worded to include indemnity. For example, Mr. Z may have told Mr. Y "Let X have the goods; I will see you get paid" or more precisely, "Let X have the goods I will pay you." In either of the two, Mr. Z is telling Mr. that X should collected the goods after which Mr. Y should turn in back to him (Z) for payment, and this is known as contract of indemnity. Mr. Z is thus accepting primary responsibility and the legal implication is as if he had collected the goods himself. In actual fact, Mr. X, in collecting the goods to be taken as an agent of Mr. Z the seller, Mr. Y, has no legal obligation to ask Mr. X for payment and Mr. Z's legal obligation to pay for the goods is not dependent on Mr. X's default. It was brought in the case of *Wautheir* v. *Wilson (1911)* that an indemnity is a clear undertaking the person giving it is a principal in his own right and primary and independent debtor as opposed to a guarantor whose liability is secondary. Such contract need not be in writing as verbal undertaking will suffice. In *Mount Stephen* v. *Lakeman (1872),* the Chairman of a local council said to a contractor: "do the job and I will see you paid" He in fact had not been authorised by the council to award the contract and on completion, the council refused to pay. When turned to by the contractor for payment, the Chairman refused to pay contending that he gave only verbal guarantee which is unenforceable as it was not in writing. The Court held that the assurance given by the Chairman was an indemnity which did not have to be in writing and that he was accordingly liable to the contractor for payment.

A guarantee is, on the other hand, "written undertaking by principal debtor is a minor and the debt is on luxury goods one party (called the guarantor) to be answerable for the debt, default or miscarriage of another party (called the principal debtor) who must be under legal obligation to repay the debt or perform the act in question."

Like another guarantee, there are three parties to a bank guarantee:

i. the principal debtor (i.e. the borrower who is the bank's customer);
ii. the creditor (i.e. the bank);
iii. the guarantor or surety (i.e. the third party who accepts secondary responsibility of the debt). He may have no other interest in the

contract between the principal and the bank other than that he accepted to repay the debt if the principal debtor fails to pay.

Here, instead of accepting primary liability by way of indemnity, Mr. Z accepts liability only to the extent that Mr. X (the principal debtor) does not pay. He may say, for example, give Mr. X the goods; if he does not pay, I will pay you. The operational phrase that distinguishes a contract of guarantee here from a contract of indemnity is "if he does not pay" and with those few words, additional obligations have been imposed on Mr. Y, the seller He has to discharge his part in the contract by selling the goods to Mr. X He has to make demand for payment on Mr. X. it is only if and when Mr. X does not pay that Mr. Z becomes liable. In other words, the guarantor's liability is contingent liability and does not crystallise or become actual liability until the principal debtor defaults. The liability of guarantor is dependent upon the obligation of a principal debtor and the guarantee is enforceable only to the extent that he guaranteed obligation is itself enforceable. Thus, where there is no primary debt, there can be no secondary liability. For example, if the principal debtor is a minor and the debt is on luxury goods for which the creditor normally not to able to sue or if the creditor waives his right against the debtor, the guarantee is to be liable. Also default of the principal debtor is required for guarantor to be liable. Since the guarantor assumes only secondary liability, he cannot be sued or compelled to rectify the debt of the principal debtor until and unless a default has actually been committed.

However, once a default has been committed, the guarantor becomes immediately liable even if notice of default has not been served on him. Default is construed in its literal sense in matter relating to guarantee. It is assumed t have occurred once the principal debtor fails to meet his promise like failing to meet a pre-agreed loan repayment program once default has occurred, it is not necessary for the creditor to request the principal debtor to pay or to sue the principal debtor before commencing recovery action against the guarantor. In the case of *Moschi* v. *LEP Air Service Limited (1973),* it was held that, it is the guarantor, and not the principal creditor, who has the obligation to see that the principal debtor pays since failure of the principal debtor to pay will automatically imply a default for which he (the guarantor) becomes automatically and immediately liable.

Also, if the principal debtor dies, the guarantor becomes liable without the personal representatives of the deceased being asked to pay.

In *African Continental Bank* v. *Kembi and Talabi (1974),* the defendants gave a guarantee in the bank's favour to secure a customer's debt. The customer later died and the bank demanded repayment from the guarantors and not from the deceased's personal representatives. In an action against them following their non-payment, the defendants contended that as the plaintiff bank did no demand payment from the deceased's personal representatives before demanding on them, they are discharged from the obligation under the guarantee. Adefarasin, C.J. rejected their contention and give a judgment for the plaintiff bank. The Court held further that notice of the principal debtor's default need to be given the guarantor and that "the liability of a surety under a contract of guarantee arises when the principal debtor makes default and except otherwise agree notice of the debtor's default need not be given to the surety and he is liable even if he has not been requested to pay. When the principal debtor dies after defaulting the guarantor remains liable without the deceased's personal representatives being required to pay." The liquidation of a statutory body or corporation will also make the guarantor be primarily liable *(Western Nigeria Finance Corp.* v. *Aladesanmi (1970).*

The case of *Reader* v. *Kingham (1862)* brought about a clearer distinction between a guarantee and an indemnity. In his case, it was decided that for a contract of guarantee to be enforceable, a principal debtor must be in contemplation and that the liability of the guarantor is conditional on the failure of the principal debtor to perform his obligations. In case if indemnity, this is not so. The principal debtor need to be in contemplation.

Also, unlike an indemnity where oral promise will suffice, a guarantee must be in writing as Section 4 of Statute of Frauds Act 1677 provides that; no action shall be brought to charge a person upon any special promise to answer for the debt, default or miscarriage of another persons, unless the agreement upon which such action is to be brought or some sufficient memorandum or note thereof is written, signed by the party to be charged therewith or his agent.

Although a bank guarantee form is usually comprehensive and with many clauses to make it legally water-tight, ordinary written memorandum, letter, or note will suffice and the size, colour or wordings employed are immaterial nor does it actually need to be types or printed as much as it sufficiently signifies that a guarantee is being given, and it is signed by the guarantor or his duly authorized agent. In the Ugandan case of *Gravson and Compan Limited v. A. H. Wardle (Uganda) Ltd. (1963)* decided by Sir Justice Udo Udoma when he was Chief Justice of Uganda and before he came to the Bench of the supreme court of Nigeria, some parties reached an oral agreement with a financier that they would give a guarantee fi facilities to the defendant company were increased. This agreement was later confirmed in writing, but the financier's standard guarantee form was not executed. The parties later sought to escape liability pleading that the letter was not guarantee but merely intention to give a guarantee at a later date. The contention was rejected and the Court held that the letter amounts to guarantee under which they were liable.

It must be borne in mind that the word 'surety' applies to all forms of security where a third party holds himself to be possibly liable, either himself personally or in respect of his property charged to secure another person's obligations or both (*Re only 1938*). However mere pledging of one's property to secure another person's debt does not involve pledging of personal credit and does not therefore amount to a guarantee other than to the extent that the property so deposited can be realised to satisfy the unsatisfied debt of the customer unless a separate guarantee has been given. In *Edu* v. *National Bank of Nigeria Limited (1971)*, the appellant deposited his title deed on a landed property to secure the amount of a limited company. At the High Court, it was held that by providing the security, he was deemed to have pledged his personal liability and that he contended on appeal to the Supreme Court that he was under no personal liability and that his liability was limited to the land comprised in the title deed submitted. The Supreme Court allowed the appeal and upheld the pleas of the appellant. The Court held that; a person who becomes a surety or guarantor in the sense of having provided a pledge or other security for the debt of another without undertaking liability beyond his pledge or other security is not deemed to have pledge personal credit.

A guarantee and third party mortgage or charges are separate and independent obligations even though given by the same person. It is important therefore that no withstanding that a third party pledges his assets, he must be made to sign separate guarantee to make him personally liable should the value of his security be insufficient to satisfy the debt guaranteed.

8.2 DIFFERENCES BETWEEN GUARANTEE AND INDEMNITY

(i) A guarantee must be in written. In case of indemnity, ordinary oral agreement will suffice.

(ii) In a contract of indemnity, there are only two parties; the indemnifier and the indemnified; whereas there are three parties in a contract of guarantee; the creditor, the principal debtor and the guarantor. In other words, while an indemnity is a two-party contract, a guarantee is three-party.

(iii) A guarantor assumes only a secondary liability and the guarantee is enforceable only if and when the principal debtor fails. The liability of an indemnifier to the indemnified is direct and independent and does not depend on the failure of any party.

(iv) A guaranty gives rise to accumulation of at least three sub-contracts: between the debtor and the creditor, between the creditor and the guarantor, between the guarantor and the debtor and if more than one guarantor, between/among the co-guarantors. On the other hand, there is only one contract in a contract of indemnity: between the indemnifier and the indemnified.

(v) The legal position in a contract of guarantee is that the guarantor gives the undertaking at the request of the principal debtor, but as an indemnity is a direct Contract between the indemnified and the indemnifier, the indemnity is not given at anybody's request but on the volition of the indemnifier.

(vi) In contract of guarantee, the guarantor, having met his obligation under the guarantee, steps into shoes of the creditor and can take legal action against the debtor to recover his loss. An indemnifier may have no third party to sue, to recover is loss unless he has assignment charge or counter-indemnity in his favour Professional indemnities like banks, therefore obtain security and counter-indemnity on a customer's behalf.

8.3 HINTS ON GUARANTEE AS SECURITY

There are two main factors that the bank must take into account in accepting guarantee as security for bank advance, these are:

(i) the value of the guarantee;

(ii) the validity of the guarantee, and the bank must subject all guarantees to the canons of a good banking security discussed earlier because of the intricate and slippery nature of guarantee.

Chapter 9

LAW OF AGENCY

OUTLINE

- Definition of Agency
- Types of Agency
- Kinds of Agency
- Terminating an Agency

Specific Learning Objectives

9.1 Definition of Agency
9.2 List the types of Agents
9.3 Discuss creation of an Agency
9.4 Enumerate kinds of Agency
9.5 Analyse Termination of an Agency

Adesany and Ayodele define agency as "a consensual relationship" existing between two parties by which the agent is 'expressly or impliedly' to act on behalf of another, 'the principal', when dealing with a third party. Friedman gives a more comprehensive definition of agency as follows:

> It is the relationship that exist between two persons where one called the principal, in such a way as to be able to effect the principal's legal disposition in respect of strangers to the relationship by making of contracts on the disposition of property.

The above definition consists of:

i. the Principal;
ii. the Agent;
iii. the Third Party;

The important things to be seen here is the concept of power which si different from authority. It is to see whether the person appointed is acting under his authority or not.

9.1 TYPES OF AUTHORITY

a. Actual or Real Agent

This is that which the principal confers to the agency by agreement. It includes not only the authority expressly stated in agreement (whether written or verbal), but implied actual authority.

b. Ostensible or Apparent Authority

Where a person been given authority to act either expressly or impliedly.

By virtue of power, the agent can enter a contract with a third party and the principal is liable as stated in the case of *Bamboye* v. *University of Horin & Others (1991) 8 NWIR.*

Agent as Distinguished from a Servant

i. A servant is a person employed to render services under the instruction of direction of his master. Whereas the agent is employed or appointed to arrange a contract between the principal and a third party.
ii. An agent may act in a dual capacity i.e. he may act as well as a servant.

An Agent as Distinguished from a Trustee

a. Relationship between an agent and a principal is based on their consent while consent does not exist in trust.
b. An agent is always appointed by principal while trustee is appointed by settler.
c. An agent represent his principal while trustee is not in any way representing the beneficiary.

9.2 TYPES OF AGENTS

1. Mercantile Agent

This is defined in section 1 of the Factories Act 1889 as a person having in the customary course of his business as such agent authorised either to sell or consign goods for the purpose of sale or to buy goods or to raise money for the security of goods.

2. Factor

This is not defined anywhere in the Act, but under common law, he is a mercantile agent entrusted with possession of goods for the purpose of sale.

3. Broker

This is a mercantile agent employed to negotiate contract on behalf of another, for the sale or purpose of property called brokerage.

4. Auctioneers

This is an agent licensed by law and authorised to sell goods or property for another at a public sale called auction.

5. Estate Agent

This is an agent engaged by an estate owner for the purpose of buying and selling houses or piece of land in consideration of payment of commission, etc.

Consideration is immaterial in agency. Capacity is of paramount importance i.e. a minor can be an agent but a principal and consent should not be with duress, fraud or undue influence.

9.3 CREATION OF AGENCY

i. Capacity to act as Principal

The general rule governing the capacity to enter into a contract also governs the right of a person to act as principal.

ii. Capacity to act as Agent

An agent does not enter an agreement on his behalf but on behalf of his principal. It is not necessary that he should have full contractual capacity. All persons of sound mind including infants and others of limited or no capacity to contract on their behalf are competent to act as agents.

No formality such as writing or deed is required for a valid appointment of an agent. In other words, there is no particular form required to create the principal-agent relationship. An appointment can be verbal i.e. by words or mouth.

9.4 KINDS OF AGENCY

1. Estoppels

This is a bar preventing a person from making allegation or denial on what someone has stated as truth. Example of estoppels arises where an employee of Y, had for some years managed a ship belonging to Y. he ordered in Y's name from Z and Y duly paid for them. X absconded and he called on Z and brought goods in Y's name and took them away. It was held that Y was liable for the price of the goods. Since he accepts purchase made by X in an unusual manner, even though it was made fraudulently by X. see *Summer* v. *Solomon (1857) 7. E and B 879.*

2. Between Husband and Wife

Where husband and wife live together and maintained a household establishment, there is presumption that the wife has authority to pledge the husbands credit for necessities suitable to the style in which they live in respect of those matter usually entrusted to the management of the wife. An authority emanates not from the fact of marriage, but from the fact of cohabitation.

3. Necessity

This is not created by consent or conduct by the parties, but by necessities. It is applicable in marine transactions where there is a contract between owner of goods in a ship and the captain of the ship. Where there is an apprehension, i.e. fear of something bad will happen, the captain can dispose the good and sell it is binding on the owner of the goods. *(See Colonial Bank* v. *John Candy).*

Condition for Agency by Necessities

i. There should be a kind of emergency development.
ii. There should be apprehension of the goods.

iii. The owner will sustain irreparable loss.
iv. There must be a bona fide intention and not a *mala fide* intention.

Essentials of Agency of Necessity

a. That the agent cannot communicate to the principal about the position which has arisen.
b. That the sale of such commodity has become a necessity.
c. Whatever he is doing is in the interest of the principal.

Agency by Ratification

This is created where A purports to act for B either having no authority at all or no authority to do that particular act. The subsequent adoption by B of A's act has the same legal consequences as if B had originally authorised the act (an act done without precedent authority become the act of the principal, if subsequently ratified by him. i.e. ratify means to give formal approval of something. Example of ratification: A without B's authority lent money to C and the money belonged to B, but subsequently where he paid some money as interest to B, he accepted it. It means the conduct of B showed that he has satisfied his act. In this situation, the principal is liable for the act of the agent.

Condition for ratification

i. That the act which is to be ratified must be done on behalf of the principal.
ii. Competence of the principal.

Kinds of acts that are not ratified

i. Illegal, void and ultra vires act cannot be ratified
ii. If there is an act which may be injurious to the third party
iii. If there is something done in breach of statutory obligation;
iv. Knowledge of fact must be there.

9.5 DUTIES OF AN AGENT

The duties of an agent are:

i. to execute the mandate of the principal;

ii. to exercise reasonable care and diligent skills;
iii. to avoid conflict of interest;
iv. not to delegate. By this, it means he cannot delegate power of agency to another person. This is explained in a Latin maxim *delegatus non potest delegare* - which means a delegated power cannot be redelegated.
v. No taking of secret profit.

TERMINATION OF AGENCY

a. By revocation.
b. Lapse of time.
c. Agency coupled with interest.
d. Where the principal is adjudged to be insolvent.
e. Completion of business.
f. It may be renounced, i.e., proper notice must be given.

Chapter 10

PARTNERSHIP

OUTLINE

Nature of Partnership
Partnership and Company Distinguished
Types of Partners
Rights and Duties of Partners

Specific Learning Objectives

10.1 Discuss Partnership
10.2 Analyse the nature of Partnership
10.3 Distinguish between partnership and company
10.4 List the types of partners
10.5 Enumerate the rights and duties of partners

10.1 INTRODUCTION: NATURE OF PARTNERSHIP

Section 1(1) of the Partnership Act, 1890, defines partnership as a relation that subsists between persons carrying on a business with a view of making profit.

10.2 FOUR ESSENTIAL ELEMENT OF THE DEFINITION

a. There must be a business.
b. The business must be in existence to make profit.
c. The business must be carried out by or on behalf of the partners.
d. The business must be varied out by two or more persons.

A business is defined in section 45 as to include trade, occupation or profession. Such definition must be constructed to mean commercial enterprise where services or goods or both services and goods are rendered or sold for profit.

Partnership cannot be formed by only one person. Persons here mean artificial persons. A man and a corporation can enter into a partnership. Two corporations can form a Partnership being two artificial persons. See *Cox* v. *Hickam.*

10.3 PARTNERSHIP AND COMPANY DISTINGUISHED

i. The partners have right in partnership property whereas companies exclusively own its properties.
ii. The debt of the company belongs to the company while partners are responsible for the debt of partnership to the last kobo.
iii. Liabilities of partners cannot be limited except in limited partnership while the liability of company is limited.
iv. The death or retirement of a member causes the dissolution of partnership whereas it does not cause dissolution of a company.
v. Every partner has the right to share in the management of the partnership while owner ship and management may be separate from company property.
vi. Shareholders and directors may contract in companies whereas partners may not contract in partnership.
vii. Activities of companies are restricted by object clause while the business in partnership can be changed at anytime by mutual agreement as illustrated in the case of *Solomon* v. *Solomon (1897) A. Co 22.*

The advantage of forming a company rather than partnership is mainly laid in the extent of personal liability of partnership to dissolutive on death or retirement.

Article or Partnership

i. Particulars: Full name and addresses must be stated
ii. Place of Business
iii. Name and style
iv. Nature of Business
v. Commencement of Business
vi. Duration
vii. Capital

viii. Property
ix. Bankers and signatories to bank accounts
x. Profits and drawings
xi. Salary
xii. Account
xiii. Power, right and duties
xiv. Retirement
xv. Expulsion and suspension

Dissolution of Partnership

a. By Act of the parties, that is:

i. By notice;
ii. Illness;
iii. Special clause in the agreement.

b. By Operation of Law

i. Expiration of term
ii. Death or bankruptcy
iii. Termination of undertaking
iv. By court order

Advantages of Company over Partnership

a. Limitation of liabilities of members
b. Legal personality and perpetual succession
c. Number of members
d. Formalities
e. Capacity to sue and be sued
f. Borrowing

Legal Requirements of Partnership

a. Legality in respect of business and of the partners
b. The minimum number of partners is 2 and the maximum is 20 as stated in section 19(1) of the Companies and Allied Matters Act (CAMA) and S. 19(2) provides that partnership consists of professionals such as lawyers, doctors, accountant etc. it may exceed 20.

c. Capacity, i.e. infant unless he is with two adults, unsound mind, bankrupt, alien unless registered with the Investment and Security Commission; National Investment Commission, etc.

10.4 TYPES OF PARTNERS

There are three types of partners, they are:

i. Active Partners
ii. Dormant Partners
iii. Nominal Partners

a. Active Partners

If the partners are actively participating in the business of the partnership, they are regarded as active partners.

b. Dormant Partners

If one partner shares in the profit of the business but his name does not feature in the business of the partnership. He is called a dominant partner.

c. Nominal Partner

This relates to a person who lends his name to a business without any interest in it.

10.5 RIGHT AND DUTIES OF PARTNERS

i. All partners are entitled to share equally in the capital of the business, and must equally constitute towards losses.
ii. Firms must indemnify every partner in respect of payment made.
iii. Partners are entitled to interest at the rate of five per cent per annum from the date of payment.
iv. A partner is not entitled to interest on capital subscribed by him.
v. Every partner must take part in the management of the partnership business.
vi. No partner shall be entitled to remuneration for acting in partnership business
vii. No person may be introduced as partner without the consent of existing partners.

Chapter 11

FRAUD IN THE BANKING INDUSTRY
IMPERATIVES FOR AN ANTI-FRAUD COURT IN NIGERIA

OUTLINE

- Legal framework against banking frauds
- Advanced fee fraud (419)
- Money laundering
- Criticisms of Regular Courts
- Special Courts and the Legal System
- Justification for an Anti-Fraud Court

INTRODUCTION

Nigeria has been associated with various forms of transactional frauds and organized crimes. Nigerians are believed to operate cells in the US, Britain, Canada, Hong Kong, Australia, Japan and in some African countries, with the assistance of other various syndicates or criminal networks within Nigeria (GUP, 1995). In 1997, for example, British Police Received from members of the public 68,000 reports of "419" letters sent by Nigerian criminal network. Also, in the mid-1990s, US authorities estimated that 58% of fraudulent insurance claims in the country were made by Nigerian and that Nigerian fraudsters were responsible for some 20 to 26 billion dollars' worth of fraud each year in the US alone (UNODC, 2005).

Recently in the exercise of its supervisory role under the Central Bank Act and the Banks and other Financial Institutions Act (BOFIA), the Central Bank of Nigeria looked into the risk management portfolio and corporate government issues in the banks. The two stage audit reports claimed the jobs of the no fewer than eight bank Chief Executive Officers (CEO) with various criminal charges slammed, on them by the Economic and Financial Crimes Commission (EFCC), some of them have been arraigned before the courts.

Frauds in the banking industry have assumed a frightening dimension. These are perpetrated either by the bank fraudsters or angst the bank or against some innocent individual customers of the bans.

The Nigerian Banking Act defines bank as any person who carried out banking on business and including a commercial bank, an acceptance house, discount house, financial institutions and merchant bank (section 43). The same section goes further to define "banking business" as: The business of receiving monies from outside sources as deposit, irrespective of payment of interest or the granting of money and acceptance of credits or the purchase of bills or the purchase or sale of securities for the writing obligations, to acquire claims in respect of a loan prior to the maturity or the applying of guarantee and other warranties for other or the effecting of transfer and clearing and such other transactions as the Minister may, on the recommendation of the Central Bank by order in the *Gazettes*. Section 43.

From the above statutory definition, it becomes clear that a bank has a wide operational capacity and dimension and this could make it susceptible to fraud. This bring us to the issue of "what is a bank fraud?" This has been defined by the *Black Law Dictionary* 8th Edition, p. 685 as "the criminal offence knowingly executing or attempting to execute a scheme or attempt to defraud a financial institution by means of false or fraudulent pretences, representation or promise."

Statistics have shown that frauds or collectively called offences against property take a high index in crime rates in the country (see Table 5).

Accordingly, the need to stem the tide of fraud in the banks calls for a special anti-fraud court to dispense speedily in view of the critical role played by the banks in the macro and micro economy of the country. Fraud against banks could take the form of advanced fee fraud, money laundering, economic crimes, dud cheques, etc. the present dispensation where the Federal High Court assumed the jurisdiction of fraud in the banking industry has occasioned delay in the trials and dispensation of cases thereby defeating the deterrent effect of punishment in fraud cases.

11.1 LEGAL FRAMEWORK AGAINST BANKING FRAUDS

Just as there are several types of banking fraud as discussed therein, there are also various legal frameworks that have been put in place to check banking frauds. These are in form of laws that have been enacted with a view to stemming and possibly stopping the menace of bank frauds. Some of the most important ones are as follows: (Also see Table 1).

i. **Penal and Court Codes**

ii. **Economic and Financial Crimes Commission Act No. 1 of 2004**

Section 14 of this Act provides for offences relating to financial malpractice where it provides.

A person who, being an officer of a bank or other financial institution or designated non-financial institution.

a. Fails or neglects to secure compliance with the provision of the Act; or
b. Fails to neglects to secure authenticity of any statement submitted commits an offence liable on conviction to imprisonment for a term not exceeding five years or to a fine of Five Hundred Thousand Naira (₦500,000) or both such imprisonment and fine.
c. The act also provides for the punishment of those who may collude with bankers or staff of financial institutions when it provides in section 18 for offences in relation to economic and financial crimes and penalties. Thus, the combined effect of section 14 and 18 clearly aims at the banks and other financial institutions.

11.2 ADVANCED FEE FRAUD (419)

Advance Fee Fraud (419) is one of the financial crimes identified in the Economic and Financial Crimes Act 2004, the other being money laundering, counterfeiting, illegal change transfer, future market fraud, fraudulent cashing of negotiable instruments, computer credit card fraud and contract dimension and this is why it is considered among transnational organized crimes.

Advanced Feed Fraud refers to an upfront payment by a victim to a fraudster to allow the victim to take part in a much larger financial transaction which he believes would either bring him profit or will result in credit being extended to him. In its simple form, advanced fee fraud involves a trick against prospective victims into parting with funds by persuading them that they will receive substantial benefit in return for providing some modes payment in advance.

Advanced Fee Fraud takes a variety of forms and falls into the following categories:

a. transfer of funds from over voiced contracts;
b. contract fraud (cash on delivery goods and services);
c. conversion of hard currency (black money).

11.3 MONEY LAUNDERING

Money laundering involves the processing or dealing with the proceeds of criminal activities in order to conceal or disguise their origin. Goredema (2000) defines it as

> the concealment of unlawfully acquired assets to make them appear to be lawfully acquired. It includes both the process/effort involved in concealment. In Nigeria, part II Section 14(1) of the Money Laundering (Prohibition) Act 2004 states that the offence is committed where person converts or transfer resources or properties derived directly or indirectly from illicit traffic in narcotic drugs and psychotropic substances or any other crime or illegal act with the aim of either concealing or disguising the genuine nature, origin, location disposition, movement or ownership of the resources, property or rights thereto derived directly from illicit traffic in narcotic drugs or psychotropic substances or other crime or illegal act. In a simple language, money laundering involves the act of "turning dirty money into clean money."

It is designed to make the origin and ownership of tainted funds; that is such monies or proceeds of human, arms and rugs trafficking, corruption, embezzlement of public funds, financial fraud, tax evasion, etc.

11.4 CRITICISMS OF REGULAR COURTS

The Regular courts have been criticized severally. Critics are quick to point out that regular courts actually undermine respect for the law through the haphazard way they handle affairs, Dambazau (2006); Silberman, C.E. (1980) criticized regular courts. "Files are misplaced; jailed defendants are brought to court on the wrong day; victims and witnesses are not notified on the date of which they are to appear (and unless they are notified, they arrived in court to find out that the case has been postponed). Prosecutors and defence lawyers are badly prepared. If the criminal courts are to contribute to a reduction in crime, it would not be stuffing more people into already overcrowded prisons or jails.

Above is the sample of the numerous criticisms of regular courts. This has leads to the creation of special courts in the legal system of many countries including Nigeria.

11.5 SPECIAL COURTS AND THE LEGAL SYSTEMS

Special courts are not viewed in our legal system. In fact, they have been found to be effective as a system in bringing the desired result in that they are special cases. Presently, the Nigerian legal system operates the following special courts that run alongside the regular courts:

i. Juvenile Courts

Where a young person or a child is charged with either indicatable or non-indictable offence other than a capital offence, it is the juvenile court that has the jurisdiction to try him, Magaji (2010). Under Young Persons Act 2004, young persons are under the age of 17 and above 14 years. Other features of the court include non-publicity of its trails, non-use of terminologies such as conviction and sentence, etc.

ii. Election Tribunal

Tribunals are special features of our judicial system. They provide speedy dispensation of justice devoid of protracted delays and undue technicalities. The 1999 Constitution recognizes tribunals when it provides for the establishment of election tribunals to be known as the National Assembly Election Tribunals which to the exclusion of any other courts have original jurisdiction to hear and determine petitions bordering on election to the National Assembly in section 283 Constitution of the Federal Republic of Nigeria 1999. There are also State Election Tribunals known as Governorship and Legislative House Election Tribunals.

iii. Military Court Martials

These courts are constituted for the trail of persons subject to military law for civil offences (Armed Forces Act, 1993). A court martial is a military court which exercise jurisdiction on members of the military who are subject to military laws. It is a service machinery set aside for serious offences under services law (Magaji B., 2007).

iv. Code of Conduct Tribunal

Under the Code of Conduct Bureau and Tribunal Act No. 1 of 1989, it provides for the establishment of the Code of Conduct Bureau and Tribunal to deal with complaints of corruption by public servants and for the breaches of its provisions. Section 20 provides for the establishment of the tribunal known as the Code of Conduct Tribunal.

11.6 JUSTIFICATION FOR AN ANTI-FRAUD COURT

a. High Volume of Fraud Cases

In the Nigerian Police Abstract of Crime Statistics (NPACS), offences have been categorized according to their frequencies as follows:

i. offences against persons;
ii. offences against property;
iii. offences against lawful authority; and
iv. offences against Local Act (Danbazau, 2008).

Thus offences relating to property, i.e. fraud is second in the listings. This shows that the volume of fraud related cases are high. Table 4 shows it occupies second place in the listings. Table 5 shows it occupies first place in frequency and volume. Also, Table 3 shows that convicted persons on fraud related cases are on the very high side (see Table 3).

b. Failure of Legal and Institutional Framework (Table 1 and 2)

Table 2 shows the institutional framework that has been put in place to check banking fraud. These includes the Nigerian Police, the Economic and Finance Crime Commission, the Independent Corrupt Practice and Other Related Offences Commission, Code of Conduct Bureau and Tribunal, State and Federal High Court; despite these, the menace of bank frauds continues. This is an indication of the need for further intervention mechanisms in the system by way of special anti-fraud court.

c. Overloading of the Federal High Court

Jurisdiction on bank related cases bothering on fraud is conferred on the Federal High Court for determination in its original jurisdiction. Section 251(1) of the 1999 Constitution of the Federal Republic of Nigeria provides inter alia that the Federal Hig section 36 h Court shall have jurisdiction to the exclusion of any other court in matters " connected with or pertaining to banking, banks or other financial institutions, including any action between the bank and another, any action by or against the Central Bank of Nigeria arising from banking, foreign exchange, coinage, legal tender, bills of Exchange, Letters of credit, promissory notes and other fiscal measures.

This is an addition to other matters and cases which are exclusive to the Federal High Court as provided and itemized in section 251(1) a-s and its additional jurisdiction in section 251(2-3) relating to criminal offences of treason, treasonable felony and allied offences. It is pertinent to observe that the volumes of jurisdiction tend to overload the Federal High Court thereby inhibiting speedy determination of cases bordering on the bank frauds.

CONCLUSION

The banking sector is key to the economic growth of the country. The massive nature of the frauds perpetrated against banks can, if not checked, ruin the economy with disastrous consequences to the country. The colossal amounts purported to have been stolen by some of the bank chiefs recently removed are staggering. In order to decisively deal with the menace, a special court would be necessary to speedily dispense justice.

Just as election is key to a democratic government deserving a special election tribunal, banks are key to the economy and the economy is the pillar of the country therefore deserving of a special court to protect it against frauds.

It is pertinent to note that a special court is not a licence for disregard to the rule of law. The constitutional guarantees to affair trial as contained in section 36 of the Constitution would be adhered to. This provision has guided criminal trials in all the special courts that are in existence in our legal system.

All the legal and institutional frameworks that have been put in place to check bank frauds need to be complemented by the establishment of a special court.

Chapter 12

INTRODUCTION TO ISLAMIC BANKING

INTRODUCTION

Islamic banking, also known as Sharia-compliant banking, has been gaining popularity in Nigeria in recent years. With a predominantly Muslim population, the demand for Islamic banking services has been on the rise. In this paper.

Islamic banking is a banking system that operates in accordance with Islamic law, also known as Sharia. The Sharia prohibits the charging of interest or *riba*, as it is considered unethical and exploitative. Instead, Islamic banks operate on the basis of profit and loss sharing (PLS), where the bank and the customer share the profits or losses of a business venture. This ensures that the bank and the customer have a mutually beneficial relationship and share the risks involved.

In Nigeria, Islamic banking was introduced in 2011 with the establishment of Jaiz Bank, the first Islamic bank in the country. Since then, other Islamic banks such as Stanbic IBTC Bank and Sterling Bank have also introduced Islamic banking services to cater to the growing demand. These banks offer a range of Sharia-compliant products and services such as current accounts, savings accounts, and financing for businesses and individuals.

One of the main advantages of Islamic banking is that it promotes ethical and socially responsible financing. As the Sharia prohibits the financing of activities that are harmful to society, such as gambling and alcohol, Islamic banks are more likely to invest in socially responsible projects such as renewable energy and affordable housing. This promotes sustainable development and contributes to the overall well-being of the society.

Another advantage of Islamic banking is that it promotes financial inclusion. As the PLS system allows for greater flexibility and risk-sharing, Islamic banks are more likely to offer financing to small and medium-sized enterprises (SMEs) and individuals who may not have access to traditional banking services. This promotes economic growth and reduces poverty by providing financial support to those who need it the most.

Despite the advantages of Islamic banking, there are also some challenges that need to be addressed. One of the main challenges is the lack of awareness and understanding of Islamic banking among the general population. Many people are not aware of the principles and practices of Islamic banking, which hinders its growth and adoption.

Another challenge is the lack of regulatory framework for Islamic banking in Nigeria. While the Central Bank of Nigeria has issued guidelines for Islamic banking, there is a need for a comprehensive regulatory framework to ensure the stability and growth of the industry.

Islamic banking has the potential to promote ethical and socially responsible financing, financial inclusion, and economic growth in Nigeria. With the growing demand for Sharia-compliant banking services, it is important for the government and financial institutions to address the challenges and provide a conducive environment for the growth of Islamic banking in Nigeria.

MAJOR STATUTES RELATING TO ISLAMIC BANKING IN NIGERIA

The following statutes provide a legal framework for the operation of Islamic banking in Nigeria and ensure that Islamic financial institutions are subject to the same regulatory and legal requirements as traditional financial institutions

i. Banks and Other Financial Institutions Act (BOFIA) 1991: This Act regulates all banking and financial institutions in Nigeria, including Islamic banks.
ii. Central Bank of Nigeria (CBN) Guidelines for Islamic Banking in Nigeria: This guideline was issued by the CBN to provide a regulatory framework for the operation of Islamic banking in Nigeria.

iii. Companies and Allied Matters Act (CAMA) 2020: This Act provides for the registration and regulation of companies in Nigeria, including Islamic financial institutions.
iv. Investment and Securities Act (ISA) 2007: This Act regulates the issuance, offering, and trading of securities in Nigeria, including *Sukuk* bonds, which are Sharia-compliant financial instruments.
v. National Insurance Commission (NAICOM) Guidelines on Takaful (Islamic insurance) Operations in Nigeria: This guideline was issued by NAICOM to provide a regulatory framework for the operation of Takaful insurance in Nigeria.
vi. Pension Reform Act (PRA) 2014: This Act regulates the operations of pension funds in Nigeria, including Sharia-compliant pension schemes.
vii. Nigerian Tax Laws: The Nigerian tax laws also apply to Islamic financial institutions, and they are subject to the same tax obligations as traditional financial institutions.

HISTORY TO ISLAMIC BANKING

Islamic banking in Nigeria has a relatively recent history that can be traced back to the early 2000s. Nigeria, with its significant Muslim population, sought to establish an alternative banking system that adhered to Islamic principles and catered to the financial needs of Muslims.

The establishment of Islamic banking in Nigeria was primarily driven by the Jaiz Bank, which was licensed as a full-fledged Islamic bank in 2011. This milestone marked a significant advancement for Islamic finance in Nigeria. Jaiz Bank operates in accordance with Islamic principles, such as the prohibition of interest (*riba*) and investment in sectors deemed unethical or non-compliant by Islamic law.

The Islamic banking industry in Nigeria has experienced notable growth since its inception. Several conventional banks in the country have also introduced Islamic banking windows, which offer Shariah-compliant financial products and services alongside their existing offerings.

The Central Bank of Nigeria (CBN) has played a pivotal role in promoting Islamic banking in the country. It has developed guidelines and frameworks to regulate the operations of Islamic banks and has encouraged conventional banks to establish Islamic banking windows. Additionally, the CBN has issued *Sukuk* (Islamic bonds) and Takaful (Islamic insurance) guidelines, facilitating the development of these sectors.

Nigeria's Islamic banking sector provides a variety of financial products, including *Murabaha* (cost-plus financing), *Musharaka* (partnership), *Ijarah* (leasing), and *Mudarabah* (profit-sharing). These products cater to the needs of individuals, businesses, and the government, offering alternatives to conventional banking services.

The growth of Islamic banking in Nigeria has fueled demand for Islamic finance education and awareness. Various institutions now offer Islamic finance courses, and professionals with expertise in Shariah-compliant finance are emerging.

Islamic banking in Nigeria continues to evolve, and the country remains determined to develop its Islamic finance industry further. The focus is now on expanding the reach of Islamic banking services, enhancing regulatory frameworks, and fostering innovation in the sector to meet the increasing demand for Shariah-compliant financial solutions.

RELEVANCE OF ISLAMIC BANKING

The following are some of the mints of Islamic Banking in Nigeria:

i. Catering to the Muslim population: Nigeria has a substantial Muslim population, and Islamic banking provides a financial system that aligns with their religious beliefs. It offers Muslims a viable alternative to conventional banking, allowing them to manage their finances in a manner consistent with Islamic principles.
ii. Enhancing financial inclusion: Islamic banking plays a crucial role in promoting financial inclusion by providing accessible financial services to individuals who previously may have been excluded due to religious reasons or preference. It allows Muslims to participate in the formal financial system and access a range of Shariah-compliant products and services.
iii. Ethical and socially responsible finance: Islamic finance emphasizes ethical and socially responsible practices. In Islamic banking, interest-based transactions (*riba*) and investing in sectors considered morally

unacceptable (such as gambling, alcohol, or pork) are prohibited. Therefore, Islamic banking promotes responsible financing and encourages investments in sectors that have a positive social impact.

iv. Infrastructure development: Islamic banking, through the issuance of *Sukuk* (Islamic bonds), has played a role in financing infrastructure projects in Nigeria. These bonds raise funds from investors in a Shariah-compliant manner and direct the proceeds towards infrastructure development, contributing to the country's economic growth and development.

v. Economic diversification: Islamic banking provides an avenue for diversifying Nigeria's financial sector. By introducing Shariah-compliant financial products and services, the sector attracts new market players and encourages competition, leading to innovation and a broader range of choice for consumers.

vi. Supporting small and medium-sized enterprises (SMEs): Islamic banking offers financing solutions, such as Musharaka (partnership) and Mudarabah (profit-sharing), which are particularly suited for SMEs. These products provide alternative financing options for startups, entrepreneurs, and small businesses, helping to stimulate economic growth and job creation.

vii. Global integration: Islamic banking in Nigeria aligns with the global Islamic finance industry, connecting the country to the international Islamic banking network. This fosters international economic integration, provides opportunities for cross-border investments and collaborations, and positions Nigeria as a participant in the global Islamic finance market.

In summary, Islamic banking in Nigeria is relevant in terms of catering to the needs of the Muslim population, promoting financial inclusion, encouraging ethical finance, supporting infrastructure development, diversifying the financial sector, supporting SMEs, and facilitating global integration.

NEED FOR ISLAMIC BANKING IN NIGERIA

i. Religious compliance: Nigeria has a significant Muslim population, and Islamic banking provides a financial system that adheres to Shariah principles. It addresses the need for Muslims to conduct their financial transactions in a manner consistent with Islamic beliefs, such as the prohibition of interest (*riba*) and involvement in unethical activities.

ii. Financial inclusivity: Islamic banking recognizes and caters to the financial needs of individuals who may have previously been excluded from the conventional banking system due to their religious beliefs or preferences. It helps to promote financial inclusion by providing accessible and inclusive financial services to a wider population.

iii. Ethical and socially responsible finance: Islamic banking operates on the principles of ethical and socially responsible finance. It avoids interest-based transactions and prohibits investments in sectors considered morally unacceptable, such as gambling, alcohol, or pork. This appeals to individuals and businesses seeking ethical investment and responsible financial practices.

iv. Alternative banking options: Islamic banking provides an alternative to conventional banking services, offering a diverse range of Shariah-compliant products and services. This gives individuals and businesses more choices and allows them to select financial products that align with their values and beliefs.

v. Infrastructure financing: Islamic banking facilitates infrastructure financing through the issuance of *Sukuk* (Islamic bonds), which direct funds towards infrastructure development in a Shariah-compliant manner. This is crucial in a country like Nigeria, where infrastructure development is vital for economic growth and overall development.

vi. SME support: Islamic banking offers financing solutions specifically tailored to the needs of small and medium-sized enterprises (SMEs). Products such as *Musharaka* (partnership) and Mudarabah (profit-sharing) can provide alternative financing options to support the growth and development of SMEs, which play a vital role in the Nigerian economy.

vii. Economic diversification: Islamic banking provides an avenue for diversifying Nigeria's financial sector. It attracts new market players, encourages competition, and fosters innovation. This diversification can contribute to a more resilient and inclusive financial system and support efforts to reduce reliance on conventional banking practices.

In conclusion, the need for Islamic banking in Nigeria arises from the desire for religious compliance, financial inclusivity, ethical finance, alternative banking options, infrastructure financing, support for SMEs, and economic diversification. It addresses the specific needs and preferences of individuals and businesses seeking Shariah-compliant financial services, promoting a more inclusive and diverse financial landscape in the country.

LANDMARK CASES ON ISLAMIC BANKING IN NIGERIA

Islamic Banking is relatively new in Nigeria, however, there are a number of landmark cases as follows:

i. *Stanbic IBTC Bank Plc* v. *Financial Reporting Council of Nigeria (FRCN) & The Central Bank of Nigeria (CBN)*: This case involved a legal dispute over the recognition and treatment of Islamic banking products by Nigerian regulatory authorities. The judgment clarified the legal framework and regulatory framework of Islamic banking in Nigeria.

ii. *Jaiz Bank Plc* v. *Abdul-Raheem Ahmed Zakari & Anor*: This case was brought before the National Industrial Court of Nigeria and involved issues related to employment discrimination based on religious beliefs within an Islamic banking institution. It explored the legal implications and rights of employees in Islamic banking institutions.

iii. *The Central Bank of Nigeria (CBN)* v. *Nigerian Deposit Insurance Corporation (NDIC):* This case pertained to the regulatory framework for Islamic banking in Nigeria, including matters related to licensing, supervision, and the financial stability of Islamic banks. The judgment provided insights into the CBN's role in regulating Islamic banking operations in Nigeria.

APPENDICES

Appendix 1

BANKS AND OTHER FINANCIAL INSTITUTIONS ACT
ARRANGEMENT OF SECTIONS
PART I
Banks

Establishment of Banks, etc.

SECTION

1. Functions, powers and duties of the Central Bank of Nigeria
2. Banking business
3. Application for grand of licence
4. Investment and release of prescribed minimum paid-up share capital
5. Power to revoke or vary conditions of licence
6. Opening and closing of branches
7. Restructuring, re-organisation, merger and disposal, etc. of bank
8. Operation of foreign banks in Nigeria
9. Minimum paid-tip share capital of banks and compliance with minimum paid-up share capital requirement.
10. Shareholder's voting rights to be proportional to shareholding
11. Restriction of legal proceedings in respect of shares held in the name of another
12. Revocation of licence
13. Minimum capital ratio
14. Non-compliance with capital ratio requirement
15. Minimum holding of cash reserves, specified liquid assets, special deposits and stabilization securities.

Duties of Banks

16. Maintenance of reserve fund
17. Restriction on dividend
18. Disclosure of interest by directors, managers and officers
19. Prohibition of employment of certain persons and inter-locking directorship, etc.
20. Restriction on certain banking activities
21. Acquisition of shares in small and medium-scale industries, agricultural enterprises and venture capital companies
22. Restriction on operations of merchant banks
23. Display of interest rates

Books of Account

Supervision

General and Supplemental

Miscellaneous Matters

BANKS AND OTHER FINANCIAL INSTITUTIONS ACT

An Act to regulate Banking and other Financial Institutions and for mattes connected therewith

[1991 No. 25] ;

[20th June, 1991]

[Commencement]

Part I

Banks

Establishment of Banks, etc.

1. Functions, power and duties of the Central Bank of Nigeria

(1) The Central Bank of Nigeria (hereafter in this Act referred to as the "the Bank") shall have the functions and powers conferred and the duties imposed on it under this Act, subject to the overall supervision of the Minister.

[1997 No. 4]

(2) The Bank shall in addition to the functions and powers conferred on it by this Act, have the functions and powers conferred and the duties imposed on the Bank by the Central Bank of Nigeria Act.

[1997 No. 4. Cap. C4.]

(3) The Bar may authorise or instruct any officer or employee of the Bank to perform any of the functions, exercise any powers, or discharge any of its duties under this Act.

(4) The Bank may, either generally or in any particular case, appoint any person who is not an officer or employee of the Bank, to render such assistance as my specify in the exercise of its powers, the performance of its functions, or the discharge of duties under this Act, or exercise, perform or discharge the functions and duties on behalf of and in the name of the Bank.

(5) For the purpose of this Act, a person shall be deemed to be receiving features as deposits.

(a) If the person accepts deposits from the general public as a features of its business of it issues an advertisement or solicits for such deposit.

(b) Notwithstanding that it receives moneys as deposits which are limited to fixed amounts or that certificates or other instrument are issued in respect of any such amounts providing for the repayment to the holder thereof either conditionally or unconditionally of the amount of the deposits are specified or unspecified dates or for the payment of interest in dividend on the amounts deposited specified intervals or otherwise, or that such certificates a transferable.

(6) Notwithstanding anything contained in this section to the contrary, the receiving moneys against any issue of shares and debentures offered to the public in accordance with any enactment in force within the Federation shall not to constitute receiving moneys deposits for the purpose if this Act.

2. Banking Business

(1) No person shall carry on any banking business in Nigeria except if it is company duly incorporated in Nigeria and holds a valid banking licence under this Act.

(2) Any person who transacts banking business without a valid licence under this Act is guilty of an offence and liable to imprisonment for a term not exceeding ten years to a fine of ₦2.000.000, or to both such imprisonment and fine.

[1998 No. 38]

3. Application for Gran Licence

(1) Any person desiring to undertake banking business in Nigeria shall apply in writing to the Governor for the grant of licence and shall accompany the application with the following

(a) A feasibility report of the proposed bank;

(b) A draft copy of the memorandum and articles of association of the proposed bank;

(c) A list of the shareholders, directors and principal officers of the proposed bank and their particulars;

(d) The prescribed application feed; and

(e) Such other information, documents and reports as the Bank may, from time to time, specify

(2) After the applicant has provided all such information, documents and report as the Bank may require under subsection (1) of the section, the shareholders of the proposed bank shall deposit with the Bank a sum equal to the minimum paid-up share capital that may be applicable under section 9 of this Act.

(3) Upon the payment of the sum referred to in subsection (2) of this section, the Governor may issue a licence with or without conditions or refuse to issue a licence and the Governor need not give any reasons for the refusal.

(4) Where an application for licence is granted, the Bank shall give written of that fact to the applicant and the licence fee shall be paid.

(5) An application for a licence shall be forwarded to the Governor and all licenses to be issued shall be with the prior approval of the Minister.

(1997 No.4)

4. Investment and Release of Prescribed Minimum Paid-up share capital

The Bank may invest any amount deposited with its pursuant to section 3(2) of this Act in treasury bills or such other securities until such a time as the Governor shall decide whether or not to grant a licence, and where the licence is not granted the Bank shall repay the sum deposited to the applicant, together with the investment income after deducting administrative expenses and tax on the income.

5. Power to Revoke or Vary Conditions of Licence

(1) The bank vary or revoke any conditions subject to which a licence was granted or may impose fresh or additional conditions to the grant of a licence.

(1998 No. 38)

(2) Where the grant of licence is subject to conditions, the bank shall comply with those conditions to the satisfaction of the Bank within such period as the Bank may deem appropriate in the circumstances.

(3) Any bank which fails to comply with any of the condition of its licence is guilty of offence under this section and shall be liable on conviction to a fine not exceeding ₦450,000 for each day ring which the condition is not complied with.

(4) Where the Governor proposes to vary, revoke or impose fresh or additional conditions on a licence, eh shall, before exercising such power, give notice of the intention to the bank concerned and give the bank an opportunity to make representation to him thereon.

(5) Any bank which fails to comply with any fresh or additional conditions imposed in relation to its licence is guilty of offence and liable on conviction to fine not exceeding ₦500,000 and to an additional fine of ₦45,000 for each day during which the offence continues.

6. Opening and Closing of Branches

(1) No bank may open or close any branch office anywhere within or outside Nigeria except with the prior consent in writing of the Bank

(2) Any bank which contravenes the provisions of subsection (1) of this section in guilty of offence and liable to fine a not exceeding ₦2,000,000 and the closure in case of the opening of a branch office and the re-opening in the case of in closure of a branch office and in addition to a fine of ₦100,000 for each day during which the offence continues.

(1998 No. 38)

7. Restructuring, Re-organisation, Mergers and Disposal, etc. of Bank

(1) Except with the prior consent of the Governor, no ban shall enter into an agreement or arrangement

(a) Which results in a change in the control of the bank

(b) For the sale, disposal or transfer howsoever, of the whole or any part of the business of the bank;

(c) For the amalgamation or merger of the bank with any other persons

(d) For the reconstruction of the bank

(e) To employ a management agent or to transfer its business to any such agent.

(2) Any person who contravenes the provisions of subsection (1) of this section is guilty of an offence and liable to a fine not exceeding

₦1,000,000 and in the case of a continuing offence to an additional fine of N10,000 for each day during which the offence continues.

(1998 No. 38)

8. Operation of Foreign Banks in Nigeria

(1) Except with the prior approval of the Bank, no foreign bank shall operate branch offices or representative office in Nigeria.

(1998 No. 38)

(2) The bank may, subject to such conditions as it may impose, from time to time, grant to any bank registered in Nigeria or a foreign bank a licence to undertake off-shore banking business from Nigeria.

(1998 No. 38)

(3) Subject to the provision of subsection (1) of this section, nothing in the provisions of the Nigerian Investment Promotion Commission Act or any other law or enactment shall be construed as authorising any pa-sort, whether as a citizen of Nigeria or a non-Nigeria, to carry on any banking business in without a valid banking licence by the bank under this Act.

(1998 No. 38)

(4) Any person who contravenes the provisions of subsection (1) or (3) of this section is guilty of an offence and liable to conviction to a fine not exceeding ₦1,000,000 and in the case of continuing offence to an additional fine of ₦10,000 for each day during the offence continues.

(1998 No. 38)

9. Minimum Paid-Up Share Capital of Banks and Compliance with Minimum Paid-Up Share Capital Requirement

(1) The bank shall, from time to time determines the minimum paid-up share capital requirement of each category of Banks licensed under this Act.

(1998 No. 38)

(2) Any failure to comply with the provisions of this section of this Act within such period as may be determined by the Bank, from time to time, shall be a ground for the revocation of any licence issued pursuant to the provisions of this Act or any other Act repealed by it.

(1998 No. 38)

10. Shareholder's Voting Rights to be Proportional to Shareholding

Notwithstanding the provisions of the Companies and Allied Matters Act or any agreement or contract, the voting rights of every shareholder in a bank shall be proportional to his contribution to the paid-up share capital of the bank.

(Cap. C20)

11. Restriction of Legal Proceedings in Respect of Shares Held in the Name of Another.

Notwithstanding anything contained in any law or in any contract or instrument, no suit or other proceedings shall be maintained against any persons registered das the holder of a share in a bank on the ground that the title to the said share tested in any person other than the registered holder.

Provided that nothing in this section shall bear suit or other proceedings on behalf of minor or person suffering from any mental illness on the ground that the registered holder holds the share on behalf of the minor or person suffering from the mental illness.

12. Revocation of Licence

The Governor may, with the approval of the Board of Directors and by notice published in the Gazette, revoke any licence granted under this Act if a bank;

(a) Ceases to carry on in Nigeria the type of banking business for which the licence was issued for any continuous period of six months or period aggregating six months during a continuous period of twelve months;
(b) Goes into laudation or is wound up or otherwise dissolved;
(c) Fails to fulfil or comply with any condition subject to which the licence was granted.
(d) Has insufficient assets to meet is liabilities
(e) Fails to comply with any obligation imposed upon it by under this Act or the Central Bank of Nigeria Act.

13. Minimum Capital Ration

(1) A bank shall maintain, at all times, capital funds impaired by tosses, in such ration to all or any assets or to all or any liabilities or to both such assets and of the bank and all its offices in and outside Nigeria as may be specified by the Bank.
(2) Any bank which fails to observe any such specified ratio may be by the Bank from
(a) Advertising for a accepting new deposits;
(b) Granting credit and making investment
(c) Paying cash dividends to shareholders

(3) In addition, the bank may be required to draw within a specified time a capital reconstitution plan acceptable to the Bank.

14. Non-Compliance with Capital Ratio Requirement

(1) Failure to comply with the provisions of section 13 of this Act may constitute a ground for the revocation of the licence of the Bank under this Act.

(2) Where the Bank proposes to revoke the licence of any bank pursuant to subsection (1) of this section, the Bank shall give notice of its intention to the bank and the bank may within 30 days make representation (if any) to the Bank in respect thereof.

(1999 No. 40)

15. Minimum Holding of Cash Reserves, Specified Liquid Assets, Special Deposits and Stabilisation Securities

(1) Every bank shall maintain with the Bank cash reserves, and special deposits and hold specified liquid assets or stabilisation securities, as the case may be, not less in amount than as may, from time to time be prescribed by the Bank or virtue of section 40 of the Central Bank of Nigeria Act.

(Cap. C4.)

(2) Where both assets and liabilities are due from and to other banks, they be offset accordingly, and any surplus of assets or liabilities shall be included or deducted, as the case may be, in computing specified liquid assets.

(3) In the case of the long-term advances to a bank or by an overseas branch or office of a bank, the advances may, with the approval of the Bank, be excluded from the demand liabilities of the Bank.

(4) Every bank Shall

(a) Furnish within a reasonable time any information required by the Bank to satisfy the Bank that the bank is observing the requirements of subsection (1) of this section;

(b) Not allow its holding of cash reserves, specified liquid assets, special deposits and stabilisation securities to be less than the amount which may, from time to time, be prescribed by the Bank;

(c) Not during the period of any deficiency, grant or permit increases in advances, loans or credit facilities to any person without the prior approval in writing of the Bank.

(5) Any bank which fails to comply with any of the provisions of subsection (4) of this section is guilty of an offence and liable to fine of

(a) In the case of paragraph (a) ₦500,000 for every month during which a default under that paragraph (a) exists;

(1999 No. 40)

(b) In the case of paragraph (b) ₦500,000 for each month of the offence.

(1999 No. 38)

(c) In the case of paragraph (c) ₦500,000 for each month of the offence.

(1999 No. 38)

And the Bank may also, during the period when the bank fails to comply with any of the requirement of subsection (4) as aforesaid, withdraw any privileges or facilities that are normally accorded the Bank.

(6) For purpose of this section, specified liquid assets, provided they are freely transferable and free from any alien or charge of any kind, shall, without prejudice to the provisions of section 40 of the Central Bank of Nigeria Act 1991, consists of all or any of the following:

(i) Currency notes and coins which are legal tender in Nigeria.

(ii) Balances at the Bank

(iii) Net balances at any licensed bank (excluding uncleared effects) and money at call in Nigeria;

(iv) Treasury bills and treasury certificates issued by the Federal Government

(v) Inland bills of exchange and promissory notes rediscountable at the bank;

(vi) Stocks issued by the Federal Government with such dates of maturity in mat be approved by the Bank

(vii) Negotiable certificates of deposit approved by the Bank; and

(viii) Such otter negotiable instruments as may, from time to time be approved by the Bank for the purpose of this subsection.

Duties of Banks

16. Maintenance of Reserve Fund

(1) Every bank shall maintain a reserve funds and shall, out of its net profits for each year (after the provision made for taxation) and before any dividend is declared, where the amount of the reserve fund is

(a) Less than the paid-up share capital, transfer to the reserve fund a sum equal to not less than per cent of the net profits; or

(b) Equal to or excess of the paid-up share capital, transfer to the reserve fund sum equal to not less than fifteen per cent of the net profit;

(c) Provided no transfer under this subsection shall be made until all identifiable have been made good.

(2) Any bank which falls to comply with the provisions of subsection (1) of the section is guilty of an offence and liable on conviction to a fine of ₦500,000.

(3) Notwithstanding paragraph (a) and (b) of subsection (1) of this section, the Bank may from time to time, specify different proportions of the net profits of each year, being either lesser or greater than the proportion specified in paragraph (a) and (b), to be transferred to the reserve fund fo a bank for the purpose of ensuring that the amount of the reserve fund of such bank is sufficient for the purpose of its business and adequate in relation of lost liabilities.

17. Restriction on Dividend

(1) No bank shall pay dividends on its share until

(a) All its preliminary expenses, organisational expenses shares selling commission, brokerage, amount of losses incurred and other capitalized expenses not represented by tangible assets have been completely written off;

(b) Adequate provisions have been made to the satisfaction of the Bank for actual and contingent losses on risk assets, liabilities, off-balance sheet commitments and such unearned incomes as are derivable therefrom;

(c) It has complied with any capital ration requirement as specified by the Bank pursuant to section 13 (1) of this Act.

(2) Any director, manager or officer who fails to comply with the requirements of this section of this Act is guilty of an offence are liable on conviction to a fine of five per cent of the dividend paid or to imprisonment for a term not exceeding three years or to both such fine and imprisonment.

(1998 No. 38)

18. Disclosure of Interest by Directors, Managers and Officers

(1) No manager or any other officer of a bank shall

(a) In any manner whatsoever, whether directly or indirectly, have personal interest in any advance, loan or credit facility; and if he has any such personal interest, he shall declare the nature of his interest to the bank;

(b) Grand any advance, loan or credit facility to any person, unless it is authorised in accordance with the rules and regulations of the bank;

and where adequate security is required by such rules and regulations such security shall, prior to the grant, be obtained for the advance, loan or credit facility and shall be deposited with the bank;

(c) Benefit as a result of any advance, loan or credit facility granted by the bank.

(2) Any manager or officer who contravenes or fails to comply with any of the provisions of subsection (1) of this section is guilty of an offence under this section and liable on conviction to a fine of ₦4,100,000 or to imprisonment for a term of three years; and in addition, any gains or benefits accruing to any person convicted under this section by reason of such contravention, shall be forfeited to the Federal Government, and the gains or benefit shall vest accordingly in that Government.

(3) It shall be the duty of a director a bank who is in any way, whether directly or indirectly, interested in the grant of an advance, loin or credit facility with the bank to declare the nature of his interest at a meeting of the Board of Directors of the Bank.

(4) In the case of a proposed "advance, loan or credit facility, the declaration, required by this section of this act shall be made at the meeting of the Board of Directors of the Bank at which the request for the advance, loan or credit facility is first taken into consideration or if the director was not present on the date of the meeting at which the matter was discussed he shall state his interest in the proposed advance, 'loan or credit facility at the next meeting of the board of directors of the Bank held after: he becomes so interested, and in a case; where the director becomes interested in any advance, loan or credit facility after it is granted, the declaration shall be made at the first meeting of the board of directors of the bank held after he becomes so interested.

(1998 No. 38)

(5) For the purpose of this section of this Act, a general notice given to the leans of directors of a bank by a director of the effect that he is a member of company or firm seeking an advance, loan or credit facility for the Bank shall be as a declaration of his interest in the grant of the advance, loan or facility which may, after the date of the notice, be granted to that r or firm, and shall be deemed to be a sufficient declaration of interest in to any such advance, loan or credit facility so granted.

Provided that any such notice shall not have effect unless it is given at a meeting of the board of directors of the bank which shall be required to do all things reasonably necessary to ensure that it is brought up and read at the next meeting of the board of directors of the bank after it is so given.

(1998 No. 38)

(6) The provisions of subsection (3) of this section shall not apply in any case.

(a) Where the interest of the director consists only of being a person holding less than five per cent of the shares of the company which is seeking and advance, loan or credit facility from the bank; or

(b) If the interest of the director may properly be regarded by the Banks as immaterial.

(1998 No. 38)

(7) For the purpose of subsection (5) of this section, a general notice given to the board of directors of a bank by a director shall be deemed to be a sufficient declaration of interest in relation to any advance, loan or credit.

(a) The notice specifies the nature and extent of his interest in the company or firm;

(b) Such interest is not different in nature to or greater in extent than the nature and extent specified in the notice at the time any advance, loan or credit facility is made; and

(c) The notice is given at the meeting of the board of directors of the bank or the director takes reasonable steps to ensure that it is brought up and at the next meeting of the board of directors of the bank after it is given.

(1998 No. 38)

(8) Every director of a bank who holds any office or possesses any property whether directly or indirectly duties or interests might be created in conflict with his duties or interest as a director of a bank, shall declare at a meeting of the board of directors of the Bank, the fact and the nature, and extent of the interest.

(9) The declaration referred to in subsection (8) of this section shall be acquired to be made at the first meeting of the board of directors of the bank held.

(a) After he becomes a director of the bank; or

(b) If already a director, after he came into possession of the property

(1998 No. 38)

(10) The secretary of the bank shall cause to be brought up and read any declaration made under subsection (3) or (8) of this section at the next meeting of the board of directors of the bank after it is made and shall record any declaration made under this section of this Act in the minutes of the meeting at which it was made or at the meeting at which it was brought up and read.

(1998 No. 38)

(11) Any director who contravene the provision of subsection (3) or (8) of this section is guilty of an offence liable on conviction to a fine of ₦100,000 or imprisonment for a term of three years or to both such fine and imprisonment.

(1998 No. 38)

19. Prohibition of Employment of Certain Persons and Interacting Directorship, etc.

(1) No bank shall

(a) Employ or continue the employment of any person who is or at any time has been adjudged bankrupt or has suspended payment to or has compounded with his creditors or who is or has been convicted by a court for an offence involving fraud or dishonesty, or professional misconduct;

(b) Be managed by a management agent except as may be approved by the Bank.

(2) Except with the approval of the Bank, no bank shall have as a director any person who is a director of

(a) Any other bank;

(b) Companies which among themselves are entitled to exercise voting rights in excess often per cent for the total voting rights of all the shareholders of the bank.

(3) No bank shall be managed by a person who is

(a) A director of any other company not being a subsidiary of the bank, or

(b) Engaged in any other business or vocation

(4) Every director of a bank shall sign a code of conduct in such form or manner as the Bank may, from time to time prescribe.

(5) The Chief Executive of a bank shall cause all the officers of the bank to sign code of conduct as may be approved by the board of directors.

20. Restrictions on Certain Banking Activities

(1) A bank shall not, without the prior approval in writing of the bank, grant

(a) To any person any advance, loan or credit facility or give any financial guarantee or incur any liability on behalf of any person so that the total value of the person is at any time more than twenty per cent of the shareholders fund unimpaired by losses or in the case of a bank not more than fifty per cent of its shareholders fund by losses; and for the purpose of this paragraph all advances, loans or credit facilities extended to any person shall be aggregated and shall include all advances, loans or credit facilities extended to any subsidiaries or associates of a body corporate.

Provided that the provisions of this paragraph shall not apply to transactions banks or between branches of a bank or to the purchase of clean or documentary bills of exchange, telegraphic transfers or documents of title to goods the holder of which is entitled to payment for exports from Nigeria or to advance made against such bills transfers or documents;

(b) Any advances, loans or credit facilities against the security of its own shares or the bank's rules and regulations and where any such rules and regulations required adequate security, such security shall be provided or, as the case may require, deposited with the bank.

(2) A bank shall not, without the prior approval in writing of the Bank

(a) Permit to be outstanding, unsecured advances, loans or unsecured credit facilities of an aggregate amount in excess of ₦50,000.

(1999 No. 40)

(i) To its directors or any of them whether such advances, loans or credit facilities are obtained by its directors jointly or severally.

(ii) To any firm, partnership or private company in which it or any one or more of its directors is interested as director/partner, manager or agent or any individual firm, partnership or private company of which any of its directors is a guarantor;

(iii) To any public or private company in which it or any one or more of its directors, jointly or severally maintains shareholding of not less than five per cent either directly or indirectly.

(b) Permit to be outstanding to its officers and employee, unsecured advances, loans or unsecured credit facilities, which in the aggregate for any one officer or employee, is an amount which exceeds one year's emolument to such officer of employee;

(c) Engage, whether on its own account or a commission basis, in wholesale or retail trade, including the import or, export trade except in so far as may exceptionally be necessary in the course of the banking operations and services of that bank or in the course of the satisfaction of debts due to its; so however that nothing in this paragraph shall be construed as precluding a bank from Undertaking equipment leasing business or debt factoring provided that the foregoing provisions of this paragraph shall not apply to a bank in the circumstances permitted under section 21 of this Act;

(d) Without prejudice to the provision of section 21 of this Act, acquire or hold any part of the share capital of any financial or commercial or other undertaking, except-

(i) Any shareholding approved by the bank in any company set, up for the purpose of promoting the development of the money market or capital market in Nigeria or of improving the financial machinery for financial economic development;

(ii) Any shareholding approved by bank pursuant to sub-paragraph (1) of this paragraph, the aggregate value of which does not ar. Time exceed twenty-five per cent of the sum of paid-up share capital and statutory reserves of that bank;

(iii) All shareholding required by a merchant bank while managing an equity issue;

Provided that the aggregate value of such acquisition does not at any time exceed the sum of the paid-up share capital of that merchant bank or ten per cent of its total assets, excluding contract items, whichever is higher and that his paragraph shall not apply to any nominate company of a bank which deals in stock or shares for or on behalf of the bank's customers of clients or majority interest acquired by a merchant bank in a company while managing an equity issue;

(e) Remit, either in whole or in part, the debts owed to it by any of its directors or past director;

(f) Purchase, sell, dispose, acquire or lease any real estate for whatever purpose.

(3) Notwithstanding the foregoing provisions of this section, a bank may secure debt on any real or other property, and in default of repayment, may acquire such property and exercise any power of sale as may be provided for in any instrument or, by law prescribed, immediately upon such default or as soon thereafter as may be deemed proper.

(4) In paragraph (a) and (b) of subsection (2) of this section, the expressions "unsecured advances and loans" or "unsecured credit

facilities", mean advances, loans or credit facilities made without security, or, it respect of any advances, loans or credit value of the assets constituting the security; any part thereof which at any time exceeds the market on established market value, the value of the assets as determined on the basis of a valuation approved by the bank.

(5) In paragraphs (a) and (e) subsection (2) of this section, the expression "director", includes director's wife, husband, father, mother, brother, sister, soft daughter and their spouses.

(6) All the directors of a bank shall be liable jointly and severally to indemnify the bank against any loss arising from any loss arising from any unsecured advances, loans or credit facilities under paragraph (a) of subsection (2) of this section.

(7) Any director, manager of officer who fails to comply with the requirements of this section of this Act is guilty of an offence and liable on conviction to a fine not exceeding ₦100,000 or to imprisonment for a term of three years and shall in addition be required to repay the loan or forfeit his known assets in lieu of the unpaid loan.

(1998 No. 38)

(8) Any bank which after the commencement of this Act, enters into any transaction which is inconsistent with the requirement of subsection (7) of this section is guilty of an offence and liable on conviction to a fine of ₦1,000,000.

(1998 No. 38)

(9) Any bank which, after the commencement of this Act, enters into any transaction which is inconsistent with any of the provisions of subsection (1) or (2) of this section, is guilty of an offence and liable on conviction to pay the Bank a fine of ₦100,000 fro each day during which the transaction continues.

21. Acquisitions of Shares in Small and Medium Scale Industries, Agricultural Enterprise and Venture Capital Companies

(1) A bank may acquire or hold part of the share capital of any agricultural industrial or venture capital company subject to the following conditions, that is

(a) The venture capital company is set up for the purpose of promoting the development of indigenous technology or a new venture in Nigeria:

(b) The shareholding by the bank is in small or medium scale industry, and agricultural enterprises as defined by the Bank;

(c) The shareholding by the bank, in any medium scale industry, agricultural enterprises or venture capital company or any other business approved by the Bank shall not be more than ten per cent of the bank's shareholding fund unimpaired by losses and shall not exceed forty per cent of the paid-up share capital of the company, the shares of which are acquired or held;
(d) The aggregate value of the equity participation of the bank in all enterprises pursuant to this section does not at any time exceed, in fund unimpaired by losses or, in the case of merchant bank, not more than fifty per cent of its shareholders fund unimpaired by losses:

Provided that a bank may hold shares acquired in the course of the satisfaction of any debt owed to it.

(2) Without prejudice to the provisions of subsection (1) of this section, a bank, may hold or acquire share capital of any other business, subject to the approved of the Bank.
(3) Every bank shall, within 21 days of the acquisition of any shareholding pursuant to subsection (1) of this section, given full particulars, thereof to the Bank.
(4) Any thus which fails to comply with the provisions of subsection (3) of this section is guilty of an offence and liable on conviction to a fine of ₦10,000 for each day during which the offence continues.

(1999 No. 40)

22.Restrictions on Operation of Merchant Banks

(1) A merchant bank shall not
(a) Accept any deposit withdrawable by cheque
(b) Accept any deposit below an amount which shall be prescribed, from time to time, the bank;
(c) Hold for more than six months any equity interest acquired in a company while managing an equity issue, except "as stipulated in section 21" of this Act.
(2) Any merchant bank which acts in contravention of or fails to comply with any of the provisions of this section is guilty of an offence and liable to a fine not exceeding $25,000 for each day during with the offence continues.

(1998 No. 38)

23.Display of Interest Rates

(1) Every banks hall display at its offices it lending and deposit interest rates and shall render to the Bank information on such rates as may be specified from time to time by the Bank.

Provided that the provisions of this subsection shall not apply to profit and loss sharing banks.

(2) Any bank in breach of any of the provisions of this section is guilty of an offence and liable to a fine not exceeding $5,000 for every day during which the offence continues.

(1998 No. 38)

Books of Account

24. Proper Books of Account

(1) Every bank shall cause to be kept proper books of account with respect to all the transactions of tire bank.

(2) For the purpose of subsection (1) of this section, proper books of account shall be deemed to be kept with respect to all transactions if such books as are necessary to explain such transactions and give a true and fair view of the state of affairs of a bank, are kept by the bank and are in compliance with the standard as may be prescribed for banks.

(3) The books of account shall be kept at the principal administrative office of a bank and at the branches of each bank in the English Language or any other language approved by the Federal Government.

(4) Where the books, of account kept by a bank with respect to all its transactions are prepared and kept in such a manner that, in the opinion of the bank, they have not been properly prepared and kept, or where a bank renders return in accordance with the provisions of section 25 of this Act, in which the Bank are inaccurate, the Bank may appoint a firm of qualified to prepare proper books of account or renders accurate returns, as the case may be, for the bank and the cost of preparing the accounts and the return shall be borne by the bank.

(5) If any person being a director, manager or officer of a bank

(a) Fails to take all reasonable steps to secure compliance with any of the provisions of this section;

(b) Has by his wilful act been the cause of any default thereof by the bank, he is guilty of an offence and liable, in respect of paragraph (a) of this subsection, to a fine of ₦100,000 and in respect of paragraph (b) of this subsection, to a fine of ₦50,000 or to imprisonment for a term not exceeding ten years or to both such fine and imprisonment.

(1999 No. 40)

25.Returns by Banks

(1) Every bank shall submit to the Bank not later than 28 days after the last day of each month or such other interval as the Bank may specify, a statement showing

(a) The assets and liabilities of the bank; and

(b) An analysis of advances and other assets, at it head office and branches in and outside Nigeria in such from as the Bank may specify, from time to time.

(2) Every bank shall submit such other information, documents, statistics or return as the Bank may deem necessary for the proper understanding of the statements supplied under subsection (1) of this section.

(3) Any bank which fails to comply with any of the requirements of subsection (1) or (2) of this section is, in respect of each such failure, guilty of an offence and liable to a fine not exceeding ₦125,000 for each day during which the offence continues.

(1998 No. 38)

26. Publication of Consolidated Statements

(1) The statement and information submitted by each bank under section 25 of this Act shall be regarded as confidential;

Provided that the Bank shall furnish any such statement or information to any agency of Government as required by law.

(2) Notwithstanding anything in this section, the Bank may prepare, and publish consolidated statements aggregating the statements furnished under section 25 of this Act for each category of banks.

27.Publication of Annual Accounts of Banks

(1) Subject to the prior approval in writing of the Book, a bank shall not later than four months after the end of its financial year

(a) Cause to be published in a daily newspaper printed in and circulating in Nigeria and approved by the Bank;

(b) Exhibit in a conspicuous position in each of its offices and branches in Nigeria; and

(c) Forward to the Bank, copies of the bank's balance' sheet and profit and loss account duly signed and containing the full and correct names of the directors of the bank.

(2) Every published account of a bank, under subsection (1) of this section, shall disclose in detail penalties paid as a result of contravention of the provisions of this Act and the auditor's report shall reflect such contravention.

(3) The balance sheet and profit and loss account of a bank shall bear on their face the report of an approved auditor and shall contain statements on such matters as may be specified by the Bank, from time to time.

(4) For the purpose of subsection (3) of this section, an "approved auditor" shall be an auditor approved for the purpose of section 29 of this Act.

(5) Any bank which fails to comply with any of the requirements of this section is in respect of each such failure guilty of an offence and liable on conviction to a fine of ₦10,000 each day during which the offence continues.

(1999 No. 40)

28. Contents and Form of Account

(1) Every balance sheet and every profit and loss account of a bank shall give a true and fair view of the state of affairs of the bank as at the end of the reporting period.

(2) Every balance sheet and every profit and loss account of a bank forwarded to the Bank in accordance with the provisions of subsection (1) of this section and section 27 (1) (c) of this Act shall comply with the requirements of any circular which has been issued by the Bank thereon.

(3) Any person being a director of any bank who fails to take all reasonable steps to secure compliance with any of the provisions of this section in respect of any accounts is guilty of an offence and liable to pay to the Bank a fine of ₦1,000 or to imprisonment for five years or to both such fine and imprisonment.

(1999 No. 40)

29. Appointment, Power and Report of Approved Auditor

(1) Every bank shall appoint annually a person approved, by the Bank, in this section referred to as "the approved auditor", whose duties shall be to make to the shareholders a report upon the, annual balance

sheet, and profit and loss account of the bank and every such report shall contain statement as to the matters and such other information as may be prescribed, from time to time, by the

(2) For the purpose of this section, the approved auditor shall be an auditor who is
(a) A member of one of the professional bodies recognised in Nigeria;
(b) Approved by the Bank;
(c) Resident in Nigeria; and
(d) Carrying on in Nigeria professional practice as accountant and auditor.
(3) Any person
(a) Having any interest in a bank otherwise than as a expositor; or
(b) Who is a director, officer or agent of a bank; or
(c) Which is a firm in which a director of a bank has any interest as partner or director; or
(d) Who is indebted to a bank, shall not be eligible for appointment as the approved auditor for that bank;
(e) An a person appointed as such auditor who subsequently
(i) Acquires such interest; or
(ii) Becomes a director, officer or agent of the bank; or
(iii) Becomes indebted to a partner in a firm in, which a director of, a bank is interested as partner or director, shall cease to be such auditor.
(4) If any bank fails to appoint an approved auditor under subsection (t); of this section the Bank shall appoint a suitable person for that purpose and shall fix the remuneration to be paid by the bank to such auditor.
(5) Anh approved auditor under this section who acts in contravention of or fails deliberate or negligently to comply with any of the provisions of this section is guilty of an offence and liable on conviction to pay to the Bank a fine of not less than ₦200,000 and not exceeding ₦500,000.

(1997 No.4 1998 No. 38)

(6) The report of the approved auditor shall be read together with the report of the board of directors at the annual general meeting of the shareholders of the bank and two copies of each report together with the auditor's analysis, of bad and doubtful advances in a from specified, from time to time, by the Bank shall be sent to the Bank.
(7) If any auditor appointed under this section, in the course of his duties as an auditor of a bank, is satisfied that;

(a) There has been a contravention of this Act, or that an offence under any other law has been committed by the Bank or any other person; or
(b) Losses have been incurred by the bank which substantially reduced its capital funds; or
(c) Any irregularity which jeopardises the interest of depositors or creditors of the bank, any other irregularity has occurred; or
(d) He is unable to confirm that the claims of the depositors or creditors are covered by the assets of the bank, he shall immediately report the matter to the Bank.
(8) The approved auditor shall forward to the Bank two copies of the domestic reports on the bank's activities not later than three months after the end the bank's financial year.
(9) Any approved auditor under this section who acts in contravention or fails deliberately or negligently to comply with any of the provisions of this section of this Act is guilty of an offence and liable on conviction to a fine not exceeding ₦500,000 and where the approved, auditor is a firm, the individual partner or partners shall in addition be liable on conviction to imprisonment for a term not exceeding five (5) years and to the find required to be paid by the firm under this subsection.
(1998 No. 38)
(10) The appointment of an approved auditor shall not be determined without prior approval of the Ban.
30. Relationship with Specialised Banks and Finance Houses:
(1) As from the commencement of this Act, the Governor shall-have power to examine, from time to time the accounts and other books of the Nigeria Industrial Development Bank, the Nigeria Agricultural and Cooperative Bank, the Nigeria Bank, the Nigeria Bank for Commerce and Industry, the Urban Development Bank, all Mortgage Institutions, Community Banks and the peoples Bank and such other specialized banks.
(2) The Bank shall also have power to examine the accounts of bureaux de change, discount houses and such other financial institutions and in that regard have power to issue reports, from time to time, regarding the accounts of such financial institutions.
(3) The periodic reports and findings of the Bank in relation to the said specialized banks and other financial institutions shall be forwarded to the Head of State through the Minister.

(4) For the purpose of implementation of this section, the specialized banks and other financial institutions shall be treated in the same manner as other banks with respect to the requirements of section 24 of this Act.

(1997 No. 4)

Supervision

31. Appointment and Power of Director of Banking Supervision and other Examiner

(1) There shall be an officer of the Bank who shall be appointed by the Governor to be known as the Director of Banking Supervision or by such other title as the Governor may specify:

(2) The Director of Banking Supervision shall have power to carry out supervisory duties in respect of banks and other financial institutions and specialized banks and or that purpose shall.

(1998 No. 38)

(a) Under conditions of confidentiality, examine periodically the books and affairs of each bank.

(b) Have a right of access to all times to the books, accounts and vouchers-of banks;

(c) Have power to require from directors, managers and officers of banks such information and explanation as he deems necessary to the performance of his duties under section.

(3) The Governor shall appoint to assist the Director of Banking Supervision such other officers of the Bank as the Governor may, from time to time, decide.

(4) The officers may be designated examiners or have such other titles at the Governor may specify.

(5) For two the purpose of this section, references to examiners are references to the Director of Banking Supervision and any officer of the Bank appointed pursuant to subsection (3) of the section.

(6) In examining the affairs of any bank under this Act, it shall be tee duty of an examiner at all times to avoid unreasonable hindrance to the daily business of the bank.

(7) Every bank shall produce to the examiners at such times as the examiners may specify, all books, accounts, documents and information which they may require.

(8) If any book, document or information is not produced in accordance with the examiner, is false in any material particular, the bank is guilty

of an offence and liable on conviction to pay the Bank a fine of ₦100,000 and in addition, to a fine of ₦10,000 for each day during which the offence continues.

(1997 No. 4, 1998 No. 38)

32.Routine Examination and Report thereon

(1) The Governor shall, in the case of routine examination, forward a copy of the report arising from the examination together with the recommendations of the Bank, to the bank concerned with instruction that it be placed before the meeting of the Board of Directors of the bank specially convened for the purpose of considering the report and the recommendations thereon.

(2) The bank shall within two weeks convey to the Governor the board of director's reactions to the report and its proposal for implementing the recommendations of the bank.

(3) Any bank which fails to comply with the provisions of subsection (1) or (2) of this section is guilty of an offence and liable to the Bank for a fine not exceeding ₦25,000 for each day during which the offence continues and if the offence continues for more than 30 days, the Bank may in addition to the fine, withdraw any privilege or facility granted to that bank by the Bank.

33. Special Examination

(1) The Governor shall have power to order a special examination or investigation of the books and affairs of a bank where he is satisfied that;

a) It is in the public interest so to do; or
b) The bank has been carrying on its business in a manner detrimental to the interest of its depositors and creditors; or
c) The bank has "sufficient" assets to cover its liabilities to the public; or
d) The bank has been contravening the provision of this Act; or
e) An application is made therefore by:

(i) A Director or Shareholder of the bank; or
(ii) A Depositor or Creditor of the bank

Provided that in the case of paragraph (e) of this subsection, the Governor may not order a special examination or investigation of the books and affairs of a bank if he is satisfied that it is not necessary to do so.

(2) For the purpose of subsection (1) of this section, the Governor shall have power to appoint one or more qualified persons other than the officer of the Bank to conduct special examination or investigation,

under conditions of confidentiality, or the books and affairs of the bank.

(3) Nothing in this section or in any other section of this Act shall be construed as precluding the Governor from appointing one or more officers of the Bank as examiners apart from those mentioned in section 32 of this Act and ascribing to such officers such other designations as he deems fit, and from directing or requiring all or any of the officers to exercise all or any of the powers of the Director of Banking Supervision under this Act.

(4) The Governor shall have power to order that all expenses of or incidental to an examination or investigation be paid by the bank examined or investigated.

34. Power to Examine Books of Other Financial Institutions and Specialized Banks

(1) Notwithstanding the powers of the Bank specified in this Act, as amended, the Bank shall have power, from time to time, to examine the books and affairs of:

(a) The Nigerian Industrial Development Bank;
(b) The Nigerian Agricultural and Co-operative Bank;
(c) The Nigerian Export Import Bank;
(d) The Nigerian Bank for Commerce and Industry;
(e) The Urban Development Bank;
(f) The Federal Mortgage Bank of Nigeria and all primary mortgage institutions;
(g) Community banks;
(h) Peoples Bank of Nigeria;
(i) Bureaux de change;
(j) Discount houses

And such other financial institutions and specialized banks as may be specified, from time to time, by the Bank.

(2) The periodic reports and findings of the Bank in relation to the other financial institutions and specialized banks together with the recommendations of the Bank shall, in specific cases, be forwarded to the appropriate Minister for necessary action.

(3) For the purposes of implementation of this section of this Act, the other financial institutions and specialized banks shall be treated in the same manner as other banks with respect to the requirements of section 24 of this Act.

(1998 No. 38)

35. Failing Bank

(1) Where bank informs the Bank that

(a) It is likely to become unable to meet its obligations under this Act; or

(b) It is about to suspend payment to any extent; or

(c) It is insolvent; or

(d) Where, after an examination under section 33 of this Act or otherwise howsoever, the Bank is satisfied that the bank is in a grave situation as regards the matters referred to in section 33(1) o this Act, the Governor may by order in writing exercise any one or more of the powers specified ins subsection (2) of this section.

(2) The Governor may by order in writing linger subsection (1) of this section

(a) Prohibit the bank from extending any further credit facility for such period as may be set out in the order, and make the prohibition subject to such exceptions, and impose such conditions in relation to the exceptions as may be set out in the order, and from time to time, by further order similarly made, extend the aforesaid period;

(b) Require the bank to take any steps or any action or to do or not to do any act or thing whatsoever, in relation to the bank or its business or its directors or officers which the Bank may consider necessary arid which is set out in the order, within such times as may be stipulated therein;

(c) Remove for reasons to be recorded in writing with effect from such date as may be set out in the order, any manager or officer of the bank, notwithstanding anything in any written law, or any limitations contained in the memorandum and articles of association of the bank;

(1999 No. 40)

(d) In respect of a bank, notwithstanding anything in any written law or any limitations contained in the memorandum and articles of association of the bank, and in particular, notwithstanding any limitation therein as to the minimum number of directors, for reasons to be recorded in writing;

(a) Remove from office, with effect from such date as may be set out in the order, any director of the bank; or

(b) Appoint any person or persons as a director or directors of the bank, arid provide in the order for the person or persons so appointed to be arid by the bank such remuneration as may be set out in the order;

(e) Appoint any person to advise the bank in relation to the proper conduct of its business, and provide in the order for the person so appointed to be paid by the bank such remuneration as may be set out in the order.

36. Control of Failing Bank

If after taking such of the steps stipulated in section 35 of this Act or such other measures as in the opinion of the Bank may be appropriate in the circumstance, the state of affairs-of the bank concerned does not improve, the bank may turn over control and management of such bank to the Nigeria Deposit Insurance Corporation (hereinafter in this Act referred to as "the Corporation") on such terms and conditions as the Bank may stipulate from time to time.

37.Power Over Significantly Under-capitalized Bank

Where the Corporation has assumed control over a bank as provided under section 36 of this Act and such bank is significantly under-capitalized to the extent that its risk weighted assets ratio is below five per cent but above two per cent, the Corporation may;

(a) Require the bank is submit a recapitalization plan acceptable to the Corporation within a stipulated period; or

(b) Prohibit the bank from extending any further credit and incurring any additional capital expenditure without the approval of the Corporation; or

(c) Notwithstanding the provisions of section 7 of this Act, require the bank to take such steps or to do or not to do any act or thing whatsoever in relation to the business of the bank or its directors or officers, which the Corporation may consider necessary within such time as the Corporation may stipulate; or

(d) With the approval of the Bank remove, for reasons to be recorded in writing and with effect from any date as may be specified, any director, manager, officer or employee of the bank; or

(e) Appoint, with the approval of the Bank, any person or persons as a director, or directors of the bank and cause their remuneration to be provided by the Bank.

(1998 No. 38)

38. Management of Failing Bank

(1) Where-the Corporation has assumed control of the business of a bank pursuant to section 36 of this Act, the Corporation shall remain in control of and continue to carry on the business of the bank in the

name and on behalf of the bank until such a time as in the opinion of the Bank, it is no longer necessary for the Corporation remain in control of the business of the bank.

(1998 No. 38)

(2) Accordingly, the cost and expenses of the Corporation or remuneration of an appointed person of the bank shall be a first charge on the assets of the bank.

39. Power of the Bank to Revoke Licence or Apply to Court

In the event that the bank over which the Corporation has assumed control cannot be rehabilitated, the Corporation may recommend to the Bank other resolution measures which may include the revocation of the bank's licence.

(1990 No. 40, 1998 No. 38)

40. Application to the Federal High Court for Winding Up

Where the licence of a ban has been revoked pursuant to section 39 of this Act, the Corporation shall apply to the Federal High Court for a winding up order of the affairs of the bank.

(1998 No. 38)

41. Legal Proceedings etc.

(1) Notwithstanding anything to the contrary contained in any law or enactment, not suit shall be instituted against a bank whose control has been assumed by the Corporation.

(2) If any such proceeding is instituted in any court or tribunal against the bank, it shall abate, cease or be discontinued without further assurance other than this Act.

(1998 No. 38)

42. Corporation to Forward Returns

Corporation shall while acting as the liquidator of licensed bank, forward to the Bank copies of any return which it is required to make, from time to time, by the Bank.

(1998 No. 38)

General and Supplemental

43. Restrictions on the Use of Certain Names

(1) Except with the written consent of the Governor:

(a) No bank shall as from the commencement of this Act, be registered or incorporated with a name which includes the words "Central" "Federal", "Federation", "Nation", "Reserve", "State", "Christian", "Islamic", "Muslim", "Quranic", or "Biblical";

(b) No person other than a bank licensed under this Act shall or continue to use the word "bank" or any of its derivatives, either in English or in ny other language in the description of title under which the person is carrying on business in Nigeria

Provided that paragraph (b) of this subsection shall not apply to banking institutions referred to in section 53 of this Act.

(2) Every bank shall use as part of its description or title the word "bank" or any one or more of its derivatives, either in English or in some other language.

(3) Subsection (1) of this section shall be apply to any registered association of banks, bankers or bank employee formed for the protection of their mutual interest or in furtherance or promotion of education and training of personnel for financial institutions in Nigeria.

(4) Any person who acts in contravention of this section is guilty of an offence and liable on conviction to a fine not exceeding ₦50,000 for each day during which the offence continues.

(1997 No. 4, 1998 No. 38)

44. General Restriction on Advertisement for Deposits

(1) No person other than a bank or any other person authorised to take deposits shall issue any advertisement inviting the public to deposit money with it.

(2) Any person who issues an advertisement in contravention of the provisions of subsection (1) of this section is guilty of an offence and liable on conviction to a fine of ₦500,000 or to imprisonment for, a term of ten years or to both such fine and imprisonment.

(1997 No. 4, 1998 No. 38)

(3) Where any bank proposes to issue any advertisement, the bank shall deliver to the Bank the text of the proposed advertisement together with the bank's latest published accounts, and shall thereafter comply with such directives and conditions as the Bank may prescribe and such text shall be regarded as confidential information.

(4) Any bank which fails to comply with the provisions of subsection (3) of this section is guilty of an offence and liable to a fine of ₦50,000 and the bank shall in addition pay a fine of ₦1,000 for every day during which an advertisement issued in contravention of subsection (3) of this section continues.

(5) In this Act, "advertisement" includes any form of advertising whether in publication or by the display of notice or by means of circular or

other document of by any exhibition of photographs or cinematograph or by way of sound broadcasting or television or loudspeaker or other public address systems and references to the issuing of an advertisement shall be contused accordingly; and for the purposes of this Act, an advertisement issued by any person by way of display or exhibition in a public place shall be, treated as issued by him on every day on which he causes or permits it to be so displayed or exhibited.

(6) An advertisement which contains information calculated to lead directly or indirectly to the deposit of money by the public shall be treated as an advertisement inviting the public to deposit money.

(7) An advertisement issued by any person on behalf of or on the order of another person shall be treated as an advertisement issued by that other person and for the purpose of any proceedings under this Act, and advertisement inviting the public to deposit money with a person specified in the advertisement shall be presumed, unless the contrary is proved, to have been issued by the person.

45. Power of the President to proscribe trade union

(1) If the president is satisfied that the trade union, the member of which employed in a bank, has been engaged in act calculated to disrupt the economy of Nigeria, he may be order published in the Gazette proscribe that union (hereafter in this section referred to as "a proscribed union") which shall, as from the date of the order, cease to exist.

(2) A proscribed union shall, not later than fourteen (14) days from the date of the order under subsection (1) of this section, surrender its certificate of aeration to the to the Registrar who shall take such steps in relation to the distribution of the assets of the union as he deems necessary or in accordance with the registered rules of the union.

(3) No person who immediately before the date of an order under this section was an officer of a proscribed union shall at any time after that date be an officer of any trade union any of the members of which are employed by a bank.

(4) If the certificate of registration f a proscribed union is not delivered to re-Registrar as required under subsection (2) of this section, every person who immediately before the proscription of the union was an officer thereof is guilty of an offence and liable on conviction to a fine of ₦5,000 or to imprisonment for six months or to both such fine and imprisonment.

(5) Any person who contravenes subsection (3) of this section is guilty of an offence and liable on conviction to imprisonment for a term of five years without an option of a fine.

(6) In this section "officer" in relation to a union means any person "aiding official position in that trade union and accordingly include in particular, president, secretary or treasurer thereof and every member of the committee of management however described. "Registrar" means the Registrar of Trade Unions appointed under section 46 of the Trade Union Act.

(Cap. T14)

46. Closure of Bank during a Strike

(1) No bank shall incur any liability to any of its customers by reason only of failure on the part of the bank to open for business during a strike.

(2) If as a result of a strike, a bank fails to open for business, the bank shall, 24 hours of the beginning of the closure, obtain the approval of the Bank for continued closure of the bank.

47. Prohibition of the Receipt of Commissions etc. by Staff of Ban

(1) Any Director, Manager, Officer or employee of a bank or any other person receiving remuneration from the bank, who asks for, receives, consents agrees to receive any gift, commission, employment, service, gratuity, mom property or thing of value for his own personal benefit or advantage for that of any his relations, from any person.

(a) For procuring or endeavouring to procure for any person an advance bans or credit facility from the bank.

(b) For the purpose of discount of any draft, note, cheque, bill of exchange or other obligation by that bank; or

(c) For permitting any person to overdraw any account with that bank without proper authority or compliance with rules and guidelines for the purpose is guilty of an offence and liable on conviction to pay to the Bank a fine of ₦50,000 or imprisonment for a term of five years or to both such fine forfeited imprisonment and in addition any such gift or any other commission shall be forfeited to the Federal Government.

(2) The provision of subsection(1) of this section shall not in any manner derogate from, and shall be without prejudice to any other written law relating to corruption or illegal gratification.

48. Disqualification and Exclusion of Certain Individual from Man Agreement of Banks

(1) Every bank shall, before appointing any director or chief executive seek and obtain the bank's written approval for the proposed appointment.

(2) No person shall be appointed or shall remain a director, secretary or an officer of a bank who.

(a) Is of unsound mind or as a result of ill health is incapable of carrying out his duties; or

(b) Is declared bankrupt or suspends payments of compound with his creditors including his bankers; or

(c) Is convicted of any offence involving dishonesty or fraud; or

(d) Is guilty of serious misconduct in relation to his duties; or

(e) In the case of possessed of professional qualification, is disqualified or suspended (otherwise than of his own request) from practicing his profession in Nigeria by the order of any competent authority made in respect of him personally.

(3) No person who has been a director of or directly concerned in the management of bank which has been wound by the Federal High Court shall, without the express authority of the Governor, act or continue to act as a director of, or be directly concerned in the management of any other bank.

(4) Any person whose appointment with a bank has been terminated or who has been dismissed for reasons of fraud, shall not be employed by any bank in Nigeria.

(5) Any bank which knowingly acts in contravention of subsection (1), (2), (3) or (4) of this section is guilty of an offence and liable on conviction to a fine of ₦100,000.

(6) Where an offence committed by a bank under subsection (4) of this section is proved to have been committed with the knowledge or connivance of any director, manager or any other officer of the bank, he, as well as the bank, is guilty of an offence and the director, manager or any other officer of the bank shall on conviction be liable to imprisonment for a ten or not less than five years or a fine of ₦50,000 or to both such imprisonment and fine.

(1990 No. 40)

(7) It shall not be a defence for any director, manager or officer of a bank to claim that he is not aware of the provisions of subsection (4) of this section, except if he can prove that he had obtained prior clearance of such a person from the secretary of the Banker's Committee who

maintains a register of terminal, dismissed or convicted staff of banks on the ground of fraud or dishonesty.

Miscellaneous Matters

49. Offences by Companies, etc. and by Servant and Agents

(1) Where any offence against any provision of this Act has been committed by a body corporate or firm, any person who was a director, manager, secretary or other similar officer of the body corporate or firm purporting to act in such capacity shall, in addition to the body corporate or firm, be deemed to be guilty of that evidence unless he proves that the offence was committed without his consent or connivance and that he exercised all such diligence to prevent the commission of the offence as he ought to have exercised having regard to the nature of his functions in that capacity and to all the circumstances.

(2) Where any person would be liable under this Act to any punishment or penalty for any act, omission, neglect, or default, he shall be liable to the same punishment or penalty for every such act, omission, neglect or default of any clerk, servant or agent or the clerk observant of such agent.

Provided that such act, omission, neglect or default was committed by the clerk or servant in the course of his employment or by the agent when acting in the course of his employment in such circumstances that had the act, omission, neglect or default been permitted by the agent, his principal would have been liable under this section.

50. Offences by Directors and Managers of Banks

Any person, being a director or manager of a bank, who fails to

(a) Take all reasonable steps to secure compliance by the bank with the requirements of this Act; or

(b) Take all reasonable steps to secure the correctness of any statement submitted under the provisions of this Act, is guilty of an offence and liable on conviction to a fine not exceeding ₦50,000 or to imprisonment for a term of three years or both such fine and imprisonment.

(1997 No. 4, 1998 No. 38)

5.1 Penalties for Offences not otherwise provided for

Any bank which contravenes or fails to comply with any of the provisions of this Act or any regulations made thereunder for which an offence or penalty is not expressly provided is guilty of an offence and liable on conviction to a fine not exceeding ₦50,000.

52.Sharing Revenues for Penalties

All revenues collections as result of penalties imposed by this Act or any other penalties for which the Bank is responsible for collection shall be shared in the ratio of 20 per cent to the Bank, 10 per cent to the Nigeria Deposit Insurance Corporation and 70 per cent to the Consolidated Revenue Fund.

(1997 No. 4)

53. Protection Against Adverse Claims

(1) Neither the Federal Government nor the Bank nor any office of that Government or Bank, shall be subject to any action, claim or demand by or liability to any person in respect of anything done or omitted to be done in good faith in pursuance or in execution of, or in connection with the execution or intended execution of any power conferred upon that government, the bank or such office, by this Act.

(2) For the Purpose of this section, the ministry or any officer duly acting on his behalf shall be deemed to be an officer of the Federal Government and the Governor, and Deputy governor of the bank, or other employee thereof or any person holding any office therein, or appointed by the Bank, under subsection (2) of section 33 of this Act, shall be deemed to be an officer of the Bank.

54. Priority of Local Deposit Liabilities.

Where a bank is unable to meet its obligations or suspends payment, the assets of the bank in the Federation shall be available to meet all the deposit liabilities of the bank and such deposit liabilities shall have, priority over all other liabilities of the bank.

55.Application of Companies and Allied Matters Act

(1) The provisions of this Act shall apply without prejudice to the provisions of the Companies-and Allied Matters Act in so far-as- they relate to banks, and to winding up by the federal High Court.

(2) Where any of the provisions of the Companies and Allied Matters act are inconsistent with the provisions of this Act shall prevent.

56. Application of Nigeria Deposit Insurance Corporation Act

The provisions of this Act shall apply without prejudice to the provisions of the Nigeria Deposit Insurance Corporation Act and were any of the provisions of this Act are inconsistent with any provisions of that Act, the provisions of this Act shall prevent.

(Cap. N102)

57. Power to make Regulations

(1) The Governor may make regulations, published in the Federal Gazette, to give full effects to the objects and objectives of this Act.

(2) Without prejudice to the provisions of subsection (1) of this section, the Governor may "Make" rules and regulations for the operations and control of all institutions under the supervision of the Bank.

PART II

Other Financial Institutions

58. Prohibition of Unlicensed Financial Institution

(1) Without prejudice to the provisions of Part 1 of Act, no person shall carry on other financial business in Nigeria and holds a valid licence granted under section 59 of this Act.

(2) Any person or institution which, before, the commencement of this Act was carrying on such other financial business as are referred to under subsection (1) of this section, shall apply in writing to the Bank for a licence with six months form the date of commencement of this Act.

(3) Any person or institution which fails to apply as provided in subsection (2) of this section, shall cease to carry on such financial business.

59. Application for Licence

(1) Any person or institution wishing to carry on other financial business other than insurance and stock broking in Nigeria shall apply in writing to the Bank for the grant of a licence and shall accompany the application with the following

(a) A draft copy of the memorandum and articles of association of the proposed financial business.

(b) Such other information, documents and reports as the Bank may from time to time. Specify: and

(c) The prescribed application fee.

(2) Altor the applicant has provided all such information, documents and reports is the Bank may require under subsection (1) of this section, the Bank may grant the licence with or without conditions or refuse to grant the licence.

(3) Where an application for a licence is granted, the Bank shall give written notice of that fact to the applicant and the licence fee shall be paid.

(4) The Bank may vary or revoke any conditions subject to which a licence was granted or may impose fresh or additional conditions to the grant of a licence.

(5) Where the Bank proposes to vary, revoke or impose fresh or additional conditions, the Bank shall before exercising such power, give notice of it to the person or institution concerned and give such a person or an opportunity to make representation to the Bank thereon.

(6) Any person who transacts business without a valid licence under section 58 of this Act or subsection (2) of this section, whether in the case of an individual or in the case of a body corporate, is guilty of an offence and liable

(a) In the case of a bony corporate, to a fine of ₦1,000,000; and

(b) In any other ease, to a fine not exceeding ₦1,000,000 or

(c) Imprisonment for a term not exceeding five years or to both such fine and imprisonment

[1999. No, 40.]

60. Failure to Comply with Conditions of Licence

(1) Any person who fails to comply with any of the conditions of its licence is guilty of an offence and liable on conviction to a fine not exceeding ₦5,000 for each day during which the condition is not complied with.

[1997 No. 4. 1998 No. 38.]

(2) Every person or institution carrying on such financial business- as are referred to in section 56 of this Act shall:

(a) Comply with the Monetary Policy Guidelines and other directives as the Bank may, from time to time, specify;

(b) Furnish within the stipulated time any statistical and other return as the Bank may, from time to time require.

(3) Any person who fails to comply with paragraph (a) or (b) of subsection (2) of s section is guilty of an offence and liable on conviction to imprisonment for a term CSS than two years and not exceeding three years or to a fine of ₦5,000 for each day during which such failure occurs.

[1997 N 4. 1998 No.38]

(4) Persistent failure to comply with the guidelines or other directives or their persistent refusal to supply returns in the prescribed form may be a ground for the revocation of a licence.

61. Supervisory Power of the Bank

(1) The Bank shall have power to

(a) Supervise and regulate the activities of other financial institutions and specialized banks;

(b) Prescribe the minimum paid-up capital requirement of other financial institutions and specialized banks.

[1998 No. 38.]

(2) The Bank may appoint examiners and any other person to carry out regular or other routine examination of the books and affairs of other financial institutions.

(3) Where the Governor is satisfied that it is in the public interest so to do he may, in addition to the routine or regular examination, order a special examination or investigation of the books and affairs of any other financial institution and for that purpose, the Governor shall have power to appoint one or more qualified persons other than the officers of the Bank to conduct special examination or investigation, under conditions of, confidentiality, of the books or affairs of such other financial Institution.

(4) The cost and expenses of the Bank or the remuneration of the person so appointed, as the case may be, shall be payable from the fund and property of the financial institution.

62. Control of Failing Other Financial Institutions

(1) Measures as in the opinion of the Bank may be appropriate in the circumstance, the state of affairs of the other financial institution concerned does not improve, the Bank may turn over the control and management of such other financial institution to an appointed person oh such terms and conditions as the Bank may stipulate, from time to If, after taking such of the steps stipulated in section 35 of this Act such other time.

(2) If after taking such steps as specified in subsection (1) of this section as r the opinion of the Governor may be appropriate in each circumstance, the. 532 of affairs of the other financial institution concerned does not improve, the Bank shall have power to revoke the licence of such other financial institution.

[1998 No. 38.]

(3) Any other financial institution whose licence is revoked subsection (2) of this section shall be wound up by a person appointed by the pursuant 10 pursuant to the Bank.

[1998 No. 38]

(4) The cost and expenses of the Bank or the remuneration of the person so appointed pursuant to subsection (1) of this section shall be payable from the fund and property of the financial institution.

[1998 No. 38.]

63. Application of Act to Other Financial Institutions

The provisions of section 35 of this Act shall apply with such necessary modification to other financial institutions.

[1999 No. 40.]

PART IN

MISCELLANEOUS AND SUPPLEMENTARY

64. Failure to Comply with Rules, etc.

(1) Notwithstanding any of the provisions of this Act, the Governor may impose a person not exceeding ₦2,000,000 or suspension of any licence issued to a bank or any other financial institution for the bank's or other financial institution's failure to comply with any rules, regulations, guidelines or administrative directives made, given or issued by the Bank under this Act.

[1998 No. 38.]

(2) The Governor may suspend any licence issued or given to any bank or any other financial institution which fails to comply with any rules, regulations, guidelines or administrative directives made, given or issued to it by the Bank under this Act.

[1997 No. 4.]

65. Powers as to Offences and The Attorney-General's Fiat

(1) The Governor of the Bank may compound any offence punishable under this Act by accepting such sums of money as he thinks fit, not exceeding the amount of maximum fine to which that person would have been liable if he had been convicted of the offence.

[1998 No. 38.]

(2) Any monies paid to the Governor pursuant to subsection (1) of this section, shall be paid into the Bank's penalty account which shall be established for that purpose.

[1999 No. 40.]

(3) No prosecution in respect of any offence under this Act shall be instituted without the consent in writing of the Attorney-General of the Federation.

[1998 No. 38.]

66. Interpretation

In this Act unless the context otherwise requires "associate" means a company in which another company owns not less than twenty per cent of the shares;

"Bank" means a bank licensed under this Act;

"Bank" means the Central Bank of Nigeria;

"banking business" means the business of receiving deposits on current account, savings account or other similar account. Paying or collecting cheques drawn by paid in by customers; provision of finance or such other business as the Governor may, by order published in the Federal Gazette, designate as banking business:

"Chief executive" in relation to a bank means a person by whatever name called. Who either individually or jointly with one or more other persons is responsible. Subject to the authority of the board of directors, for the conduct of the business and administration of the bank;

"Commercial bank" means a bank in, Nigeria whose business includes the acceptance of deposits withdrawable by cheques;

"Community bank" means a bank whose business is restricted to a specified geographical area in Nigeria;

"Deposit" means money lodged with any person whether or not for the purpose of any interest or dividend and whether of not such money is repayable upon demand upon a given period of notice or upon a fixed date;

"Deputy Governor" means a Deputy Governor of the Central Bank of Nigeria:

"Director" includes any person by whatever name he may be referred to carrying out or empowered to carry out substantially the same functions of a director in relation to the affairs of a company incorporated under the Companies and Allied Matters Act

[Cap. C20.]

"factoring" means the business of acquiring debts due to any person:

federation" means. the Federal Republic of Nigeria:

*Governor" means the Governor or any or the Deputy Governors of the Central Bank of Nigeria;

"leasing" means the business of letting or sub-letting movable property on hire for the purpose of the use of such property by the hirer or any other person in any business whatsoever and where the lessor is the owner of the property regardless of whether the letting is with or without an option to purchase the property.

"licence" means a licence issued under this Act;

"Merchant bank" means a bank whose business includes receiving deposits on deposit account, provisions of finance, consultancy and advisory services relating to corporate and investment matters, making or managing investments on behalf of any person;

"other financial institution" means any individual, body, association or group of persons, whether corporate or unincorporated, other than the banks licensed under, this Act, which carries on the business of a discount house, finance company and money brokerage and whose principal objects include factoring, project financing equipment leasing, debt administration, fund management, private ledger services, investment management, local purchases, order financing, export finance, project consultancy, financial consultancy, pension fund management and such other business as the Bank may, from time to time, designate;

[1998 No.38]

President" means the President of the Federal Republic of Nigeria;

"profit and loss sharing bank" means a bank which transacts investment or commercial banking business and maintains profit and loss sharing accounts;

relation of person" includes father, mother, child, brother, sister, uncle, aunt and cousins where applicable, and their spouses;

"Shareholders funds" means the aggregate of paid-up share capital, statutory and all other reserves;

"Specialized banks" includes Nigerian Industrial Development Bank, Nigerian Agricultural and Co-operative Bank, Nigerian Export Import Bank, Nigerian Bank for Commerce and Industry, the Urban Development Bank, Federal Mortgage Bank of Nigeria and all Primary Mortgage Institutions, Community Banks, Peoples Bank of Nigeria and such other banks as may be designated from time to time;

[1998 No. 38.]

State "means any of the States of the Federation.

67.Short Title

This Act may be cited as the Banks and Other Financial Institutions Act.

APPENDIX 1-B

BANKS AND OTHER FINANCIAL INSTITUTIONS ACT SUBSIDIARY LEGISLATION

No Subsidiary Legislation

BANK (MOTOR VEHICLE LOANS) (MISCELLANEOUS PROVISIONS) ACT

ARRANGEMENT OF SECTIONS

BANKS (MOTOR VEHICLE LOANS) (MISCELLANEOUS PROVISIONS) ACT

An Act to prohibit the sale, disposal or parting with possession of a motor vehicle or which a bank loan is still outstanding and to require the licensing authority to enter al particulars on the loan in the register.

[1979 No. 14.]

[4th April, 197]

[Commencement.]

1. Offences and Penalty for Unauthorized Sale of a Motor Vehicle on Which Loan is Outstanding

(1) As from the commencement of this Act, it shall be an offence for any person to sell, dispose or otherwise part with the possession of a motor vehicle on which a (1) obtained from a bank is still outstanding without first obtaining the consent in writing of the bank prior to the sale or disposal.

(2) Any person who fails to comply with the provisions of subsection (1) of this section shall be guilty of an offence and liable on conviction to a fine of ₦200 or six months imprisonment or to both such fine and imprisonment.

2. Disclosure of Certain Particulars to the Licensing Authority

(1) As from the commencement of this Act, any person who purchases a motor vehicle with a loan granted by a bank shall disclose to the

licensing authority the particulars of the other participant of the loan, the name and address of the bank making the loan, the name and address of the bank making the load and such other particulars as may be prescribed:

Provided that where such a person fails or refuses to disclose such particular within thirty days from the purchase of the motor vehicle the bank may itself supply the particulars concerned to the licensing authority which shall register the latter particulars in substitution for any other entry made in the revenant register.

(2) It shall be duty of the licensing authority to which the particulars stipulated in subsection (1) of this section are given to cause the particulars or, as the case may require, the substituted particulars to be entered in the appropriate register relating to the motor vehicle and to endorse on the motor vehicle licence the name of the bank making the loan or such endorsement on the motor vehicle licence that clearly shows that a loan is still outstanding on motor vehicle.

(3) No change of ownership of the motor vehicle shall, prior to the full repayment or settlement of the loan, be registered by the licensing authority without a certificate of discharge or consent in writing issued by the bank offering the loan to purchase the motor vehicle.

(4) Any registration made contrary to the provision of this section shall be void and shall have no effect whatsoever on the right of ownership or the right to recover possession of the motor vehicle by the bank which had granted the ear for the purchase of such motor vehicle.

3. Issue and Effect of Discharge Certificate

(1) Immediately after full settlement or repayment of a loan (including any interest thereon) is made by the borrower to the bank, the bank shall issue a discharge certificate to the person who obtained the loan and shall send a copy of the discharge certificate to the licensing authority.

(2) On the receipt of the discharge certificate, the licensing authority shall make an entry in that behalf in the register relating to the motor vehicle and thereafter the Owner of the motor vehicle shall be free to dispose of the motor vehicle without having to comply with the requirements laid down in the foregoing provisions of this Act.

4. Interpretation

In this Act, unless the context otherwise requires

"bank" has the meaning assigned thereto by section 66 of the Banks and Other financial Institutions Act;

[Cap. B3]

"motor vehicle" means a mechanically propelled vehicle intended or adopted for use on roads;

"prescribed" means prescribed by the Minister charged with responsibility for finance.

5. Short Title

This Act may be cited as the Banks (Motor Vehicle Loans) (Miscellaneous provisions) Act.

APPENDIX II

CENTRAL BANK OF NIGERIA ACT, 2007
ARRANGEMENT OF SECTIONS

32. Incidental Powers.
33. Power to require or share information.
34. Prohibited activities.
35. Publication of monetary policy rate.
36. Service to the Federal Government.
37. Federal Government's usage of other banks Stale Treasuries.
38. Advances to Federal Government.
39. Power to act as banker to State Governments, etc.
40. Power to act as agent for Federal, State or Local Governments.
41. Banker to other banks.
42. Co-operation with banks in Nigeria.
43. Establishment of Financial Services Regulation Co-ordinating Committee.
44. Objectives of the Committee.
45. Reserve requirements.
46. Appointment of other banks as agent.
47. Payment and settlement systems.
48. Financial Year.
49. Audit
50. Publication of annual accounts and reports.
51. Power to make regulations.
52. Protection against adverse claims.
53. Exemption of the bank from the payment of tax.
54. Proceeding of the Board and Monetary Policy Committee.
55. Exclusion of the application of the Companies and Allied Matters Act, 1990.
56. Liquidation.
57. Power to licence and regulate credit Bureaux.
58. Savings Cap. 192 LFN 1990.
59. Repeal.
60. Interpretation.
61. Citation.

SCHEDULES
CENTRAL BANK OF NIGERIA ACT; 2007
2007 ACT, NO 7

An Act to repeal the Central Bank off Nigeria Act 1991
and to Re-enact the Central Bank off Nigeria Act; and for Related Matters

(25th Day of May, 20071)

ENACTED by the National Assembly of the Federal Republic of Nigeria

1.(1) There is established for Nigeria a body known as Central Bank of Nigeria (hereinafter in this Act referred to as the

(2) The Bank shall be a body corporate with perpetual succession and a common seal and nay sue and be sued in a corporate name.

(3) In other to facilitate the achievement of its mandate under this Act and the Banks and Other Financial Institutions Act and in line with the objective of promoting stability and continuity in economic management the Bank shall be independent body in the discharge of the functions.

(4) Subject to limitations in this Act, the Bank may acquire, hold and dispose of moveable and immoveable property for the purpose of its functions.

2. The Principle objective of the Bank shall be to-

(a) Ensure monetary and price stability;

(b) Issue legal tender currency in Nigeria;

(c) Maintain external reserves to safeguard the international value of the legal tender currency.

(d) Promote a sound financial system in Nigeria, and

(e) Act as banker and provide economic and financial advice to the Federal Government.

(3) The Bank shall have its Head Office in any location which is by law the capital of the Federal Republic of Nigeria and may open branches in any part of Nigeria and appoint agents and correspondents abroad in accordance with the decisions of the Board.

(4) (1) The authorised capital of the Bank shall be one hundred billion naira,

(2) All the capital of the Bank shall be subscribed and held only by the Federal Government.

(3) The authorised and paid-up capital may be increased by such amount Board may, from time to time, determine with the approval of the

President, and shall be subscribed by the Federal Government and paid up at par,

5.(1) The Bank shall -

(a) In respect of each financial year, determine its operating surplus which shall be the remaining sum from its income and other receipts after meeting all expenditure as approved by the Board.

(b) As approved by the Board for that year, make provision for the contribution to staff pension fund in accordance with the Pension Reform Act 2004 and for any other purpose approved by the Board.

(2) The Bank shall establish a general reserve fund and shall allocate thereto at the end of every financial year one-quarter of its operating surplus for the year.

(3) The balance of operating surplus shall be paid to the Federal Government half-yearly,

6. (1) There shall be for the Bank a Board of Directors (in this Act referred to as "the Board") which shall be responsible for the policy and general administration of the affairs and business of the bank.

(2) The Board shall consist of-

(a) A Governor who shall be the Chairman;

(b) four Deputy Governors;

(c) The Permanent Secretary, Federal Ministry of Finance;

(d) five Directors; and

(e) Accountant-General of the Federation.

(3) The Board shall be responsible for-

(a) The consideration and approval of the annual budget of the Bank.

(b) The approval of the audited and management accounts and the consideration of the management letter from the external auditors;

(c) The formulation and implementation of exchange rate policy

(d) Making recommendation to the President for the appointment of Auditors in accordance with section 49 of this Act, the provision of the necessary facilities and the rates of remuneration;

(e) The establishment and closing of branches and currency centres; and

(f) Carrying out of such activities as are necessary and expedient for the purpose of achieving the objective of the Bank.

(4) The Board shall approve the detailed responsibilities of each of the Deputy Governors on the recommendation of the Governor.

(5) Without prejudice to Sub-section (4) of this section, the Board may, on the recommendation of the Governor, assign or re-assign the Deputy

Governors from time to time, as may be expedient for the performance of the Bank's functions under or pursuant to this Act.

7.(1) The Governor or in his absence, one of the Deputy Management Governors nominated by him shall be in charge of the day-to-day management of the Bank and shall be answerable to the Board for his Acts and decisions.

(2) The provisions of the section 6 (1) of this Act shall apply in relation to the general policy pursued on any administrative matters including staff pensions, salaries, allowances and any other similar matters

8.(1) The Governor and Deputy Governors shall be persons of recognised financial experience and shall be appointed by the President subject to confirmation by the Senate on such terms and conditions as may be set out in their respective letters of appointment.

(2) The Governor and Deputy Governors shall be appointed in the first instance for a term of five years and shall each be eligible for re-appointment for another term not exceeding five years:

Provided that, of the first four Deputy Governors to be so appointed, one shall in the first instance be appointed for three years and two shall in the first instance be appointed for four years.

(3) The salaries fees, wages or other remuneration or allowances including pension and other allowances payable to the Governor and to the Deputy Governors shall be as stipulated from time to time by the Board subjected to the approval for the president.

(4) The Governor shall appear before the National Assembly at semi-annual hearings as specified in sub-section (5) regarding-

(a) Efforts, activities, objectives and plans of the Board with monetary policy, and

(b) Economic development and prospect for the future described in the report required in the sub-section (5)(b) of this section.

(5) The Governor shall, from time to time-

(a) Keep the President, informed of the affairs of the Bank including a report on its budget; and

(b) Make a formal report and presentation on the activities of the Bank and the performance of the economy to the relevant committees of National.

9. The Governor and Deputy Governors shall devote the whole of their time to the service of the Bank and while holding office shall not engage in any full or part time employment or vocation whether

remunerated or not except such personal or Charitable causes as may be determined by the board and which do not conflict with or detract from their full-time duties:

Provided that the Governor or any of the Deputy Governors may, by virtues of his office, be appointed with the approval of the Board to:

(a) Act as member of any Commission established by the Federal Government to enquire into any matter affecting currency or banking in Nigeria;

(b) Become Governor, Director or members of the Board or by whatever name called, of any international bank or international monetary institution to which the federal Government shall have interest or give support or approval;

(c) Become Director of any corporation in Nigeria in which the Bank may participate under section 31 of this Act.

10.(1) The five directors of the bank shall be appointed by the president subject to confirmation by the senate and in appointing five external directors of the bank, the president shall have due regard to at fair representation of the financial, agricultural, industrial and commercial interests and the principle of Federal Character.

(2) A Director appointed pursuant to this section shall be a person of recognized standing and experience in any of economics, law, public administration, business administration, accounting, banking and finance, but while a Director of the Bank, he shall not hold office as a Director on the Board of any Federal, State or Local Government of any other body:

Provided that he may hold office as a Director of any private commercial, financial, agricultural, industrial, or other organization or institution so long as his duties in respect the of do not conflict with his duties as a Director of the Bank.

A Director appointed pursuant to this section shall-

(a) Hold office for four years and shall be eligible for re-appointment for another term of four years.

(b) Be entitled to such fees and allowances as may be prescribed by rules made in that behalf by the Board and approved by the president.

11. (1) A person shall not remain a Governor, Deputy Governor or Director of the Bank if he is

(a) A member of any Federal, or State legislative house; or

(b) A director, officer or employee of any bank licensed under the Banks and other Financial Institutions Act.

(2) The Governor, Deputy Governor or Director shall cease to hold office in the Bank if he-

(a) Becomes of unsound mind or, owing to ill health, is incapable of carrying out his duties;

(b) Is convicted of any criminal offence by a court of competent jurisdiction except for traffic offences or contempt proceedings arising in connection with the execution of any power or duty conferred under this Act or the Banks and Other Financial Institution Act;

(c) Is guilty of a serious misconduct in relation to his duties under this Act;

(d) Is disqualified or suspended from practising his profession in Nigeria by order of a competent authority made in respect of him personally;

(e) Become bankrupt;

(f) Is removed by the President:

Two-thirds majority of the senate praying that he be so removed.

(3) The Governor or any Deputy Governor may resign his office by giving at least three months' notice in writing to the President of his intention to do so and any Director may similarly resign by giving at least one month's notice in writing to the president of his intention to do so.

(4) If the Governor, any Deputy Governor or Director of the Bank dies, resign or otherwise vacates his office before expiry of the term for which he has been appointed, there shall be appointed a fit and proper person to take his place on the Board for the unexpired period of the term of appointment in the first instance if the vacancy is that of

(a) The Governor or a Deputy Governor, the appointment shall be made in the manner prescribed by the section (8) and (2) of this Act: and

(b) Any Director, the appointment shall be made in the manner prescribed by section 10(1) and (2) of this Act.

12. (1) In order to facilitate the attainment of the objective of the price stability and to support the economic policy of the Federal Government, there shall be a Committee of the Bank known as Monetary Policy Committee (in this Act referred to as "the MPC).

(2) The MPC shall consist of-

(a) The Governor of the Bank who shall be the Chairman;

(b) The four Deputy Governors of the Bank;

(c) Two members of the Board of Directors of the Bank;

(d) Three members appointed by the President; and

(e) Two members appointed by the Governor

(3) The MPC shall have responsibilities within the Bank for formulating monetary and credit policy

(4) The appointment of a member of the MFC pursuant to sub-section 2 (d) and (e) of this section, the remuneration, filling of temporary vacancies, qualification, tenure of office and disqualification shall be subject to the same terms as are stipulated for a Director under sections 10 and 11 of this Act.

(5) The provision of the second Schedule to this Act shall have effect with respect to proceedings of the MFC

13.(1) Meeting of the Board shall take place as often as may be required, but not less than six times in every year of the Bank.

(2) The Governor shall preside at every meeting of the Board and in his absence a Deputy Governor designated by him shall preside at such meeting.

(3) Five Members of the Board, three of whom shall be directors other than the Governor of the Deputy Governors, shall form a quorum at any meeting.

(4) Unless otherwise provided in this Act, decision shall be by a simple majority of the votes of the members present, but in case of any equality of vote, the person presiding shall have a casting vote.

14. (1) There shall be for the Boards a Secretary who shall be-

(a) Appointed by the Board; and

(b) Be responsible to the Board through the Governor.

(2).The secretary shall be responsible for-

(a) Convening, on the authority of the Chairman, meetings of the Board

(b) Recording the minutes of all the meeting of the Board and such other meetings as the Board may direct;

(c) Acting as Secretary to any Committee of the Board;

(d) Maintaining and keeping minute books and register of the Directors of the Bank;

(e) Keeping in safe custody the common seal of the

(f) Keeping in safe custody all title documents relating to the Bank properties;

(g) Keeping in safe custody all agreements entered into by the bank with any third party; and

(h) Carrying out such other duties and responsibilities as may be assigned to him, from time to time, by the Governor.

(3) The Secretary to the Board shall be a lawyer, with at least, 10 years cognate experience.

(4) Appointment of employees of the Bank shall only be in respect of positions created by the Bank and on such terms and conditions as may be laid down by the Board:

Provided that the appointment and removal of staff of the grade of Assistant Director and above shall be with the approval of the Board.

(5) A salary, fees, wage, allowance and other remuneration paid by the Bank shall not be computed by reference to the operating surplus of the Bank.

(6) The salaries, fees, wages, or other remuneration payable to or in respect of employees of the Bank, other than the Governor or Deputy Governors, shall be as stipulated, from time to time, by the Board

15. The unit of currency in Nigeria shall be the Naira which shall be divided into one hundred kobo.

16. The exchange rate of the Naira shall be determined, from time to time, by a suitable mechanism devised by the Bank for that purpose.

17. The Bank shall have the sole right of issuing currency notes and coins throughout Nigeria and neither the Federal Government nor any State Government, Local Government, other person or authority shall issue currency notes, bank notes or coins or any documents or tokens payable to bearer on demand being document or token which are likely to pass as legal tender.

18. The Bank shall -

(a) Arrange for the printing of currency notes and coins;

(b) Issue, re-issue and exchange currency notes and coins at the Bank's offices and at such agencies as it may, from time to time, established appoint;

(c) arrange for the safe custody of un-issued stocks of currency notes and for the preparation, safe custody and destruction of plates and paper for the printing of the currency notes and disc for the minting of coins; and

(d) Arrange for the destruction of the currency notes and coins withdrawn from circulation under the provision of section 20 (3) of this Act or otherwise found by the Bank to be unfit for use.

19.(1) The currency notes and coins issued by the Bank shall be-

(a) In such denomination of Naira or fraction thereof as shall be approved by the President on the recommendation of the Board; and
(b) Of such forms and designs and bear such advises as shall be approved by the President on the recommendation of the Board.
(2) The standard weights and composition of coins issued by the Bank and the amount of remedy and variation shall be determined by the President on the recommendation of the Board.
20.(1) The currency notes issued by the Bank shall be legal tender in Nigeria at their face value for the payment of any amount.
(2) The coins issued by the Bank shall, if such coins have not been tempered with be legal tender in Nigeria at their face value up to such amount or amounts as may be determined, from time to time, by the Bank.
(3) Notwithstanding Sub-sections (1) and (2) of this section, the Bank shall have power, if directed to do so by the President and after giving reasonable notice in that behalf, to call in any of its notes or coins on payment of the face value thereof and any note or coin with respect to which a notice has been given under this sub-section shall, on the expiration of the notice, cease to be legal tender, but, subject to section 22 of this Act, shall be redeemed by the Bank upon demand.
(4) It shall be an offence punishable by a term of imprisonment of not less than years for any person to falsity, make or counterfeit any bank note or coin issued by the Bank which is legal tender in Nigeria.
(5) A person who refuses to accept the Naira as a means of payment is guilty of an offence and liable on conviction to a fine of ₦50,000 or 6 months imprisonment:
Provided that the Bank shall have powers to prescribe the stances and conditions under which other currencies may be used as medium of exchange in Nigeria.
21.(1) A person who tempered with a coins or notes by the Bank is guilty offence and shall on conviction stable to imprisonment for a term not less than six month or to not less than ₦50,000 or to both such fine for and a term imprisonment.
(2) A coin or note shall be deemed to have been tampered with if the coin or note has been impaired, diminished or lightened otherwise than by fair wear and tear and has been defaced by stumping, engraving, mutilating, piecing, stapling, writing, 3 soiling, squeezing or any other

form of deliberate and wilful abuse whether the coin or note has or has not been thereby diminished or lightened.

(3) For the avoidance of the doubt, spraying of dancing or matching of the Naira or any note issued by the Bank during social occasions or otherwise howsoever shall constitute an abuse and defacing of the Naira or such note and shall be punishable under sub-section (1) of this section.

(4) It shall also be an offence punishable under Sub-section (1) of this section for any person to hawk, sell or otherwise trade in the Naira notes, coins or any other note issued by the Bank.

(5) In This Section-

(i) "Matching" includes spreading, scattering or littering of any surface with any Naira notes or coins and stepping thereon, regardless of the value, volume, occasion or intent.

(ii) "Spraying" include adorning, decorating or spraying anything or any person any part of any person or the person of another with Naira notes or coins or sprinkling or sticking of the Naira note or in a similar manner regardless of the amount, occasion or intent.

22.(1) A person shall not be entitled to recover from the Bank the value of any lost, stolen, mutilated or imperfect note or coin.

(2) The circumstances in which, and the conditions and limitations subject to which, the value of the lost, stolen, mutilated or imperfect notes or coins may be refunded ex-gratia shall be within the absolute discretion of the Bank.

23.The Bank shall not be liable for payment of any stamp duty under the Stamp Duties Act in respect of its notes issued as currency.

24.The Bank shall at all time maintain a reserve of external assets consisting of all or any of the following-

(a) Gold coin or bullion;

(b) Balance at any Bank outside Nigeria where the currency is freely convertible and in such currency, notes, coins money at call and any bill of exchange bearing at least two valid and authorized signatures and having a maturity not exceeding ninety days exclusive of days of grace.

(c) Treasury bills having a maturity not exceeding one year issued by the Government of any country outside Nigeria whose currency is freely convertible;

(d) Securities of, or guarantee by, a government of any country outside Nigeria whose currency if freely convertible provided such securities shall mature in a period not exceeding ten ears from the date of acquisition and are of such investment grade as may be determined by the Board from time to time;

(c) Securities of, or guarantees by, international financial institutions if such securities are expressed in currency freely convertible, in the form of investment grade assets as may be determined by the Board and maturity of the securities shall not exceed five years;

(f) Nigeria's gold tranche in the International Monetary Fund;

(g) Allocation of Special Drawing right made to Nigeria by international monetary fund;

(h) Investment by way of loans or debenture in an investment bank or development. Financial institutions within or outside Nigeria for a maximum period of five years in so far as-

(i) The amount invested is not more than 5% of the total foreign reserve,

(ii) The reserve level at the time of investment is more than such amount as will sustain twenty-four months of import and

(iii) The loan debenture is denominated in foreign currency:

Provided the investment bank or development financial institution referred to in paragraph (h) of this section carries such a rating by rating: as may be prescribe from time to time by the Bank; and

(iv) Such other securities and investment as may be approved from time to time by the Board:

Provided they are liquid foreign currency assets that are of investment and in the form of freely convertible currencies.

25. The bank shall use it best endeavour to maintain external reserves level Nigeria.

26. The Bank shall issue and redeem on demand at its Head Office, Nigeria currency against other currencies eligible for inclusion in the reserve of external assets under this Act,

27. The Bank may-

(a) Issue demand drafts and effect other kinds of remittance payable as its own offices or at the offices of agencies or correspondent;

(b) Open accounts for and accept deposits from the Federal, State and Local Governments, and from funds, institution and corporations of all such Government banks and other credit or financial institutions;

(c) Maintain accounts with central banks and other banks outside Nigeria;

(d) Act as correspondent, banker or agent for any central banks or other monetary authority established under government auspices;
(e) Accept from customers, for custody securities and other articles of Value; and
(f) Undertake on behalf of customers and correspondents, the purchase, sale, collection and payment of securities, currencies and credit instrument in Nigeria or abroad and the purchase of the sale of Gold or silver.

28. The bank may
(a) Purchase and sell gold coin bullion;
(b) Purchase, sell, discount and rediscount inland bills of exchange and promissory notes arising out of bona fide commercial transactions bearing two or more valid and authorized signatures and maturing within ninety days exclusive of days of grace, from the date of acquisition;
(c) Purchase, sell, discount and rediscount inland bills of exchange and promissory notes bearing two or more valid and authorized signature drawn or issued for purpose of financing seasonal agricultural operation or marketing of crops, semi-manufacturing or manufacturing operation designed for export or marketing of these products and maturing within 180 days, exclusive of days exclusive of days of grace, from the date of acquisition;
(d) Purchase, sell, discount and rediscount treasury bills of Federal Government which have been publicly offered for sale and are to mature within 364 days;
(e) Purchase, sell, discount or rediscount treasury certificate maturing within such a period as may be determined by the Federal Government and specified by an instrument made by the Federal Government;
(f) Discount and rediscount project-tied bonds issued by State Governments; Local Governments, corporations owned by the Federal or State Governments, being bond which have been publicly offered for sale and with maturity not exceeding three years;
(g) Purchase and sell securities of the Federal Government maturing in not more than twenty-five years which have been publicly offered for sale or form part of an issue which is being made to the public at the time of acquisition, so that the total amount of such securities of maturity exceeding two years in the ownership of the Bank other than securities

held in terms of paragraph (h) of this section or held by the Bank as collateral under section 29 (1) (b) shall not together at any time exceed seventy five per cent of the total demand liabilities of the Bank;

(h) Invest in securities of the Federal Government for any amount and to mature at any time, on behalf of staff pension funds and other internal funds of the Bank;

(i) Purchase and sell foreign currencies and purchase, sell, discount rediscount bills of exchange and treasury bills drawn in or on places abroad and maturing within 184 days exclusive of days of grace from the date of acquisition;

(j) Purchase and sell securities guaranteed by any government whose currency is freely convertible or securities issued by international financial institutions, of which Nigeria is a member, which are also expressed in currencies which are freely convertible and are of investment grade; and

(k) Hold redeemable bond for the purpose of regularizing any currency exchange exercise.

29.(1) The Bank may:

(a) Grant advances for fixed period not exceeding three months against publicly issued treasury bills of the Federal Government;

(b) Grant advance for fixed period not exceeding one year at a minimum rate of interest of at least one per cent above the Banks's Monetary policy rate against:

(i) Gold coin or billion,

(ii) Securities of the Federal Government which have been publicly offered for sale and are to mature within a period of twenty-five years:

Provided that no advances so secured shall at any time exceed seventy-five per cent of the market value of the security pledged and that the total of secured securities held by the Bank is within the limitation imposed by section 28 (g).

(iii) Such bills of exchange and promissory notes as are eligible for purchase, discount or rediscount by the Bank up to seventy five per cent of their nominal value.

(iv) Warehouse warrants or their equivalent (security possession of goods), in respect of staple commodities or other goods duly insured and with a letter of hypothecation from the owner.

Provided no such advances shall exceed seventy five per cent of the current market values of the commodities in question, or

(v) Treasury certificate issued by the Federal Government:

Provided that no advances so secured shall at any time exceed seventy-five per cent of the market value of the certificate pledged;

(c) Notwithstanding the provision of section 34(d) of this Act, grant temporary advances to banks within the meaning of the Banks and Other Financial Institutions Act which participate in bank clearing in respect of temporary debit balance on their accounts at such rate of interest and under such terms as the Bank may, from time to time determine;

(d) Grand advances to any authority:

(i) For fixed period not exceeding one year at a rate of interest which shall be at least one per cent above the Bank's monetary policy rate, and

(ii) Except as prescribed in sub-section (1) (c) of this section, upon such conditions as the Bank may specify or as prescribed to ensure payment thereof with interest;

(e) Grant advances referred to in subsection (1) (d) of this section in any particular case where a guarantee in writing is given by the Federal Government to the Bank on behalf of any such authority so that:

(i) The total advance which may, subject to provisions of this section, be granted shall not exceed an amount considered by the Bank to be adequate for the authority to commence its operations at the beginning of the crop or produce season,

(ii) Such advances shall be secured so soon after the advances have been granted as may be agreed by the Bank (either in part or in whole) as prescribed in subsection (1) (a) and (b) of this section and the said provisions shall be so construed;

(f) Any advance which may be granted by virtue of the provisions of subsection (1) (d) and (e) of this section shall be used solely for the purpose of financing:

(i) The purchasing and marketing operations authorized to be undertaken by any such authority by the law under which the authority was by the law under which the authority was established or as may be approved by the Bank, and

(ii) With the approval of the Bank, other operations as may be incidental thereto.

Provided that any such authority may, if it is so wishes, make advances to any licensed buying agent (within the meaning of any law under which the authority was established) for the purchase of produce for sale to the said authority, provided also that the quality of produce to be so purchased is included in the estimated tonnage of crops against which total advances are to be made by the Bank.

(2) Paragraph (d) to (f) subsection (1) of this section relate to any authority of the Federal Government, State Government or two or more State Governments including an interim authority established for such purpose by any law in operation in Nigeria.

(3) The reference in paragraph (d) to (f) of subsection (1) of this section to granting of advances includes a reference to the provision of credit facilities.

30. The Bank shall have power;

(a) To carry out open market operations of maintaining monetary stability in the economy of the country, and without prejudice to the generality of the foregoing, the Bank may also for that purpose issue, place, sell, repurchase, amortise or redeem securities (which shall constitute the obligations) and the securities shall be issued at amortization, negotiability and redemption as the Bank may deem appropriate;

(b) To issue other forms of securities including treasury bills as the Bank may deem necessary for purpose of liquidity management;

(c) To sell or place allocation to each Bank any securities issued under paragraph (a) or (b) of this section; and

(d) To repurchase, amortise or redeem in such manner as the Bank may deem appropriate, any such securities.

31. The Bank may subscribe to, hold and sell shares of any Corporation or company or debentures thereof set up with approval of or under the authority of the Federal Government for the purpose of promoting the development of money or capital market in Nigeria or stimulating financial or economic development so however that in any such case, the total value of the holding of share, or as the case may be, debenture to which this section applied shall not at any time exceed ten times the aggregate of the Bank's paid up capital and the general reserve fund of the Bank.

32. (1)The Bank may, subjected as is expressly provided in this Act generally conduct business as a bank, and do all such things as are incidental to or consequential upon the exercise of its power or the discharge of its duties is under this.

(2) The Governor may, at any time in his direction and by previous notice in writing lodged with the Board, decide that the power conferred by

section 28 (d), (g), (h), 29 (1) (b) and 30 of this Act be extended to the treasury bills and treasury certificate or the securities, as the case may be, of any State Government with which the Bank appears substantially to have establish relationship of banker, or to any specified treasury bills and treasury certificates or securities of such a State Government subject to the conditions as specified in those paragraphs and subject to limitations specified in section 28 (g) which limitations shall then apply to the aggregate values of the Federal and State Government securities so dealt with.

33.(1) In addition to any of its power under this act, the

(a) Require persons and institution having access thereto, at all reasonable time, to supply, in such forms as the Bank may from time to time direct, information relating to or touching or concerning matters affecting the economy of Nigeria and

(b) Issue guidelines to any person and any institution under its supervision

(2) The Bank shall take account of matters of confidential nature supplied to the Bank under this section, but where the Bank is satisfied that it is in the national interest and that the person supplying the information does not object to a proposal to publish it within a reasonable time of becoming aware of it, the Bank may, from any information in its possession, compile and publish statistical data and anything relevant thereto, on the national economy.

(3) Where any person lawfully required to supply information for the purpose of this section:

(a) Supplies information which he knows to be false or supplies the information recklessly as to its truth or falsity; or

(b) Without reasonable excuse (the proof of the reasonableness to lie on him) fails to comply with any requirement of the Bank under subsection (1) (a) of this section the supply or failure to supply, as the case may be, as provided, shall be an offence under this section.

(4) An offence under this section is punishable on conviction by

(a) Imprisonment not exceeding three years of with a fine not exceeding ₦10,000,000 for every false information or with both such imprisonment and fine;

(b) A fine not exceeding ₦2,000,000 for failure to comply with the requirement of the Bank;

(5) A person or institution that fails to comply with any guidelines issued under subsection (1) (b) of this section shall be liable on conviction

(a) In the case of institution, to a fine not exceeding ₦10,000,000; and
(b) In the case of person, to imprisonment for a term not exceeding three years to a fine of not less than ₦50,000 and not exceeding ₦2,000,000 or to both such imprisonment and fine;
(6) The Bank may, in the exercise of its power and on the basis reciprocity, enter into agreement or arrangements with other regulate authorities in Nigeria or in other countries exercising similar responsibilities for
(a) The promotion of mutual co-operation; and
(b) The exchange of information for a purposes of enhancing supervision and regulation of financial

Provided that the exchange of such information shall be conditional upon assurances of confidential treatment of information so given or received.

34. The Bank shall not
(a) Engage in trade or otherwise have a direct interest in any commercial, agricultural or industrial undertaking, except as provided in section 27 to 32 of this Act, or in any other undertaking, except such interest which the Bank may in any way acquire in the course of the satisfaction of debt due to it, and provided that all such interests so acquired shall be disposed of at earliest suitable time;
(b) Except as provided in section 31 of this Act, purchase the share of any corporation or company including the shares of any banking institution;
(c) Grant loan upon the securities of any shares;
(d) Subjected to the provision of section 38 of this Act, grant secured advances or advances secured otherwise than as laid down in section 29 (1) (a) and (b) of this Act.

Provided that in the event of the Bank becoming in the opinion of the Bank endangered, the Bank may secure such debt on any real or other property or the debtor and may acquire such property which shall be-resold at the earlier suitable time;

(e) Purchase, acquire or lease real property except in accordance with the provision of paragraph (d) of this section and except so far as the Bank shall consider necessary or expedient for the provision or future provision of business premises for the Bank and its agencies and any clearing house set up as provided in section 47 of this Act and residences for the Governor of the Bank;
(f) Draw or accept bills payable otherwise than on demand;

(g) Pay interest on deposits except deposit in respect of cash reserve and special deposits as stipulated in section 45 (1) (a) and (c) of this Act;
(h) Accept for discount or as security for and advance made by the Bank of the Bank;
(i) And
(j) Open accounts for accept deposit from person other than provided in section 27 (b) and (c) of this Act
35. The Banks hall make public, at all times its monetary policy rate.
36. (1) The Bank shall be entrusted with Federal Government banking and foreign exchange transactions.
(2) The Bank shall receive and disburse Federal Government moneys and keep accounts thereof.
(3) In any place where eth Bank has no branch, it may appoint another bank to act as its agent for the collection and payment of Federal Government moneys.
37. Notwithstanding the provision of section 36 of this Act, the Federal Government may;
(a) Maintain account in Nigeria with other Bank in such case and on such conditions as the Bank may determine; and
(b) Use the service of the State Treasuries for the collection and payment of Federal Government moneys in places where it may be appropriate or convenient to do so.
38. (1) Notwithstanding the provision of section 34 (d) of this Act, the Bank may grant temporary advances to the Federal Government in respect of temporary deficiency of budget revenue at such rate of interest as the Bank may determine.
(2) The total amount of such advances outstanding shall not at any time exceed five per cent of the previous year's actual revenue of the Federal Government.
(3) All advances made pursuant to this section shall be repaid:
(a) As soon as possible and shall in any event be payable by the end of the Federal Government financial year in which they are granted and if such advances remain unpaid at the end of the year, the power of the Bank to grant such further advances in any subsequent year shall not be exercisable, unless the outstanding advances have been repaid; and
(b) In such form as the Bank may determine provided that no other promise to pay at a future date or securitization by way of issuance of

treasury bills, bonds, certificate or other forms of security which is required to be underwritten by the Bank.

39. The Bank may act as banker to States and Local Governments and to funds, institutions or corporations established by Federal Governments, States and Local its

40. The Bank may act generally as agent for the Federal Government, State Governments, or Local Governments;

(a) Where the Bank can do so appropriately and consistently with the provisions of this Act and with its duties and functions as Central Bank; and

(b) On such terms and conditions as may be agreed between the Bank and the Government concerned.

41. The Bank shall act as banker to other banks in Nigeria and may also provide banking services to banks outside Nigeria.

42.(1) The Bank Shall wherever necessary seek the cooperation of and cooperation with other banks in Nigeria to:

(a) Promote and maintain adequate and reasonable financial service for the public;

(b) Ensure high standards of conduct and management through the banking system; and

(c) Further such policies not in consistent with the opinion of the Bank be in the national interest.

(2) Notwithstanding the provision of section 29 (1) and (34) (d) of this Act, the Bank may grant loans and other accommodation facilities at such rate of interest and on such terms as the Bank may determine to any bank which may be having liquidity problems.

43. (1) There is hereby establish for the purpose co-ordination the supervision of financial institutions, a Financial Regulation Co-ordinating Committee (in this Act referred to as "the Committee")

(2) The Committee shall consist of:

(a) The Governor of the Bank who shall be the Chairman;

(b) The Managing Director, Nigeria Deposit Insurance Commission;

(c) The Director General, Securities and Exchange Commission;

(d) The Commissioner of Insurance

(e) The Registrar General, Corporate Affairs Commission; and

(f) A representative of the Federal Ministry of Finance not below the rank of Director.

44. The objectives of the Committee shall be :

(a) Co-ordinate the supervision of financial institutions especially conglomerates;
(b) Cause reduction of arbitrage opportunities usually created by differing regulation and supervision standards among supervisory authorities in the economy;
(c) Deliberate on problems experience by any member in it relationship with any financial institution;
(d) Eliminate any information gap encountered by any regulatory agency in its relationship with any group of financial institutions;
(e) Articulate the strategies for the promotion of safe, sound and efficient practices by financial intermediaries; and
(f) Deliberate such other issue as may be specified from time to time.

45. (1) Bank may, from time to time, issue; by circular requiring each bank to:
(a) Maintain at all times in the form of cash reserves with the Bank, at its office, a sum equal to prescribed ratio of the Bank's deposit liabilities;
(b) Hold a minimum amount of specified liquid assets which shall be expressed as a ratio of deposit liabilities of the Bank; and
(c) Maintain as special deposit liabilities or percentage of an increase or absolute increase in such deposit liabilities over an amount outstanding on a date, and for a period as shall be specified by the Bank.

(2) For the purpose of subsection (1) (a) of this section, shall specify:
(a) The class of deposit liabilities against which the cash reserves mentioned in that paragraph shall be held; and
(b) The ratio of cash reserve which a Banks hall so maintain.

(3) For the purpose of subsection (1) (a) of this section, the cash reserves of a bank shall be determined with such period as the Bank may, from time to time, specify, on the Bank of the periodic balance of the bank's deposit liabilities and the Bank shall have power to:
(a) Require bank from time to time to prepare and deliver to the Bank in such form and within such period as Bank may specify, a true and correct statement showing the position of the deposit liabilities of the bank and the Bank may require such statement to be made at such intervals as it may specify;
(b) Require any Bank to furnish to it such information and statistics in such form and as often as the Bank may deem necessary for the purpose of

satisfying itself that the bank concerned has complied or is complying with the provision of subsection (1) of this section.

(4) For the purpose of subsection (1) (b) of this section, the Bank shall have power, in respect of the specific liquid assets which may', from time to time, be held by a bank, to vary the composition and proportion of each category.

(5) For the purpose of subsection (1) (c) of this section, the Bank shall have power to specify the class of deposits to which the provisions of that subsection shall apply and any special deposits held in accordance with that subsection (1) (b) of this section, and subject to the provisions of this subsection, the Bank may, at its direction, pay interest on such special deposits held by it.

(6) The Bank shall have power to prohibit any bank which fails to comply with directive issued under this section, from extending new loans and advances and from undertaking new investments, until the bank complies with the directive to the provision of section 13(5) of the Banks and Other Financial Institutions Act.

(7) A bank which furnishes false information to the Bank for any purpose under this section is guilty of an offence and is liable on conviction to a fine not less than ₦10,000,000 but not exceeding ₦20,0000,000.

46. The bank may appoint as its agents any bank in Nigeria on such terms as may be agreed between the Bank and the bank concerned for the issue, re-issue, exchange and withdrawal of currency notes and coins, or for any other purpose pertaining to the Bank's functions under this Act.

47.(1) The bank shall facilitate the clearing of cheques and credit instruments for the banks carrying on business in Nigeria and for this purpose, the Bank shall at any appropriate time establish clearing house in premises provided by the Bank in such places the bank may consider necessary;

Provided that a bank may be barred from participating in clearing for such period as the Bank may deem fit for non-compliance with directive of the Bank.

(2) Notwithstanding subsection (1) of this section and in furtherance of the provision of section 2 (d) of this Act, Bank shall continue to promote and facilitate the development of efficient and effective systems for the settlement of transactions in the development of electronic payment system.

(3) The bank shall have power to prescribe rules and regulations for the efficient operation of all clearing and settlement system.
(4) In furtherance of the objective of a sound financial system and notwithstanding the provisions of the Evidence Act, any physical or electronic record of transactions that is in a format approved by the Bank shall constitute sufficient proof of such transactions.
48. The Financial year of the Bank shall begin on 1st January and end 31st December.
49. (1) The accounts of the Bank shall be audited by auditors appointed in accordance with the provision of section 6 of this Act.
(2) The Auditor General of the Federation shall conduct an examination of the accounts of the Bank, and submit a report thereon relating to issue, re-issue, exchange and withdrawal of currency notes and coins by the Bank and the Bank shall provide all necessary facilities for the purpose of the examination.
50.(1) The bank shall, within two months after the close of each financial year, transmit to the National Assembly and President a copy of its annual accounts certified by the Auditor.
(2) A report required to be submitted to the National Assembly and the President shall be published by the Bank in such manner as the Governor may direct.
(3) The Board shall ensure that account submitted pursuant to this section shall as soon as possible be published in Gazette.
(4) The Bank shall as soon as may be practicable after the last day of each month make up and publish a return of its assets and liabilities as at the close of business on that day, or if that day is a holiday, as at the close of business on the last preceding business day.
(5) A copy of the returned to in subsection (5) of this section shall be forwarded to the President and shall be published in the Gazette.
(6) In the application of this section, the Gold tranche position at the International Monetary Fund shall from part of the external reserve assets of the Bank.
51. The Board shall have power to make and alter rules and regulations for the good order and management of the Bank.
52.(1) Neither the Federal Government nor the Bank nor any officer of the Government or Bank shall be subjected to any claim or demand by or liability to any person in respect of anything done or omitted to be done in good faith in pursuance or in execution of, or in connection

with the execution or intended execution of any power conferred upon that Government, the bank or such officer, by this Act.

(2) For the purpose of this section, the Minister or any Officer duly acting on this behalf shall be deemed to be an officer or the Federal Government and the Governor, any Deputy Governor of the bank or other employee shall be deemed to be an Officer of the Bank.

53.(1) The Bank shall be exempted from the payment of income tax under the Companies income Tax Act or nay subsequent amendment thereto.

(2) The Bank shall not be liable for the payment of the tenement rate, ground rent or such other property tax imposed under any legislation dealing with real property.

54. The provisions contained in the First and Second Schedules to this Act shall have effect with respect to the proceeding of the Board and monetary Policy Committee respectively and the other matters contain therein and the Board and shall have power to amend the provision of the Schedules as it may deem necessary.

55.The provision of the Companies and Allied Matters Act 1990 or any amendments thereto shall not apply to the Bank.

56. The Bank shall not be placed in liquidation except ant legislation enacted in that behalf and then only in the way directed by the legislation.

57. (1) In furtherance of the provision of section 2 (d); Act, Bank shall have power to licence, and regulate credit bureau to collect, in such manner as the Bank may deem fit, credit information on the customers of banks and other all institutions.

(2) For the purpose of subsection (10 of this section, the Bank shall have power to collect in such manner as the Bank may deem fit for any person or any such credit bureaux, credit information on the customer of banks and other financial institutions and the Bank may disclose the information so collected in such manner as may be deemed appropriate by the Bank.

(3) A bank shall before granting loan, advances or credit facility to any customer obtain from the Bank credit information on that customer where the amount of the loan, advance or credit facility is up to one million naira or such sum as may be set from time to time by the Bank.

58. Without prejudice to section 6 of the Interpretation Act, the repeal of the enactments referred to in subsection 59 shall not affect anything done under or pursuant to those enactments.

59. (1) The Central Bank of Nigeria Act 1991 is hereby repealed

(2) The following amendment enactments are also consequently repealed:

(a) The Central Bank of Nigeria (Amendment) Act of 1993;

(b) The Central Bank of Nigeria (Amendment) Act of 1997;

(c) The Central Bank of Nigeria (Amendment) (No. 2) Act 1998; and

(d) The Central Bank of Nigeria (Amendment) Act of 1999.

(3) The rights, interest, obligations and liabilities of the Bank existing before the commencement of this Act under any contract of instruments, or in law or in equity apart from any contract or instrument, shall virtue of this Act be assigned to and vested in the Bank.

60. In this Act:

"Bank means the Central Bank of Nigeria established under Section (1) (1) of this Act;

"bank" means a bank licence under the Bank and Other Financial Institutions Act 1991 or under the repealed Banking Act or any other prior legislation;

"Bank examiner" means a bank examiner appointed pursuant to the Banks and Other Financial Institutions Act 1991;

"Board" means the Board of Directors of the Bank established under Section 6 (1) of this Act;

"Governor" and "the Deputy Governor" means respectively Governor and the Deputy Governor of the Bank appointed in this Act;

"Officers" or "officer" of the Bank" means officer of the Central Bank of Nigeria;

"President" means the President of the Federal Republic of Nigeria

61. This Act may be as the Central Bank of Nigeria Act, 2007.

FIRST SCHEDULE

Section 54

Proceedings of the Board, etc.

1. (1) Not Less than three weeks notices shall be given of each meeting of the Board and such notice shall be sent to every Director at his registered address but where it is necessary to convene an emergency

meeting, all reasonable step shall be taken to give notice to every Director who is at the time in Nigeria.

(2) A person other than the Directors and the Secretary shall not attend meetings of the Board of the Chairman may request the presence of officers of the Bank when technical matters are under consideration.

2. (1) The Board shall cause minutes to be duly entered in a book provided for that purpose:

(a) Of all appointment of Officers made by the Board;

(b) Of the name of all Directors present at each meeting of the Board; and

(c) Of all the resolutions and proceedings of each meeting

(2) A copy of the minutes shall be circulated at that or succeeding meeting and after approval by the Board, signed by the Chairman.

3. The common seal of the Bank shall fixed under such conditions as may be determined, from time to time, by a resolution of the Board.

4. A Director shall, on appointment or re-appointment, sign a declaration as in form 1 in the Annex to this Schedule affirming his allegiance and service to the Bank and pledging himself to observe strict secrecy respecting all transaction of the Bank.

5. A Director having any interest, directly or indirectly in any dealing or business in which the Bank is concerned shall disclose such interest at the meeting of the Board at which the dealing or business is discussed and in no circumstances shall he vote on the matter. If required by the Board to

6. (1) A Director, Officer and other employee of the Bank shall indemnified by the Bank against all losses, cost and expenses incurred by him by reason of any contract entered into or act or deed done in the proper and careful discharge of his duties. The Bank shall pay all such costs, losses and expenses.

(2) No Director, Officer or other employee of the Bank shall be liable to the Bank for any losses, cost or expenses incurred by the Bank by the insufficiency or deficiency of value of, or title to, property or securities acquired or taken on behalf of the Bank or by the insolvency, bankruptcy or wrongful act of any customer or debtor of the Bank, unless due to wilful default in the execution of his duties.

7. In consultation with the Board, the Governor and Deputy Governor be responsible for:

(a) Fixing the rate or rates of discount or rediscount and the rate or rates of interest on advances to Government and to other customers of the Bank;
(b) Devising suitable mechanisms to determine the rate of exchange at which the Bank shall buy and sell foreign currency under section 16 of this Act;
(c) The appointment of auditors in accordance with section 49 of this Act, the provision of the necessary facilities and the rate of remuneration;
(d) The establishment and closing of branches and currency centres;
(e) The appointment of Branch Controllers and Currency Officers; and
(f) The appointment of officers and other employee:

Provided that the Governor shall have authority to make such appointment as de deems appropriate without consultation with the Board in relation to officers and employees whose salaries do not exceed Central Bank Services Scale 06.

8. (1) The Governor and Deputy Governor shall have special responsibility for:
(a) The organization of the management of the Bank at its Head Office, branches and currency centres;
(b) Causing:
(i) True account to be kept of all transactions entered into by Bank and off the assets and liabilities of the Bank and of all valuable entrusted to the Bank;
(ii) The compilation, form and publication of account in accordance with section 50 (2) of this Act;
(c) The safe-keeping of all the assets of the Bank and the valuable entrusted to the Bank;
(d) The discharge by officers and other employee of the Bank of duties placed upon them;
(e) The supervision of arrangement related to the issue and redemption of currency notes and coins and all matters connected with the forms, design and composition of currency notes and a

Provided that the Director of Currency Operations shall be charge with the direct responsibility under the Governor for specified matters under sub-paragraph.

(2) The Governor shall work out the detailed responsibilities of each of the Deputy Governors; and may assign any of this duties during his

absence from duty or at such other time to any of the Deputy Governors as he deems fit.

(3) Without prejudice to sub-paragraph (2) of this paragraph, the Governor shall have power to assign the Deputy Governors, from time to time as may be expedient for the performance of the Bank's function under or pursuant to this Act.

9. The books of the Bank shall be kept at the Head Office of the Bank or at such other places as the Board may, from time to time determine

10. The Governor shall formulate, the approval of the Board, general rules and any subsequent amendment thereto, providing for:

(i) The sage keeping of the common seal of the Bank;

(ii) The sage keeping of the assets of the Bank and of valuable entrusted to the bank;

(iii) The safe keeping of stocks of unissued or redeemed currency and the preparation, safe custody and destruction of plate and paper for the printing of currency notes and disc for the minting in transit;

(iv) The protection of bank notes and coins in transit;

(v) The conditions under which any Zonal Controller, Branch Controller or Currency Officer may be appointed; and

(vi) The conditions governing discounts and advances;

(vii) The exercise of dual control and general security through the Bank;

(viii) Such additional arrangement which may be made to ensure the efficient working of the Bank, through proper observance of security and the accuracy of the accounts of the Bank.

11. (1) The Board shall, from time to time as it deems fit, delegate some of its responsibilities to the Committee of Governors;

(2) Formal meeting of the Committee of Governors shall take place as often as may be required but not less than once a month.

(3) The Committee of Governor shall cause minutes to be duly entered in books provided for that purpose during each of its formal meetings.

(4) The Governor shall preside over every meeting but in his absence a Deputy Governor designated by him shall act in his place and in the absent of both the governors present shall act as Chairman.

12. The Board by resolution shall, for such purposes as it may, from time to time decides authorized the Governor, the Deputy Governor or any officer of the Bank to sign document relating to all aspects of the Bank's business provided that such documents are not required by law

or common practice to be given under seal. Any such authorizations shall forthwith be notified in the Gazette.

13. (1) An officer or other employee of the Bank shall not occupy any other office or hold any other employment whether remunerated or not except with the approval of the Board embodied in a resolution and only in the following capacities

(a) As member of any economic research institution or of any commission establish by the Federal Government to enquire into any matter affecting currency or banking in Nigeria or into such other subjects relating to the functions of the Bank under this Act;

(b) As Director or member of the Board or by whatever name called, of any international bank, international monetary authority or economic institution to which the Federal Government shall have interest or give support or approval;

(c) As Director or alternate Director of corporation in Nigeria in which the Bank may participate under section 31 of this Act;

(d) As members of other agency of the Federal, State and Local Government.

(2) A remuneration to which any officer or other employee of the Bank is entitled in respect of any appointment made by virtue of the provisions of this Schedule shall be paid direct to the Bank.

(3) This Schedule shall not prevent the Bank from employing, at the Board's discretion and subject to such terms and conditions as shall be laid down by the Board, part-time advisers for particular purposes and for specific periods of time.

14. All officers and employee of the Bank shall be required to sign declarations as in Form 2 in the Annex to this Schedule affirming their allegiance and service to the Bank and pledging themselves to observe strict secrecy respecting all transactions of the Bank.

15. (1) The appointment of a legal practitioner to the Bank and change in that appointment shall be made by the Board on the recommendation of the Governor

(2) Plaints, writs, statement, affidavits and all other documents connecting with legal proceedings may be signed and verified on behalf of the Bank by any officer empowered by or under paragraph 12 of this Schedule.

16. The Board may require any officer or other employee to give the Bank, in such manner as it may require, such security as it may regard reasonable for the faithful discharge of his duty.

17. In this Schedule:

"Committee of Governor" means a committee of the Governor and the Deputy Governors of the Central Bank of Nigeria.

"Director" means a member of the Board of Director of the Central Bank of Nigeria.

SECOND SCHEDULE

Section 12 (5) and 54

Proceeding of the Monetary Policy Committee

1. The MFC shall meet a least four times in a year
2. The Governor (or in his absence, the Deputy Governor responsible for monetary policy) may summon meeting on giving not less than 7 days notice.
3. The quorum shall be six members two of whom shall be the Governor and a Deputy Governor or two Deputy Governor.
4. The chair shall be taken by the Governor or, if he is not present, the F Deputy Governor responsible for monetary policy.
5. Decisions shall be taken by a vote of all those present at the meeting.
6. In the event of a tie, the Chairman shall have a second or casting
7. The MFC shall submit periodic report of its meeting and activities to the Board of the Directors of the Bank.

I certify, in accordance with section 2 (1) of the Acts Authentication Act, Cap. 4, Law of the Federation of Nigeria 1990, that this is a true copy of the Bill passed by both Houses of the National Assembly.

Nasiru Ibrahim Ardo
Clerk to the National Assembly
25th Day of May, 2007

EXPLANATORY MEMORANDUM

This Act repeals the Central Bank of Nigeria Act, 1991, re-enacts as a new Central Bank of Nigeria Act, 2007 and establishes the Central Bank of Nigeria for the promotion of sound financial system in Nigeria and to act as banker and provide economic and financial advice to the Federal Government.

APPENDIX III

REGULATORY AND SUPERVISORY GUIDELINES FOR MICRO FINANCE BANKS (MFBS) IN NIGERIA
TABLE OF CONTENTS

1. INTRODUCTION

1.1 Background

The growing awareness of the potential of microfinance in poverty reduction, economic growth and development, couple with the emergence of several highly successful and fast growing Micro Finance Institutions (MFIs), has effectively put the issue of microfinance on the political agenda of most developing countries. Consequently, the supervisory authorities of such institutions have taken active measures to address the issue of microfinance by developing an appropriate regulatory and supervisory framework based on the particular features and risks associated with this activity.

The challenge that supervisors face, which is sometimes complicated by a multitude of Legal initiative in this area, is how to accommodate or reasonably encourage microfinance within a frame work of generally accepted norms and prudential standards for the financial services industry. In general, a frame work that does not adequately address the features and risks of microfinance would neither effectively serve the institutions nor the people who depend upon them. Therefore, bank supervisors strive to ensure that the supervisory framework in place is such that would result in innovative, rapid and balance growth of the industry as well as being consistent with accepted banking practices. The issue of savings of deposits is central to the regulation and supervision of microfinance. Specifically, supervisory authorities are expected to ensure that the poor clients who constitute the bulk of the consistency of microfinance institutions do not lose their savings if such institutions fail.

A new challenge for developing an appropriate regulatory and supervisory framework for microfinance lies in the great diversity of institutions offering microfinance service. A comprehensive framework which significantly base on the micro lending activity should, therefore, be developed and made applicable to all supervised institutions offering this service, regardless of whether they are licensed as a bank or as new institutions created specifically for microfinance the regulation should be defined to include standards for portfolio classification, loan documentation, loan loss provisioning, and write-offs for all microfinance operation.

It is significant to note that the characteristics of microfinance clients are distinct, their credit methodology is different and, in many cases, the ownership structure of the institutions is not the same as that typically found in conventional financial institutions. These and other factors give rise to unique risk profile which needs to be addressed through the regulatory framework and supervisory shall be implemented which would focus mainly on:

(a) An effective governance and ownership structure;
(b) A responsive lending methodology;
(c) Accurate and up-to-date knowledge of borrower characteristics;
(d) A appropriate management information system;
(e) Adequate internal control mechanisms and procedures

A simple and rational regulatory and supervisory framework which would achieve a balanced growth, promote transparency, control the risks faced by institutions engaged in microfinance, eliminate barriers and unnecessary requirements has, therefore, been developed and would be implemented for the sector.

1.2 Power to Regulate

These supervisory regulatory guidelines being issued by the Central Bank of Nigeria (hereinafter referred to as CBN or the Bank) in exercise of the powers conferred on it by the provisions of Section 28 subsection (1) (b) of the CBN Act No. 24 of 1991 (as amended) and in pursuance of the provisions of sections 56-60A of the Banks and Other Financial Institutions Act (BORA) No. 25 of 1991 (as mended). The guidelines are designed to regulate microfinance activities the establishment and operations of Micro-finance Bank (MFB) that sole to accept savings/deposits from members of the public and engage in microfinance intermediation services for their clients in Nigeria.

1.3 Terms and Definition

For the purpose of clarity, the following terms and definition shall be used in the applicable sections of these guideline.

(a) Micro Finance Bank

A Micro Finance Bank (MFB), unless otherwise stated, shall be construed to mean any company licensed to carry on the business of providing micro-finance services such as savings, loans, domestic funds transfer, and other financial services that are needed by the economically active poor, micro, small and medium enterprises need to conduct or expand their business as defined by these guidelines.

(b) Micro Finance Client

A client of an MFB who generally possesses the following characteristics shall qualify as a micro finance client:

(i) Has a monthly income of not more than twice the monthly per capital income of Nigeria, or minimum wage, whichever is higher.

(ii) Has a total productive assets (including those arising from loans but excluding the cost of land) of not more than five hundred thousand Naira (₦500,000.00).

(iii) Is not a regular employee of any organization;

(iv) Aged between 18 and 60 years.

(c) Poor Person

A poor person shall be defined as one who has meagre means of sustenance or livelihood and whose total income during a year is less than the minimum taxable limit set out in the law relating to income tax.

(d) Micro-Enterprises

A micro-enterprise is a business that requires micro credit/loans to operate. The operations and management are often built around the sole owner or micro-entrepreneur usually works alone or provides employment for a few people, typically the immediate family members, and does not often require formal registration to start. The management and accounting requirements of the business are usually very simple and flexible. Generally, micro entrepreneurs work formally, without business licenses or formal records of their activities of earnings. The scope of economic activities of micro-enterprises typically includes primary production and crafts, value-added processing and distributive trades.

(e) A Micro Loan

A micro loan is a facility granted to an individual borrower or a group borrowers whose principal source of income is derived from business activities involving the production or sale of goods and services. The maximum principal amount shall not exceed ₦500,000 or as may be reviewed from time to time by CBN.

Generally, a micro loan is a granted to the operators of Micro-enterprises, such as peasant farmers, artisans, fishermen, rural women, senior citizens, salaried and non-salaried workers in the formal and informal sectors. The said loans are usually unsecured, but typically granted on the basis of the applicant's character and the combined cash flow of the business and household. Ordinarily, the tenure of a micro loan is 180 days (6 months). However, in the case of crops with a longer gestation period a maximum tenure of Twelve (12) months shall be permitted. Micro loans may require joint and several guarantees of one or more persons. The repayment may be on a daily, weekly, bimonthly or monthly basis. In accordance with the amortization schedule in the loan contract.

2.0 PERMISSIBLE AND PROHIBITED ACTIVITIES

2.1 Permissible Activities

An MFB shall be allowed to engage in the provision of the following services to its clients:

(a) Acceptance of various types of deposits, including savings, time, target and demand from individuals, groups and associations, except public sector deposits (government);
(b) Provision of credit to its customers, including formal and informal self-help groups, individuals and associations;
(c) Promotion and monitoring of loan usage among its customer by providing ancillary capacity building in such areas as record keeping and small business management;
(d) Issuance of redeemable debentures to interested parties to raise funds from member of the public with the approval of the CBN;
(e) Collection of money or proceeds of banking instruments on behalf of its customer through correspondent banks;
(f) Provision of payment services, such as salaries, gratuities, and pensions for the various tiers of government;
(g) Provision of loan disbursement services for the delivery of the credit programmers of governments, agencies, groups and individuals for poverty alleviation on a non-recourse basis;
(h) Provision of ancillary banking services to their customers, such as domestic remittance of funds and safe custody;
(i) Maintenance and operation of various types of account with other banks in Nigeria;

(j) Investment of surplus funds of the MFB in suitable instruments, including placing such funds with correspondent banks and in Treasury bills;
(k) Payment and receipt of interest as may be agreed between the MFBs and their clients, in accordance with existing guidelines;
(l) Operation of micro leasing facilities, microfinance related hire purchase, and arrangement of consortium lending and supervision of credit schemes to ensure access of micro finance customer to input for their economic activities;
(m) Receiving of re-financing or other funds from the CBN and other sources, private or public, on terms mutually acceptable to both the provider of the funds and the recipient MFBs;
(n) Provision of microfinance related guarantees for MFB customers to enable them have greater access to credit and other resources;
(o) Buying, selling and supplying industrial and agricultural inputs, livestock, machinery and industrial raw materials to poor persons on credit and acting as agents for any association for the sale of such goods or livestock;
(p) Investment in shares or equity of anybody corporate, the objective of which is to provide microfinance services to poor persons;
(q) Encouragement of investment in cottage industries and income generating relating to microfinance activities;
(r) Provision of services and facilities to customers to hedge various risks relating to microfinance activities;
(s) Provision of professional advice to poor persons regarding investments in small businesses; rending managerial, marketing, technical and administrative advice to customers and assisting them in obtaining services in such fields;
(t) Mobilizing and providing financial and technical assistance and training to mircro-enterprises;
(u) Provision of loans to microfinance clients for home improvement and consumer credits; and
(v) Performance of non-banking functions that relate to micro finance business development services, such as co-operatives and group formation activities, rural industrialization and other support services needed by micro enterprises;

No MFB shall undertake any business or activity other than those permitted as stated above or as may be prescribed by the Central Bank of Nigeria from time to time.

2.2Prohibited Activities

NO MFB shall engage in the provision of the following financial services;

(a) Acceptance of public sector (Government) deposits except for the permissible activities (f) and (g) in subsection 2.1 of these guidelines;
(b) Foreign exchange transactions;
(c) International commercial papers;
(d) International corporate finance;
(e) International electronic funds transfer;
(f) Cheque clearing activities;
(g) Dealing in tend for speculative purposes;
(h) Real estate, except for its use as office accommodation;
(i) Allowing any facility for speculative purposes; and
(j) Entering into leasing, renting, and sale/purchase of any kind with its directors, officers, employees or person who, either individually or in concert with their family members and beneficiaries, own five per cent (5%) or more of the equity of the MFB, without the prior approval in writing of the Central Bank of Nigeria.

4.0 OWNERSHIP AND LICENSING REQUIREMENTS

4.1 Ownership Requirements

Microfinance banks can be established by individuals, groups of individuals, community development associations, private corporate entitles, or by foreign investors. Significantly ownership diversification shall be encouraged to enhance good corporate governance of licensed MFBs. Universal banks that intend to set up any category of the MFBs as subsidiaries shall be required to meet the prescribed prudential requirements and availability of free funds and if, in the view of the regulatory authorities, have satisfied all the requirements stipulated in the guidelines.

4.2 Licensing Requirements

Any promoters seeking a licence for a Microfinance Bank (MFB) business in Nigeria shall apply in writing to the Governor of the Central Bank of Nigeria. There shall be two (2) categories of licence available for promoters (both local and foreign) of Microfinance Banks based on geographical coverages as specified below.

(i) A Microfinance Bank licence (A.K.A Community Banks) to operate as a unit bank. The minimum capital requirement shall be ₦20.000,000 (Twenty million naira) or such amount as may be prescribed by the CBN from time to time.
(ii) A Microfinance Bank licensed to operate in a State and open branches within a specified state or Federal Capital Territory. The minimum capital requirement shall be ₦1,000,000,000 (One billion naira) or such amount as may be prescribed by the CBN from time to time.
(iii) Such application shall be accompanied with the following;
(a) A non-refundable application fee of ₦50,000.00 or ₦100,000.00 for MFBs licensed to operate in LGAs and States, respectively, in bank drafts, payable to the Central Bank of Nigeria;
(b) A deposit of the minimum capital requirements for the relevant category of MFB, which shall be in bank draft and payable to the CBN. The capital thus deposited, together with the accrued interest, shall be released to the promoters on the granting of a licence;
(c) Satisfactory verifiable and acceptable evidence of payment by the proposed shareholders of the minimum capital requirement for the category of licence being applied for, including a personal statement that capital does not originate from bank credit, any for or credit questionable sources, or any activity that relates to money laundering;
(d) A certificate of capital importation issued by an authorized dealer (banks) in the case of foreign capital.
(e) A copy of the MFBs detailed feasibility report disclosed relevant information that shall include:
(i) The objectives and aims of the proposed MFB
(ii) The justification for the establishment of the MFB
(iii) The services that the MFB intends to provide
(iv) The branch expansion programme (if any) within the first five years,
(v) The proposed training programme for staff and management's succession plan.
(vi) A five-year financial projection for the operation of the MFB indicating its expected growth and profitability
(vii) Details of the assumptions upon which the financial projections have been made
(viii) The organizational structure of the MFB, setting out in detail, the functions and responsibilities of the top management team

(ix) The composition of the Board of Directors and the Curriculum Vitae (CV) of each member, including other directorships held (if any)
(x) Appropriate management information systems, internal controls and procedures, including manuals of operations, and
(xi) The conclusions based on the assumptions made in the feasibility report.

(f) A copy of the draft Memorandum and Articles of Association;
(g) A letter of intent to subscribe to the shares of the proposed MFB, signed by each subscriber.
(h) A copy of the list of promoters/proposed shareholder in tabular form, showing their business and residential addresses (not Post Office addresses) and the names and addresses of their bankers;
(i) The names and CV's of the proposed members of the Board of Directors Each CV's must be personally signed and dated

No proposed MFB under this policy shall incorporate/register its name with the Corporate Affairs Commissions (CAC) until a written approval-in-principal (AIP) has been communicated to the promoters by the CBN, a copy of which shall be presented to the Corporate Affairs Commission.

In considering an application for a licence, the CBN shall satisfy itself thus;

(i) The promoters and the proposed Management team are "fit and proper" persons to invest in manage the financial services industry in Nigeria by regulatory standards;
(ii) The promoters have submitted the names and curriculum vitae of the top management team of the proposed MFB;
(iii) The minim paid-up capital/shareholders' funds of the relevant category being applied for its acceptable and the source is verifiable and satisfactory to the CBN;
(iv) The quality of the management of the proposed MFB is sound;
(v) The earnings prospects of the company is realizable; and
(vi) The objectives of the company as disclosed in its Memorandum and Articles of Association agree with the services listed in the relevant provision of these guidelines.

(j) The CBN shall, before the issuance of an approval-up-principal (AIP), arrange an appraisal interview for the promoters of the proposed MFB. The date and time for the interview shall be communicated to the promoters in writing.

(k) If satisfied, the Governor may grant a licence to the MFB, where the grant of licence is declined, the reason(s) for refusal shall be communicated in writing to the applicant.

(l) The CBN may at any time vary or revoke any conditions of a licence or impose additional conditions.

(m) Where a licence is granted subject to some conditions, the MFB, shall comply with those conditions to the satisfaction of the CBN within such period as the CBN may deem appropriate in the circumstances. Any MFB that fails to comply with such conditions shall be guilty of an office, under BOFIA 1991 (as amended).

(n) All licensed MFBs be required to add "Microfinance Bank (MFB) Ltd" after their names which shall be registered with the Corporate Affairs Commission as compliance with the Companies and Allied Matters Act (CAMA).

4.3 Application and Licensing Fees

The application and licensing fees, which may be varied at the instance of the CBN shall be as follows:

	Unit MFB	State MFB
(a) Non-refundable Application fee	₦50,000.00	₦100,000.00
(b) Non-Refundable Licensing Fee	₦100,000.00	₦250,000.00
(c) Change of Name fee	₦20,000.00	₦50,000.00

An MFB wishing to convert its licence status shall be required to pay the applicable

5.0 MANAGEMENT

5.1 Directors

(a) The maximum number of directors (including executive directors) on the Board of an MFB shall be seven (7), which the minimum shall be three (3). To qualify for the position of a director in an MFB, it is required that the person must not be a current employee of a bank or other financial institution, except where the MFB is promoted by a bank or other financial institution and the person is representing the interest of such institution. In the circumstance, where a current employee of a bank or other financial institution is proposed for the position of director, the consent of the employer must be given in writing to the CBN. No person serve as director in more than two (2) institution under the regulatory purview of the CBN.

(b) At least two (2) members of the Board of Directors, other than the Executive Management, shall be required to have banking or related industry experience.

(c) The appointment of new directors and management staff shall be approved by CBN.

5.2Management Requirements

The following minimum qualifications and experience are mandatory for officers who may occupy the key to top management positions in MFBs:

(a) Managing Director/Chief Executive: a recognized university degree or its equivalent and/ or professional qualification with at least 7 years post-qualification experience in banking or related industry.

(b) Departmental Head: a recognized university degree or its equivalent an/or professional qualification with at least 5 years post-qualification experience in banking or related industry.

(c) A Person with any other qualifications or experience that may be considered adequate by the CBN may hold either of the positions (a) and (b) within an MFB.

5.3 Certification Process

In recognition of the peculiarities microfinance services and the management of MFBs, it shall be required that the top management possesses the requisite certification on microfinance management from recognized certification institutions acceptable to the Central Bank of Nigeria. To fulfill this requirement, members of the top management team of an MFB shall be required to submit evidence of such certificate. Members of the executive management shall be required to possess certification on microfinance management not later than three (3) years after the take-off of the certification programme. A transition period of twenty four (24) months shall be allowed for the take-off of this program following the implementation of the microfinance policy. Failure to comply with this condition shall be a sufficient ground for the removal of the affected officer.

5.0 CONDITIONS PRECEDENT TOT EH COMMENCEMENT OF OPERATIONS

(a) The promoters of an MFB shall submit the following documents to the CBN before it is permitted to commence;

(i) A copy of the shareholders' register in which the equity interest of each shareholder is properly reflected (together with the original for sighting).
(ii) A copy of the share certificate issued to each shareholder
(iii) A certified true copy of Form CO2 (Return of Attornments) filed with the Corporate Affairs Commission.
(iv) A certified try copy of the Form CO7 (Particulars of Directors) and a writing confirmation that the Board of Directors approved by the CBN has been installed
(v) A certified true copy of the Memorandum and Articles of Association approved by the CBN and filled with the Corporate Affairs Commission
(vi) The opening statement of affairs audited by an approved firm of accountant practicing in Nigeria
(vii) A certified true copy of the certificate of incorporation of the company (together with the original for sighting purposes only);
(viii) A copy each of the letters of offer and acceptance of employment by the Management staff and a written confirmation that the Management team approved be the CBN has put in place; and
(ix) A letter of undertaking to comply with all the rules and regulations guiding the operations of MFBs.

(b) The MFB shall inform the CBN of the location and address of its Head Office in Nigeria and shall confirm that all infrastructures for take-off are in place in addition, the MFB shall show evidence that an appropriate management information system, internal controls and procedures, including manuals of operations, have been put in place.
(c) The MFB shall be informed in writing by the CBN that it may commence business after the physical inspection of its premises.
(d) The MFB shall inform the CBN in writing of the date of commencement of business after the physical inspection of its premises.

7.0 FUNDING ACCOUNTS AND RELATED MATTERS

7.1 Sources of Funds

The sources of funds of an MFB shall consist of the following;

(a) Shareholders' funds paid-up share capital and reserves;
(b) Deposits/savings of customers;
(c) Grants/donations from individuals, organizations, national government, and International sources;
(d) Fees and commissions; and

(e) Interest income

7.2 Books of Accounts

(i) The Board of Directors of an MFB shall ensure that the institution keeps proper books of account with respect to all transactions at the principal administrative office and in all its branches in English, or any other language approved by the Federal Government of Nigeria.

(ii) For the purpose of subsection (i) of this section, "proper books of account" shall contain all information necessary to explain all transaction and give a true fair view of the state of affairs of the MFB and be presented in compliance with the accounting standards issued by the Nigerian Accounting Standards Board.

(iii) Where the books of account are not properly kept, in the opinion of the CBN, the Bank shall apply the provision of section 24 (5) BOFIA, 1991 as amended.

(iv) If any person being a Director, Manager or Officer of an MFB fails to take all reasonable steps to secure compliance with any of the provisions of this section, he or she shall be appropriately, in line with the provision of these guidelines.

7.3 Portfolio-At-Risk (PAR)

(a) PAR is the outstanding principal amount of all loans that have at least one instalment past due for one or more days. The amount includes the unpaid principal balance including the accrued interest. Under PAR, loans are considered past due if payment has fallen due and remained unpaid. Loan payments are applied first to any interest due, and then to any instalment of principal that is due but unpaid, beginning with the earliest instalment. The number of days of lateness is based on the due date of the earliest loan instalment that has been fully paid.

(b) It shall be required that PAR shall not exceed 2.5% of any given time for an MFB.

(c) Past Due Micro Loans: This is any loan that has missed one day repayment in accordance with the agreed repayment term in the loan contract. Such loans, whether restructured or refinanced, shall attract appropriate provision for loan loss. The past due micro loans shall remain in the account of the MFB until it is fully repaid, or arrangements are formalized for its reactivation renewal restructuring or a collection case has been filed in court.

(d) Accrual of Interest Earned: No accrual of interest shall be allowed after the micro loan has become past due. All interest accrued and/or booked shall be revered and the accrual interest shall be allowed after the micro loan become past due as defined in (c) of this subsection.

(e) Restructured Micro Loans: These represent micro loans that have been renegotiated or modified to either lengthen or postpone the original scheduled instalment payments, or to substantially after the original terms of the loans. Restructured loans, which shall include refinanced loans (i.e. loans disbursed to enable repayment or part prepayment of prior loans that was past due). Shall be treated as non-performing and no interest income shall be accrued thereon.

7.4 Rendition of Returns

In compliance with the provision of section 58 (2) (b) of BOFIA, 1991 (as amended), the following quarterly returns shall be submitted by MFBs.

(i) Statements of Assets and Liabilities;
(ii) Profit Loss Account;
(iii) Schedule of Loans and Investments on sector basis (number and value);
(iv) Schedule of Liabilities (deposits) on maturity basis (number and value);
(v) Interest Rate Structure;
(vi) Schedule of Balances held with banks;
(vii) Returns on;
(i) Borrowings from other MFBs, other financial institution, individuals and non-financial institutions;
(ii) Credits to other MFBs, other financial institutions, individuals/non-staff and others;
(iii) Non-performing credits;
(iv) Off balance sheet engagements;
(v) Non-performing other assets; and
(vi) Other items as may be specified by the CBN

All quarterly returns must reach the Director of Other Financial Institutions Department (OFID) of the CBN, Lagos, not later than 14 days, after the end of each quarter. The Managing Director/Chief Executive Officer and the Chief Accountant (or equivalent) the MFB shall sign and attach to every return made to the CBN a declaration of the authenticity of its contents. The frequency of the return may be reviewed from time to time by the CBN.

Universal banks currently engaged in micro finance services, either as an activity or product, shall be required to submit the returns on their micro-finance activities separately, in accordance with the provisions of these guidelines.

8.0 COMPLIANCE WITH ANTI-MONEY LAUNDERING ACT AND THE "KNOW YOUR CUSTOMERS (KYC) CIRCULARS

All MFB's shall be required to comply with Anti-money Laundering Act 2004, and the principles and procedures of Know Your Customer (KYC) relevant Circulars as issued by the CBN from time to time.

9.0 PUBLICATION OF AUDITED FINANCIAL STATEMENTS

9.1 Procedure and Publication

Every MFB shall submit its audited financial statements and the abridged version of the accounts to the Director of OFID for approval not later than four months after the end of the company's financial year. The Domestic Report on the Accounts from the External Auditors shall be forwarded to the Director, OFID, not later than three months after the end of the accounting year. After approval by the Central Bank of Nigeria, the MFB shall be required to display an abridged version of its audited financial statements at its head office and all its branches. Every approved audited account shall disclose in details the penalties paid as a result of any contravention of BORA 1991 (as amended) and any policy guidelines in force during the year in question and the auditor's report shall reflect such contraventions. Any MFB that fails to comply with the above requirements shall be liable to a fine not exceeding ₦20,000.00 for each day during which the offence continues.

9.2 Penalties for Late or False/Inaccurate Returns or Other False/Inaccurate Information

(a) For lateness in submitting a return or furnishing any information required, the penalty shall be a fine of ₦20,000.00 for each day during which such failure occurs. Persistent failure/refusal (consequently for a period of six months or six times within a period of twelve months) to render returns in the prescribed form shall be a ground for the revocation of an MFB's licence.

(b) Where the Bank considers it necessary, it may appoint a firm of qualified accountants to prepare proper books of account or render accurate returns, as the case may be, for the MFB concerned and the cost of preparing eh account or rending the returns shall be borne by the MFB.

(c) If any Director or Officer of an MFB fails to take all reasonable steps to ensure that proper books of accounts are kept with respect to all transactions by the company at its Head Office and/or at its branches, the CBN may impose on him a fine not exceeding ₦20,000.00 and in addition shall be removed and black-listed. If any default in this respect is caused by the wilful act of any Director or Officer of the MFB, the CBN may impose on him/her a fine not exceeding ₦1.0 million or cause the removal of such Director or Officer in order to protect the integrity of the financial system. In addition, the Bank may impose on the MFB such other penalties as are deemed appropriate.

10.0 PRUDENTIAL REQUIREMENTS

10.1 General Prudential Requirements

Every MFB shall comply with the following requirements;

(a) Compulsory Investment in Treasury Bills: All MFBs shall be required to maintain not less than 5 per cent of their deposit liabilities in Treasury Bills (TBs).

(b) Liquidity Ratio: The operation of MFBs requires the maintenance of a high level of liquid assets to meet frequent requests for funds from clients and for field operations. All MFBs shall be required to maintain a minimum ratio of twenty per cent (20%) of their deposits liabilities, including 5% compulsory Investment in Treasury Bills in the liquid assets.

(c) Capital Funds Adequacy: An MFB shall at all times maintain a minimum capital adequacy ratio as may be prescribed by the CBN from time to time. The capital adequacy ratio shall be measured as a percentage of the capital based of an MFB to its risk-weighted asset exposure in accordance with the provisions which the CBN shall prescribe.

The minimum Capital Adequacy Ratio (Capital/Risk Weighted Assets Ratio) for each Micro Finance Institution shall be 10%. Furtherance, an MFB is expected to maintain a ratio of not less than 1:10 between its shareholders' fund unimpaired by losses and net credits.

The CBN may require an MFB to maintain additional capital as it consider appropriate in respect of specific concentration of risks or market risks or connected lending.

When any of the above ratios falls below the prescribed level, the MFB shall be prohibited from any or all of the following, until the required ratio is restored:

(i) Granting credits and undertaking further investment;
(ii) Paying dividend to shareholders;
(iii) Borrowing from the investing public; and
(iv) Opening branch/cash centres

In addition, the MFB shall be required to submit, within a specified period, a re-capitalization plan acceptable to the CBN. Failure to comply with the above may constitute ground for the revocation of the operating licence of the MFB or such other penalties as may be deemed appropriate. MFB's are enjoined to ensure that their shareholders' funds do not fall below the required minimum paid-up capital.

(d) Fixed Assets/Long-term Investment and Branch Expansion: No MFB shall be allowed to finance any the following other than from the shareholder's funds, unimpaired by losses;

(i) The acquisition of fixed assets;
(ii) Equity investments and investment in long-term debenture and
(iii) Branch expansion

In consideration of a request for any or combination of the above options, reference shall be made to be aggregate value of the listed items against the shareholders' funds, unimpaired by losses.

(e) Maintenance of Capital Funds: MFBs are generally expected to pay less emphasis on collaterals in granting credits. The impact of delinquent risk assets, which may result in capital erosion, calls for stringent maintenance of capital funds.

Every MFB shall, therefore, maintain a reserve fund into which shall be transferred out of its net profits for each year, before it declares any dividend and after it has made provision for any taxes, the following amounts;

(i) Where the amount of the MFB's reserve fund is 50 per cent (50%) or more, but less than 100 per cent (100%) of its paid-up capital, an amount which shall not be less than 25 per cent (25%) of the MFB's net profit for the year, or
(ii) Where the amount of the MFB's reserve fund is equal to 100 per cent (100%) or more of its paid-up capital, an amount equal to 12.5 per cent (12.5%) of the MFB's net profit for the year.

An MFB shall not appropriate any sum of sums from the balance in its reserve fund unless prior approval in writing is obtained from the CBN for the purpose, which may be granted for such amount and subject to compliance with such conditions as the CBN may determine.

The CBN may, from time to time, vary the proportion of net profit transferable to Statutory Reserves.

No accretion shall be made to the reserve fund shall:

(i) All preliminary and pre-operational expenses have been written off;

(ii) Adequate provisions has been made for loan loss/assets deterioration; and

(iii) All identifiable losses have been fully provided for.

(f) Restrictions on Declaration of Dividends: An MFB shall not declare or pay a dividend on its hares until it has:

(i) Completely written-off all its preliminary and pre-operational expenses;

(ii) Made the required provisions for non-performing loans and other erosions in assets values;

(iii) Satisfied the minimum capital adequacy ratio requirement; and

(iv) Met all matured obligations

1. Where the payment of dividend would result in withdrawal of any part of the free reserves due to inadequacy of the profit for the year or where the statutory report of the auditors on the Annual Accounts of the bank is not satisfactory, the MFB may declare any dividend on its shares only after obtaining the prior approval of the CBN.
2. Where an MFB declares or pays any dividend in contravention of this provision, every director and chief executive officer of the MFB shall be liable to pay to the CBN a penalty, the sum of which shall be determined by the CBN.

(g) Limit of Lending to a Single Borrower and Related Party: the Maximum loan by an MFB to any individual borrower or director, related borrowers shall not exceed one per cent (1%), while a group borrower is restricted to maximum of 5% of the MFB's shareholders' fund unimpaired by losses or as may be prescribed by the CBN from time to time.

In addition, aggregate insider-related lending shall not exceed 5% of the paid-up capital of the MFB at any time. For this purpose, loans under a staff scheme shall not apply, but shall be in accordance with the staff conditions of service.

Any contravention will attract a penalty of 1.0 million on the MFB and a fine of ₦100,000.00 of the director/manager who fails to comply.

(h) Maximum Equity Investment Holding Ratio: The aggregate value of the equity participation of an MFB in all permissible enterprises shall not exceed 7.5% of its shareholders' fund unimpaired by losses without prior approval in writing by the CBN.

(i) Provision of Classified Assets: All performing risk assets created by the MFBs shall attract 1% general provision. Provision for non-performing risk assets and other assets shall be as stated hereunder:

Requirement (No. of Days Missed Payment)	Description	Provisioning or Allowance for Probable Tosses (%)
0	Performing	1%
1-30 days	Past and watch	5%
31-60 days	Sub-standard	20%
61-90 days	Doubtful	50%
91 or more days and/ restructured loans Lost		100%

Each MFB shall review, at least one every thirty days, its loans and advances and other investments and make appropriate provisions for loan losses or assets deterioration.

Every MFB must sent to OFID every month a schedule of loans/investments showing the provisions made for losses or deterioration in the quality of the loans/investments.

(j) Contingent Items: The concept, use and treatment of Bankers' Acceptances (BAs) and Commercial Papers (CPs) by banks and discount hoses and other financial institutions shall apply to MFBs.

(k) Limit of Investment In fixed Assets: The maximum amount which an MFB can invest in fixed assets, is 20% of its shareholders' funds unimpaired by losses.

Any contravention shall attract a penalty not exceeding two (2) million or suspension of the licence.

(l) Revaluation of fixed Assets: Prior approval of the CBN must be obtained by any MFB before the recognition of the revaluation surplus on fixed assets in its books, taking into consideration that:

(i) The basis of the underlying fixed assets valuations are stated and the valuation made by qualified professional valuers whose identity and qualifications are stated:

(ii) The difference between the market and the historic values of the eligible fixed assets being revalued shall be discounted by 55%.
(iii) The revaluation of fixed assets is applicable to own premises only; and
(iv) The revaluation of fixed assets (owned premises only) is permissible within a minimum period of 5 years after the date of the purchase of the asset or the last revaluation.

10.2 Special Prudential Standards

Some regulations common in traditional banking shall be adjusted, at the full discretion of the CBN from time to time, to accommodate the peculiarities of microfinance services as detailed in this section.

(a) Unsecured Lending Limits: in accordance with the provisions of BOFIA section 20 (2) (a), any unsecured advances or loans or Credit facilities of an aggregate amount in excess of Fifty Thousand Naira (₦50,000.00) is not permitted. For the purpose of applying this regulation to an MFB, group guarantees or third parity guarantees of an individual acceptable to the MFB shall qualify as collateral for microfinance loans.
(b) Loan Documentation Requirement: Given the nature of microfinance loans, sizes and customers, collateral registration, financial statement of borrowers or evidence that those businesses are formally registered shall not be required.
(c) Restriction of Co-signers as Borrowers: The restriction prohibiting a bank from lending to someone who has co-signed or otherwise guaranteed a loan from the same banks shall not apply to a Micro Finance Bank.
(d) Reporting Requirements: The reporting requirements for microfinance banks shall be simplified to minimize administrative costs to them.
(e) Cash Requirements: The mandatory cash reserve requirements (CRR) for banks shall not apply to an MFB. Rather, an MFB shall be required to have compulsory investment of 5% of its total deposit liabilities in treasury bills which shall qualify as specified liquid asset in the computation of its liquidity ratio.

11.0 ASSESSMENT SOUNDNESS

"MFB Rating" is a standard measurement for the assessment of its performance in capital, asset quality, management, earnings, and liquidity (CAMEL), with weighing as follows:

CAMEL Factor	Weight
Capital	30%

Asset Quality	30%
Management	30%
Earnings	20%
Liquidity	10%

The factor that may affect an MFB rating are violations of the legal lending limit and judgment factors.

Judgment factors may reduce MFB's rating to "unsound" in the event of internal disputes, intervention by third parties, window dressing, unsound banking parties, financial difficulties/and other irregular banking practices. Rating is divided into four categories: sound, satisfactory, marginal, and unsound.

12.0 REQUIREMENTS FOR THE INCREASE SHARE CAPITAL

All increases in share capital in any form shall be approved by the CBN. Application in respect of this shall be supported with the following:

(i) Board resolution authorizing the increase;
(ii) Evidence of payment of stamp duty;
(iii) Corporate Affairs Commission (CAC) registration of the increase;
(iv) Form CO2 showing the additional capital;
(v) Share certificate issued by shareholders;
(vi) Photocopy of the share register showing the entries of allotment;
(vii) Evidence of payment for the new allotment of shares by the shareholders (photocopies of cheques lodged should be attached). No cash payment is allowed for significant acquisition, i.e. up 5% of the share in MFB;
(viii) Vouchers showing evidence of internal transfer or payment for the right issues allotted;
(ix) Any other information that may be required or stipulated by the CBN.

12.0 DISCLOSURE OF INTEREST BY DIRECTORS AND OFFICERS OF MFBs

Every Director and Officer of MFB, who has any personal interest, whether directly or indirectly, in an advance, loan or credit facility, or proposed advance, loan or credit facility, vendor services from the MFB(s) in which he/she is serving, shall promptly declare the nature of his/her interest in writing to the Board of Directors of the MFB and the declaration shall be circulated to all the directors.

Every Director or Officer of MFB who holds any office or possess any property whereby, whether directly or indirectly, duties or interest might be created in conflict with his duties or interest as a Director or Officer of the MFB, shall declare a meeting of the Board of Directors of the MFB, the fact and the nature, character and extent of such interests. Any director or Officer who contravenes either of these regulations shall be liable to a fine of ₦500,000.00 or removal from office.

14.0 DISCLOSE OF REQUIRED INFORMATION TO THE CREDIT REFERENCE BUREAU

Every MFB shall be required to supply information all its credit clients to the Credit Reference Bureau from time to time. An addition, all MFBs shall provide:

(a) Details of non-performing loans of credit accommodations classified as doubtful or lost in its portfolio, where the amount owed is not in dispute, the customer has not made any satisfactory proposals for repayment following formal demand, and the customer has been given at least twenty-eight days' notice of the intention to disclose that information to the Credit Reference Bureau.

(b) Information on its customer involved in financial malpractices, including dud cheques.

(c) No information other than that referred to in subsections (a) and (b) above shall be divulged by any Institution to the Credit Reference Bureau without the customer's consent.

(d) Where (i) the Credit Reference Bureau, or (ii) an institution, discloses to another institution or its officer, the Credit Reference Bureau or its officer, the information referred to in subsections (a) and (b) above in good faith in the performance of its duties, no right of action shall be accrue to or against the customer for breach for any duty of confidentiality.

(e) Any customers of an MFB has a right to know his credit status forwarded to the Credit Reference Bureau.

15.0 OPERATIONAL REQUIREMENTS AND CONTROLS

15.1 Opening/Relocation and Closing of Branches: Prior approval of the CBN is required for the opening, relocation or closing of branches or cash centres of MFBs. In the case of relocation, appropriate notice of intention to relocate the principal place of business shall be given to the general public by the MFBs, after the CBN's approval.

In contravention, the MFB shall be made to pay a fine not exceeding ₦200,000.00 and also close or reopen the branch as the case may be and, in addition, a fine of ₦20,000.00 for each day during which the offence continues.

15.2 Change of Name by Licensed MFBs: Every MFB shall be required to obtain CBN's approval before effecting a change of name as contained in its operational licence.

15.3 Display of licence: a copy of an MFB's licence shall be displayed in a conspicuous at its Head officer as well as in the branches in contravention, the MFB shall be penalized in line with section 60 (i) of the Banks and Others Financial Institutions Act (BORA 1991) as amended.

15.4 Display of Interest Rates: Every MFB shall display on a daily basis in a conspicuous place at its Head Office and branches, its rates of interest. Interest rates shall be quoted on an annual basis and not monthly. In contravention, the MFB shall be liable to a fine of ₦50,000.00 and ₦5,000.00 in addition, for every day during which the offence continues or such other penalties deemed appropriate by the CBN.

15.5 Internal Controls: Every MFB shall have an Internal Audit Unit, which shall ensure that the operations of the company conform to the law as well as to its internal rules and regulations. The Internal Auditor shall forward his report directly to the Board of Directors to strengthen corporate governance in the MFB. Every fraud or attempted fraud must be promptly reported to the Director of OFID by the head of the unit. Also, a quarterly report on frauds and forgeries affecting the company and any default in meeting any obligation to lenders or investors shall be submitted to the Director, OFID. Where no funds/forgeries and defaults occurred during quarter, a nil return shall be forwarded. The reporter report shall be made along with the quarterly returns on assets and liabilities. Failure to comply with this requirement shall attract a fine of ₦50,00.00 per quarter.

16.0 APPOINTMENTS OF CHIEF EXECUTIVE/PRINCIPAL OFFICER AND EXTERNAL AUDITOR

16.1 Appointment of Chief Executive/Principal Officer

The appointment or replacement of the Chief Executive Officer or any of the Principal Officers of any MFB shall be cleared with the CBN before such appointment is made. Where the turnover of principal and senior officers sis considered to be unduly high, or where the reason for leaving by an officer suggests an attempt to cover up a fraud or other illegal activity, or to punish the officer for attempting to prevent illegal activities, the CBN shall cause an investigation to be conducted into the matter and other affairs of the MFB as may be considered necessary. The report of such investigation or special examination shall determine the penalty to be imposed on the MFB concerned.

16.2 Appointment of External Auditor

Every MFB shall appoint and approved external auditor, whose duties shall be to make to the shareholders a report on the annual financial statements of the company, and every such report shall contain true and faire statements as to the matters and such other information as may be prescribed from time to time by the CBN.

The approved auditor shall satisfy the following requirements:

(a) A member of a recognized professional accountancy body in Nigeria;
(b) Continues in professional practice as accountant and auditor in Nigeria;
(c) No person shall be appointed as the auditor of the MFB if;
(i) He has Interest in the MFB other than as a depositor; or
(ii) He is a Director, officer or agent of such institution, or
(iii) He comes from a firm in which a director of the MFB has interest as partner, or director, or (iv) He is indebted to the MFB
(d) Any auditor who is subsequently affected by section 15 (2) (c) above shall immediately cease to continue as the auditor of the
(e) An approved auditor in the course of his duties shall immediately report to the CBN formally if it is certified that;
(i) There has been a contravention of BOFIA 1991 (as amended), or that an offence under any other law, guidelines, circulars, etc.; has been committed by the MFB or any of its officers; or
(ii) Losses have been incurred by the MFB which substantially reduce its capital funds; or
(iii) He is unable to confirm that the claims of the depositors or creditors covered by the assets of the MFB.
(f) The approved auditor shall also forward the CBN one (1) copy of the domestic report on the activities of the MFB not later than three (3) months after the end of the financial year of such MFB.
(g) The approval auditor shall have the right of access at all times to all books, accounts and vouchers of the MFB an shall be entitled to require the directors, managers and officers of the MFB all information

and explanations he considers necessary for the performance of his audit.

(h) If any MFB fails to appoint or fill a vacancy for an approved auditor, the CBN shall appoint a suitable person for that purpose and shall fix the remuneration to be paid by the MFB to such auditor.

(i) The appointment of an approved auditor shall not be determined without if prior written approval of the CBN

(j) Any approved auditor who acts in contravention of the foregoing requirements or this section shall be liable to a fine of a maximum of ₦50,000.00 or a determination of his status as an approved auditor to all financial institutions under the supervisory purview of the CBN

(k) No Audit Firm shall serve the same institution as External Auditor for a continuous period exceeding three (3) years in order to enhance transparency in reporting.

16.0 SCHEME OF ARRANGEMENT

No MFB shall enter into any "Scheme of Arrangement" with its creditors/investors without obtaining the prior approval of the CBN. Any MFB that is unable to meet its obligations to its creditors or investors shall submit its proposals to restore liquidity or viability and for eventual settlement of its outstanding obligations to the Director of OFID for consideration and approval. Failure to comply with this will attract a penalty of ₦2,500.00 for each day during which the contravention exists.

17.0 RESTRUCTURING AND REORGANIZATION

Except with the prior consent of the Governor of the CBN, no MFB shall enter into an agreement or arrangement:

(a) Which results in a change in the control of the MFB; or

(b) For the sale, disposal or transfer of the whole or any part of the business of the MFB;

(c) For the amalgamation or merger of the MFB with any other company; or

(d) To employ a management agent or to transfer its business to any such agent.

18.0 TRANSFORMATION OF OTHER INSTITUTIONS AND MICROFINANCE BANKS (MFBs)

Any financial institution under the purview of the Central Bank of Nigeria that intends to transform into a Micro Finance Bank shall apply to the Bank and ensure that the licensing requirements for MFB are met.

(a) Universal Bank: A Universal Bank can operate a microfinance bank by betting up subsidiary MFB and obtaining a licence for it. Universal Banks currently engaging in microfinance services, either as an activity or product which do not desire to set up a subsidiary, shall be required to set up a department/unit for such services and shall be subjected to the provisions of the MFB regulatory and supervisory guidelines. The department/unit shall headed by a staff of not less than a Deputy General Manager or its equivalent for the purpose. Due to the peculiarities of microfinance practice and the nature of assets formed, the micro finance department of such a bank shall be required to have the following;

(i) A Management team;

(ii) Internal Controls and Procedures, and Manuals of Operations specifically designed for microfinance;

(iii) A Management Information System (MIS) and a loan tracking mechanism;

(iv) A Dedicated unit at branch level that is equipped for deposit mobilization and credit monitoring;

(v) A reporting format and policy for income recognition for MFBs, i.e. loan loss provisions; and

(vi) A Management that has completed the Certification Programme and any other conditions that the CBN may require from time to time.

Any Universal Bank that engages in microfinance services as an activity or product shall be required to submit separate quarterly returns of its microfinance portfolio, aside from its other lending activities.

(b) Community Banks: All community banks licensed prior to the approval of this policy shall transform to microfinance bank on meeting the prescribed new capital and other conversion requirement with a period of 24 months from the date of approval of the policy. Any community bank that falls to meet the new capital requirement within the stipulated period shall cease to operate as community bank. A community bank can apply to convert to a state microfinance bank if it meets the capital and other conversion requirements of a State MFB.

Specifically, Community Banks (CBs) wishing to transform to MFBs shall meet the following requirements:

(i) The minimum capital requirement/shareholders' funds must be raised to a minimum of ₦20 million for each unit, while that of MFBs with state wide coverage shall be ₦1.0 billion;

(ii) Upgrade its management team, Internal Controls, Management Information System (MIS), and procedure and Manuals of Operations;
(iii) May which to have a branded name not limited to the catchment area of its original location;
(iv) Meet the criteria for branch network when its applies;
(v) Adopt the reporting format and policy for income recognition for MFBs i.e. loan loss provisions;
(vi) Board and Management to undergo the Certification Programme;
(vii) Board and Management to undergo re-orientation on the commercial vision microfinance banking.
(c) Non-Government Organization (NGOs) MFIs

A transforming NGO-MFI shall be required to provide an institutional assessment by a rating agency with specialization in micro financing and an audited statement of Assets and Liabilities by a firm of chartered accountants acceptable to the CBN. The Institution assessment shall include the NGO's financial status, governance structure, human resources, risk management policy, control procedures, accounting and Management Information Systems. The application for conversion to an MFB shall be supported by the following documents:
(i) Board resolution approving the transformation and stating the objectives;
(ii) Details feasibility report, including a business plan specifying what the MFB plans to achieve in the next five years;
(iii) Detailed Curriculum Vitae of the proposed board members of the MFB, commitment letters to serve as board members and subscribed capital, if any;
(iv) Draft Memorandum and Articles of Association;
(v) Proposed name of the MFB;
(vi) Details of assets and liabilities to transfer to the MFB; the transfer shall be admissible to the value assessed/determined by the audit/consulting team during the institutional assessment phase; and
(vii) Payment of the MFB application fee is specialized in these guidelines.

The institution shall be required to submit separate quarterly return of its microfinance portfolio aside from its other lending activities.

In consideration of meeting the minimum capital requirement/shareholders' funds for the transformation, an existing institution shall be exempted from deposition, the paid-up, capital requirement (as the case may be) with the Central Bank of Nigeria. Its capital shall, however, be subject to verification by the CBN for confirmation.

19.0 COLLABORATION TO REGULAR DEPOSITS/SAVINGS MOBILIZING INSTITUTIONS

In order to prevent regulatory arbitrage at the lower end of the financial market, the CBN shall collaborate with other relevant agencies of government to supervise, the activities of financial co-operation and NGOs that have significant operations due to their micro savings/deposits taking activities from their members. Any of such institutions that attains a total assets of Twenty million naira (₦20,000,000.00) and/or total membership/clients of two thousands (2000) shall be required to transform to the relevant category of MFB, to the licensing requirements provided in these guidelines.

Collaborations between the CBN, the CAC and relevant government agencies shall be promoted to reduce arbitrage in the practice of microfinance.

20.0 CONDITIONS FOR GRANTING AND REVOCATION OF LICENCE

20.1 Conditions For Granting Approval-In-Principle

The Central Bank of Nigeria, on receipt of an application, which is complete in all respects, shall process the application and, if satisfied with the overall quality of the proposal, shall grant an Approval-in-Principle for establishing the MFB within three (3) months or receipt of the application.

20.2 Conditions For Final Licence and Commencement Of Business

A proposed MFB with an Approval-in-Principle shall be granted a final operating licence after satisfying the conditions stated in subsection 3.1 of these guidelines. Before being granted approval to commence operation, a newly licensed MFB shall be required to comply with the conditions precedent to the commencement of operations as contained in subsection 3.2 of these guidelines.

20.3 Conditions for Revocation of Licence

The ground for revoking a licence granted as MFB may be any or all of the following;

(a) Submission of false information/data during and/or after the processing of the application for licence;

(b) The use of proxies or disguised names to obtain a licence for MFB;

(c) Engaging in functions/activities outside the permissible scope or its licence as specified in subsection 1.1 of these guidelines;
(d) Persistent failure to comply with request for information/data in the form required/specified by CBN;
(e) Engaging in activities prejudicial to the Nigerian economy;
(f) Failure to redeem matured obligations to customers;
(g) Unauthorized shop closure;
(h) Failure to comply with any directive issued by the CBN;
(i) Any other act(s) which in the opinion of the CBN constitute(s) a violation or a serious default;
(j) Engaging in prohibited activities as listed in these guidelines; and
(k) Such other conditions are applicable to banks and other financial institutions which constitute grounds for revocation, under the Banks and Other Financial Institutions Act (BOFIA) of 1991 (as amended).

22.0 EXIT CONDITIONS

The conditions for the exit of a licensed, MFB shall be as prescribed by the relevant sections of the Banks and Other Financial Institutions Act (BOFIA) of 1991 (as amended) as applicable to deposit taking financial institutions and the Companies and Allied Matters Act (CAMA) 1990.

22.0 GENERAL

The list of valid licences of MFBs shall be published by the CBN from time to time.

CBN Abuja
December 2005.

APPENDIX IV

MICROFINANCE POLICY, REGULATORY AND SUPERVISORY FRAMEWORK FOR NIGERIA

TABLE OF CONTENTS

LIST OF ACRONYMS

ACGS - Agricultural Credit Guarantee Scheme
BOFIA - Banks and Other Financial Institution Act
CAC - Corporate Affairs Commission
CAMA - Companies and Allied Matters Act
CBN - Central Bank of Nigeria
CBs - Community Banks
FEAP - Family Economic Advancement Programme
LGA - Local Government Area
MFB - Micro Finance Bank
MFBs - Micro Finance Banks
MFIs - Micro Finance Institutions
MSME - Micro, Small and Medium Enterprises
NACB - Nigerian Agricultural Co-operative Bank Limited
NACRDB - Nigerian Agricultural Co-operative and Rural Development Bank Limited

NAIC	-	Nigerian Agricultural Insurance Corporation
NAPEP	-	National Poverty Eradication Programme
NDE	-	National Directorate of Employment
NDIC	-	Nigeria Deposit Insurance Corporation
NEEDS	-	National Economic Empowerment Developments Strategy
NGO	-	Non-Governmental Organization
NMFCC	-	National Micro Finance Consultative Committee
PBN	-	Peoples Bank of Nigeria
ROSCAs	-	Rotating Savings and Credit Associations
RRF	-	Refinancing and Rediscounting Facility
SHGs	-	Self Help Groups
SMEEIS	-	Small and Medium Enterprises Equity Investment Scheme
VAT	-	Value Added Tax

CHAPTER 1
INTRODUCTION

1.0 INTRODUCTION

Robust economic growth cannot be achieved without putting in place well focused programmes to reduce poverty through empowering the people by increasing their access to factors of production, especially credit. The latent capacity of the poor for entrepreneurship would be significantly enhance through the provision of microfinance services to enable them engage in economic activities and be more self-reliant, increase employment opportunities, enhance household income, and create wealth.

1.2 Microfinance is about providing financial services to the poor who are traditionally hot served by the conventional financial institutions. Three features distinguish microfinance from other financial products. These are:

(i) The smallness of loans advanced and saving collected,

(ii) The absence of asset-based collateral, and

(iii) Simplicity of operations

1.3 In Nigeria, the formal financial system provides services to about 35% of the economically active population while the remaining 65% are excluded from access to financial services. These 65% are often served by the informal financial sector, through Non-Governmental

Organization - Microfinance Institutions (NGOMFIs), money lenders, friends, relatives, and credit unions. The non-regulation of the activities of some these institutions has serious implications for the Central Bank of Nigeria's (CBN's) ability to exercise one aspect of its mandate of promoting monetary stability and a sound financial system.

1.4 A microfinance policy which recognizes the existing informal institutions and brings them within the supervisory purview of the CBN would not only enhance monetary stability, but also expand the financial infrastructure of the country to meet the financial requirements of the Micro, Small and Medium Enterprises (MSME's). Such policy would create a vibrant microfinance subsector that would be adequately integrated into the mainstream of national financial system and provide the stimulus for growth and development. It would also harmonize operating standards and provide a strategic platform for the evolution of microfinance institutions, promote appropriate regulation, supervision and adoption of best practices. In these circumstances, an appropriate policy has become necessary to develop a long-term sustainable microfinance subsector.

1.5 The purpose of this policy paper, therefore, is to present a Microfinance Policy Framework for Nigeria that would enhance the provision of diversified microfinance services on a long-term, sustainable basis for the poor and low income groups. The policy would create a platform from the establishment of microfinance works; improve the CBN's regulatory supervisory performance in ensuring monetary, stability and liquidity management; and provide an appropriate machinery for tracking the activities of development partners in the microfinance subsector in Nigeria.

1.6 The policy has been prepared in exercise of the powers conferred on the Central Bank of Nigeria by the provisions of section 28, subsection (1) (b) of the CBN Act 24 of 1991 (as amended) and in pursuance of the provisions of sections 56, 50 (a) of the Banks and Other Financial Institutions Act (BOFIA) 25 of 1991 (as amended).

1.7 The policy paper has benefitted from wide consultations, through the conduct of a baseline survey on the activities of Micro Finance Institutions (MFIs) in Nigeria, National and International consultative stakeholder's for a, as well as study tour to India, Pakistan, Indonesia, Philippines and Uganda.

CHAPTER 2

OVERVIEW OF MICROFINANCE ACTIVITIES IN NIGERIA

2.0 OVERVIEW OF MICROFINANCE ACTIVITIES IN NIGERIA

2.1 The practice of microfinance in Nigeria is culturally rooted and dates back several centuries. The traditional microfinance institutions provide access to credit for the rural and urban, low-income earners. They are mainly the informal Self-Help Groups (SHGs) or Rotating Savings Credit Associations (ROSCAs) types, Other providers of microfinance services include savings collectors and co-operative societies. The informal financial institutions generally have limited outreach due primarily to paucity of loanable funds.

2.2In order to enhance the flow of financial services to Algeria's rural areas, Government has, in the past, initiated a series of publicly-financed micro/rural credit programmes and policies targeted at the poor. Notable among such programmes were the Rural Banking Programme, sectoral allocation of credits, concessionary interest rate, and the Agricultural Credit Guarantee Scheme (AGGs). Other Institutional arrangements were the establishment of the Nigerian Agricultural and Co-operative Bank Limited (NACBL), the National Directorate of Employment (NDE), the Nigeria Agricultural Insurance Corporation (NAIC), the Peoples Bank of Nigeria (PBN), the Community Banks (CBs) and the Family Economic Advancement Programme (FEAP). In year 2000, government merged the NACB with the PBN and FEAP to form the Nigerian Agricultural Co-operative and Rural Development Bank Limited (NACRDB) to enhance the provision of finance to the agricultural sector. It also create the National Poverty Eradication Programme (NAPEP) with the mandate of providing financial services to alleviate poverty.

2.3Microfinance services, particularly, those sponsored by government, have adopted the traditional supply led, subsidized credit approach mainly directed to the agricultural sector and non-farm activities, such as trading, tailoring, weaving, blacksmithing, agro-processing and transportation. Although the services have resulted in an increased level of credit disbursement and gains in agricultural production and other activities, the effects were short-lived, due to the unsustainable nature of the programme.

2.4Since the 1980s, Non-Government Organizations (NGOs) have emerged in Nigeria to champion the cause of the Micro and Rural entrepreneurs, with a shift from the supply-led approach to a demand-driven strategy, the number of NGOs involved in microfinance activities has increased significantly in recent times due largely to the inability of the formal financial sector provide the service needed by the low income groups and the poor, and the declining support from development partners amongst others. The NGOs are charity, capital lending and credit-only membership based institutions. They are generally registered under the Trusteeship Act as the sole package or part of their charity and social programmes of poverty alleviation. The NGOs obtain their funds from grants, fee interest on loans and contributions from their members. However, they have limited outreach due, largely, to unsustainable sources of funds.

CHAPTER 3
JUSTIFICATION FOR THE ESTABLISHMENT OF MICROFINANCE BANK

3.0 JUSTIFICATION FOR THE ESTABLISHMENT OF MICROFINANCE BANKS

From the appraisal of the existing microfinance-oriented institutions in Nigeria, the following facts have become evident:

3.1 Weak Institutional Capacity

The prolonged sub-optional performance of many existing community banks, microfinance and development finance institutions is due to incompetent management, weak internal controls and lack of deposit insurance schemes. Other factors are poor corporate governance, lack of well-defined operations and restrictive regulatory/supervisory requirements.

3.2Weak Capital Base

The weak capital base of the existing institutions, particularly the community banks, cannot adequately provide a cushion for the risk of lending to micro entrepreneurs without collateral. This is supported by the fact that only 75 out of over 600 community banks whose financial statements were approved by the CBN in 2005 had up to ₦20 million shareholders' funds unimpaired by losses. Similarly, the NACRDB, with a proposed authorized share capital of ₦50.0 billion, has ₦10.0 billion paid-up capital and only ₦1.3 billion shareholders' funds unimpaired by losses, as at December, 2004.

3.3 The Existence of a Huge Un-Served Market

The size of the unserved market by the existing financial institutions is large. The average banking density in Nigeria is one financial institution outlet to 32, 700 inhabitant. In the rural areas, it is 1:57,000, that is, less than 2% of rural households have access to financial services. Furthermore, the 8 (eight) leading Micro Finance Institutions (MFIs) in Nigeria were reported to have mobilized a total savings of ₦222.6 million in 2004 and advanced ₦2.624 billion credit, with an average loan size of ₦8.206. 90. This translates to about 320,000 membership based customer that enjoyed one form of credit or the other from the eight NGO-MFIs. Their aggregate loans and deposits, when compared with those of community banks, represented percentages of 23.02 and 1.04 respectively. This reveals the existence of a huge gap in the provision of financial services to a large proportion of the active but poor and low income group. The existing formal MFIs serve less than One Million out of the over 40 Million people that need their services. Also, the aggregate micro credit facilities in Nigeria account for about 0.2% of GDP and less than 1% of the total credit to the economy. The effect of not appropriately addressing this situation would further exacerbate poverty and slow down growth and development.

3.4 Economic Empowerment of the Poor, Employment Generation and Poverty Reduction

The baseline economic survey of Small and Medium Industries (SMIs) in Nigeria conducted in 2004, indicated that the 6,498 industries covered currently employ a little over one million workers. Considering the fact that about 18.5 million (28% of the available work force) Nigeria are unemployed, the employment objective role of the SMIs is far from being readied; one of the hallmarks of the National Economic Empowerment and Development Strategy (NEEDS) is the employment of the poor and the private sector, through the provision of needed financial services, to enable them engage in or expand their present scope of economic activities and generate employment. Delivering needed services as contained in the strategy would be remarkably enhanced through additional channels which the microfinance bank framework would provide. It would also assist the SMIs in wising their productive capacity and level of employment generation.

3.5 The need for Increased Savings Opportunity

The total assets of the 615 community banks which rendered their reports, out of the 753 operating community banks as at end December 2004, stood at ₦34.2 billion. Similarly, their total loans and advances amounted to ₦11.4 billion while their aggregate deposit liabilities stood at ₦21.4 billion for the same period. Also, as at end-December 2004, the total currency in circulation stood at ₦545.8 billion, out of which ₦458.6 billion or 85.12 per cent was outside the banking system. Poor people can and do save, contrary to general misconceptions. However, owing to the inadequacy of appropriate savings opportunities and products, savings have continued to grow at a very low rate, particularly in the rural areas of Nigeria. Most poor people keep their resources in kind or simply under their pillows. Such methods of keeping savings are risky, low in terms of returns, and undermine the aggregate volume of resources that could be mobilized and channelled to deficit areas of the economy. The microfinance policy would provide the needed window of opportunity and promote the development of appropriate (safe, less costly, convenient and easily accessible) savings products that would be attractive to rural clients and improve the savings level in the economy.

3.6 The Interest of Local and International Communities in Microfinancing

Many international investors have expressed interest in investing in the microfinance sector. Thus, the establishment of a microfinance framework for Nigeria would provide an opportunity for them to finance the economic activities of law income groups and the poor.

3.7Utilization of SMEEIS Fund

As at December, 2004, only ₦8.5 billion (29.5%) of the ₦28.8 billion Small and Medium Enterprises Equity Investment Scheme (SMEEIS) fund had been utilized. Moreover, 10% of the fund meant for micro credit has not been utilized due to lack of an appropriate framework and confidence in the existing institutions that would have served the purpose. This policy provides an appropriate vehicle that would enhance the utilization of the fund.

The microfinance policy would provide the needed window of opportunity and promote the development of appropriate (safe, less costly, convenient and easily accessible) savings products that would be attractive to rural clients and improve the savings level in the economy.

CHAPTER 4
THE MICROFINANCE POLICY

4.0 THE MICROFINANCE POLICY

4.1 Policy Objectives: the specific objectives of this microfinance policy are the following:

(i) Make financial services accessible to a large segment of the potentially productive Nigerian population which otherwise would have little or no access to financial services;

(ii) Promote synergy and mainstreaming of the informal subsector into the national financial system;

(iii) Enhance service delivery by microfinance institutions to Micro, Small and Medium Entrepreneurs;

(iv) Contribute to rural transformation; and

(v) Promote linkage programmes between universal/development banks, specialized institutions and microfinance banks.

4.2 Policy Targets

Based on the objectives listed above, the targets of the policy area as follows:

(i) To cover the majority of the poor but economically active population by 2020 thereby creating millions of jobs and reducing poverty;

(ii) To increase the share of micro credit as a percentage of total credit to the economy from 0.9 per cent in 2005 to at least 20 per cent in 2020; and the share of micro credit as a percentage of GDP from 0.2 per cent in 2005 to at least 5 per cent in 2020.

(iii) To promote the participation of at least two-thirds of the states and local governments micro credit financing by 2015.

(iv) To eliminate gender disparity by improving women's access to financial services by 5% annually, and

(v) To increase the number of linkages among universal banks, development banks, specialized finance institutions and microfinance banks by 10% annually.

4.3 Policy Strategies

A number of strategies have been derived from the objectives and targets as follows:

(i) Licence and regulate this establishment of Microfinance Banks (MFBs)

(ii) Promote the establishment of NGO-based microfinance institutions.
(iii) Promote the participation of Government in the microfinance industry by encouraging States and Local Governments to devote at least one per cent of their annual budgets to micro credit initiatives administered through MFBs.
(iv) Promote the establishment of institutions that support the development and growth of microfinance service, providers and clients;
(v) Strengthen the regulatory and supervisory framework for MFBs;
(vi) Promote sound microfinance practice by advocating professionalisms, transparency and good governance in microfinance institutions;
(vii) Mobilize domestic savings and promote the banking culture among low-income groups;
(viii) Strengthen the capital base of the existing microfinance institutions;
(ix) Broaden the scope of activities of microfinance institutions;
(x) Strengthen the skills of regulators, operators, and beneficiaries of microfinance initiatives
(xi) Clearly define stakeholders' roles in the development of the microfinance subsector; and
(xii) Collaborate with donors, coordinate and monitor donor assistance in microfinance in lien with the provisions of this policy.

CHAPTER 5
THE GOALS OF MICROFINANCE BANKS

5.0 THE GOALS OF MICROFINANCE BANKS

The establishment of microfinance banks has become Imperative to serve the following purposes.

(i) Provide diversified, affordable and dependable financial services to the active poor, in a timely and competitive manner, that would enable them to undertake and develop long-term, sustainable entrepreneurial activities;
(ii) Mobilize savings for intermediation;
(iii) Create employment opportunities and increase productivity of the active poor in the country, thereby increasing their individual household income and uplifting their standard of living;
(iv) Enhance organized, systematic and focused participation of the poor in the socio-economic development and resource allocation process;

(v) Provide veritable avenues for the administration of the micro credit programmes of government and high net worth individuals on a non-recourse basis. In particular, this policy ensures that state governments snail dedicate an amount of not less than 1% of their annual budgets for the on-tending activities of microfinance banks in favour of their residents; and

(vi) Render payment services, such as salaries, gratuities, and pension for various tiers of government.

CHAPTER 6
POLICY MEASURES AND INSTRUMENTS FOR THE ESTABLISHMENT OF MICROFINANCE BANKS

6.0 POLICY MEASURES AND INSTRUMENTS FOR THE ESTABLISHMENT OF MICROFINANCE BANKS

Private sector-driven microfinance banks shall be established. The banks shall be required to be well-capitalized, technically sound, and oriented towards lending, based on the cash flow and character of clients, there shall be two categories of Micro Finance Banks (MFBs), namely;

(i) Micro Finance Banks (MFBs) licensed to operate as a unit bank, and (ii) Micro Finance Banks (MFBs) licensed to operate in a state.

The recognition of these two categories of banks does not preclude them from aspiring to have a National coverage subject to their meeting the prudential requirements. This is to ensure an orderly spread and coverage of the market and to avoid, (in particular, concentration in areas already having large numbers of finance institutions). An existing NFO which intends to operate a MFB can either incorporate a subsidiary MFB, while still carrying out its NGO operations, or fully convert into a MFB.

(i) MFBs Licensed to Operate as a Unit Bank (A.K.A Community Banks) MFBs licensed to operate as unit banks shall be community based banks. Such banks can operate branches and/or cash centres subject to meeting he prescribed prudential requirements and availability of free funds for opening branches/cash centres. The minimum paid-up capital for this category of banks shall be ₦20.0 million for each branch.

(ii) MFBs Licensed to Operate in a State

MFBs licensed to operate in a State shall be authorized to operate in all parts of the state or the Federal Capital Territory in which they are registered; subject to meeting the prescribed prudential requirements and availability of free funds for opening branches. The minimum paid-up capital for this category of banks shall be ₦1.0 billion.

MFBs licensed to operate as unit banks shall be community-based banks. Such banks can operate branches and/or cash centres within the Local Government Areas in which they are registered, subject to meeting he prescribed prudential requirements and availability of free funds for opening branches/cash centres. The minimum paid-up capital for this category of banks shall be ₦20.00 million.

CHAPTER 7
ORGANIC GROWTH PATH FOR MFBs

7.0 ORGANIC GROWTH PATH FOR MFBs

7.1 This policy recognizes that the current financial landscape of Nigeria is skewed against Micro, Small and Medium Enterprises (MSMEs) in terms of access to financial services. To address the imbalance, this policy framework shall promote an even spread of microfinance banks, their branches and activities, to serve the unserved but economically active clients in the rural and peri-urban areas.

7.2 The level of spread and saturation of the financial market shall be taken into consideration before approval is granted on to an MFB to establish branches across the Local Government Area, and/or States, in fulfilment of the objectives of this policy. Specifically, an MFB shall be expected to have a reasonable spread in a Local Government Area or State before moving to another location, subject to meeting all necessary regulatory and supervisory requirements stipulated in the guidelines. This is to avoid concentration in already served areas and to ensure extension of services to the economically active poor, and to micro, small and medium enterprises.

7.3In order to achieve the objectives of an organic growth path, a microfinance bank licensed to operate as a unit bank shall be allowed to open new branches in the same State, subject to meeting the prescribed prudential requirements and availability of minimum free funds of f420.0 million for each new branch. In fulfilment of this requirement, an MFB licensed to operate as a unit bank can attain the status of a State MFB by spreading organically from one location to another until it covers at least and two-thirds of the LGAs of the State. When an MFB has satisfactorily covered a state and wishes to start operations in another state, it shall obtain approval and be required to again grow organically by having at least ₦20 million free funds unimpaired by losses for each branch to be opened in the new state.

7.4 An MFB licensed to operate in a State shall be allowed to open a branch in another State, subject to opening branches in at least two-thirds of the local governments of the State it is currently licensed to operate in, subject to the provision of ₦20.0 million free funds and, if in the view of the regulatory authorities, it has satisfied all the requirements stipulated in the guidelines.

7.5 However, an MFB may wish to start operations as a State Bank from the beginning and therefore not wish to grow organically from branch to branch. Such an MFB may be licensed and authorized to operate in all areas of the state from the beginning subject to the provision of a total capital base of ₦1 billion. In other words, the preferred growth path for MFBs is the branch by branch expression to become State Banks. But anyone wishing to start big as a state institution can do so subject to availability of ₦1 billion and proven managerial competence. An MFB licensed to operate in a State shall be allowed to open a branch in another State, subject to opening branches in at least two-thirds of the local governments of the State it is currently licensed to operate in, subject to the provision of ₦20.0 million free funds and, if, in the view of the regulatory authorities, it has satisfied all the requirements stipulated in the guidelines.

CHAPTER 8
OWNERSHIP OF MICROFINANCE BANK

8.0 OWNERSHIP OF MICROFINANCE BANKS

8.1 Microfinance banks can be established by individuals, groups of individuals, community development associations, private corporate entities, or foreign investors, significant ownership diversification shall be encourage to enhance good corporate governance of licensed MFBs.

Universal banks that intend to set up any of the two categories of MFB as subsidiaries shall be required to deposit the appropriate minimum paid-up capital and meet the prescribed prudential requirements and if, in the view of the regulatory authorities, have also satisfied all the requirements stipulated in the guidelines, shall be licensed.

8.2 Non-individual, group of individuals, their proxies or corporate entities, and/or their subsidiaries, shall establish more than one MFB under a different or disguised name.

Microfinance banks can be established by individuals, groups of individuals, community development associations, private corporate entities, or foreign investors. Significant ownership diversification shall be encouraged to enhance good corporate governance licensed MFBs.

CHAPTER 9
PARTICIPATION OF EXISTING FINANCIAL INSTITUTIONS IN MICROFINANCE ACTIVITIES

9.0 PARTICIPATION OF EXISTING FINANCIAL INSTITUTIONS IN MICROFINANCE ACTIVITIES

9.1 Universal Banks

Universal banks currently engaged in Microfinance services, either as an activity or product and do not wish to set up a subsidiary, shall be required to set up a department/unit for such services and shall be subjected to the provisions of the MFB regulatory and supervisory guidelines.

9.2 Community Banks

All licensed community banks, prior to the approval of this policy, shall transform to microfinance banks licensed to operate as a unit bank on meeting the prescribed new capital and other conversion requirements within a period of 24 months from the date of approval of this policy. Any community bank which fails to meet the new capital requirement within the stipulated period shall cease to operate as a community bank. A community bank can apply to convert to a microfinance bank licensed to operate in a State if it meets the specified capital and other conversion requirements.

9.3 Non-Governmental Organization - Micro Finance Institutions (NGO-MFIs)

The policy recognizes the existence of credit-only, membership-based microfinance institutions which shall not be required to come under the supervisory purview of the Central Bank of Nigeria. Such institutions shall engage in the provision of micro credit to their targeted population and will not mobilize deposits from the general public. The registered NGO-MFIs shall be required to forward periodic returns on their activities to the CBN. NGO-MFI's that wish to obtain the operating licence of a microfinance bank shall be required to meet the specified provisions as stipulated in the regulatory and supervisory guidelines.

9.4 Transformation of the Existing NGO-MFIs

Any existing NGO-MFIs which intends to operate an MFB can either incorporate a subsidiary MFB while still carrying out its NGO operations or fully convert into an MFB. Any NGO-MFI's that wishes to convert fully into a microfinance bank must obtain an operating licence and shall be required to meet the specified provisions as stipulated in the regulatory and supervisory guidelines.

This policy recognizes the existence of credit-only, membership-based microfinance institutions which shall not be required to come under the supervisor purview of the Central Bank of Nigeria. Such institutions shall engage in the provision of micro credits to their targeted population and will not mobilize deposits from the general public.

CHAPTER 10
JUSTIFICATION FOR THE CAPITAL REQUIREMENTS

10.0 JUSTIFICATION FOR THE CAPITAL REQUIREMENTS

10.1 The present capital base of ₦5 million for community banks has become too low for effective financial intermediation. Indeed, to set up a community bank, at least ₦5 million is required for the basic infrastructure, leaving zero or a negative balance for banking operations. From a survey of community banks, an operating fund of ₦50 million is about the minimum capital (own capital and deposits) a community bank needs to provide effective banking services to its clients. However, it is recognized that since many community banks are based on the rural areas, their promoters may not be able to effectively raise ₦50 million as shareholders' funds. Hence, the stipulation of ₦20 million as shareholders' funds for the unit microfinance banks. The banks are expected to engage in aggressive mobilization of saving from micro-depositors to shore up their operating funds.

10.2 A State coverage microfinance bank that would operate multiple branches would be expected to take off with funds sufficient to operate a full branch in at least two-thirds of the Local Government

Areas in that State. Hence, a minimum paid-up capital of ₦1.0 billion shall be required to obtain the licence to operate a State coverage MFB. Expansion to another State shall be subject to the provision of ₦1.0 billion minimum shareholders' funds unimpaired by losses, and after opening branches in at least two-thirds of the Local Government Areas of the State it is currently licensed to operate in, and if in the view of the regulatory authorities, it has satisfied all the requirement stipulated in the guidelines.

10.3 The experience of other countries sheds light on the level of capitalization required for microfinance banks. In most countries, the level of capitalization depends on the geographical coverage of the banks, and for some countries, even for a particular scope of coverage (district or province), the population and volume of business of the area further determine the level of capitalization. The capitalization requirements in other countries were also considered in arriving at the capitalization levels for the two categories of MFBs in this policy.

A minimum paid-up capital of ₦1.0 billion shall be required to obtain the licence to operate a state coverage MFB. Expansion to another state shall be subject to the provision of ₦1.0 billion minimum shareholders' funds unimpaired by losses, and after opening branches in at least two-thirds of the Local Government Areas of the State it is currently licensed to operate in, and if in the view of the regulatory authorities, it has satisfied all the requirement stipulated in the guidelines.

CHAPTER 11

FRAMEWORK FOR THE SUPERVISION OF MICROFINANCE BANKS

11.0 FRAMEWORK FOR THE SUPERVISION OF MICROFINANCE BANKS

11.1 Licensing and Supervision of Microfinance Banks

The licensing of microfinance banks shall be the responsibility of the Central Bank of Nigeria. A licensed institution shall be required to add "microfinance bank", after its name. All such names shall be registered with the Corporate Affairs Commission (CAC), in compliance with the Companies and Allied Matters Act (CAMA) 1990.

11.2 Establishment of National Microfinance Consultative Committee

A National Microfinance Consultative Committee (NMFCC) shall be constituted by the Central Bank of Nigeria (CBN) to provide direction for the implementation and monitoring this policy. Membership of the Committee shall be determined from time to time by the CBN. The

Microfinance Support Unit of the CBN shall serve as the secretariat to the committee.

11.3 Credit Reference Bureau

Due to the peculiar characteristics of microfinance practice, a credit reference bureau, which shall provide information on microfinance clients and aid decision making, is desirable. In this regard, the present Credit Risk Management System in the CBN shall be expanded to serve the needs of the microfinance sector.

11.4 Rating Agency

The CBN shall encourage the establishment of private rating agencies for the subsector to rate microfinance institutions, especially those NGO-MFIs which intend to transform to microfinance banks.

11.5 Deposit Insurance Scheme

Since MFBs are deposit-taking institutions and in order to reinforce public confidence in them, MFBs shall qualify for the deposit insurance scheme of the Nigeria Deposit Insurance Corporation (NDIC).

11.6 Management Certificate Process

In order to bridge the technical skills gap, especially among operators of microfinance banks, the policy recognizes the need to set up an appropriate capacity building programme for MFBs. To this end, the CBN shall put in place a microfinance bank management certification process to enhance the acquisition of appropriate microfinance operational skills of the management team of MFBs. A transition period of twenty four (24) months shall be allowed for the take-off of the programme, with effect from the date of launching the policy.

11.7 Apex Associations of Microfinance Institutions

The establishment of an apex association of microfinance institutions to promote uniform standards, transparency, good corporate practices and full disclosures in the conduct of MFI business shall be encouraged.

11.8 Linkage Programme

The policy recognizes the importance of the provision of wholesale funds for microfinance banks to expand their outreach Pursuant to this, the CBN shall work out the modalities for fostering linkages between universal/development banks, specialized finance institutions and the microfinance banks to enable the latter sources for whole funds and refinancing facilities for on-lending to their clients.

11.9 Establishment of a Microfinance Development Fund

In order to promote the development of the subsector and provide for the wholesale funding requirements of microfinance banks, a Micro Finance Sector Development Fund shall be set up. The fund shall provide necessary support for the development of the sub-sector in terms of refinancing facility, capacity building, and other promotional activities. The Fund would be sourced from governments and through soft facilities from the international development financing institutions a well a multilateral and bilateral development institutions.

11.10 Prudential Requirements

The CBN recognizes the peculiarities of microfinance practice and shall accordingly put in place appropriate regulatory and prudential requirements to guide the operations and activities of the microfinance banks.

11.11 Disclosure of Sources of Funds

Licensed MFBs shall be required to disclose their sources of funds, in compliance with the Money Laundering Prohibition Act 2004.

11.12 Corporate Governance for Microfinance Banks

The board of directors of MFBs shall be primarily responsible for corporate governance in the microfinance banks. To ensure good governance of the banks, the board of directors shall be responsible for establishing strategic objectives, policies and procedures that would guide and direct the activities, of the banks and the means to attain same, as well as the mechanism for monitoring Management's performance. Thus, while management of the day-to-day affairs of the banks shall be responsible of the Management team, the board of directors shall, however, be responsible for monitoring and overseeing Management's actions. Consequently, the licensed microfinance banks shall be expected to operate under diversified and professional board of directors.

In order to promote the development of the subsector and provide for the wholesale funding requirements of 'microfinance banks, a Microfinance Sector Development Fund shall be set up. The fund shall provide necessary support for the development of the subsector in terms of refinancing facility, capacity building, and other promotional activities. The Fund would be sourced from governments and through soft facilities from the internal development financing institutions, as well as multilateral and bilateral development institutions.

CHAPTER 12
REGULATORY INCENTIVES

12.0 REGULATORY INCENTIVES

12.1 The new window of opportunity for the merging microfinance banks in bringing financing services to people who never had access to such services before, would require the support of government and that of regulatory authorities. The CBN shall collaborate with the appropriate fiscal authorities in providing a favourable tax treatment of MFBs' financial transactions, such as exemption from Value Added Tax (VAT) on lending, or tax on interest income or revenue.

12.2 similarly, the principle of exemption from profit tax shall be applied to any MFB that does not distribute its net surplus but ploughs it back and reinvest the surplus to finance more economically beneficial micro, small and medium entrepreneurship.

12.3 Furtherance, a Rediscounting and Refinancing Facility (RRF) shall be made available to MFBs for purposes of providing liquidity assistance to support and promote microfinance programmes. This would enable MFBs that have met the CBN prudential requirements to, on a sustainable basis, provide and render micro-credits and other services to their clients.

The new window of opportunity for the emerging microfinance banks in bringing financial services to people who never had access to such services before, would require the support of government and that of regulatory authorities. The CBN shall collaborate with the appropriate fiscal authorities in providing a favourable tax treatment of MFBs financial transactions, such as exemption from Value Added Tax (VAT) on lending, or tax on interest income or revenue.

CHAPTER 13
THE ROLES AND RESPONSIBILITIES OF STAKEHOLDERS

13.0 THE ROLES AND RESPONSIBILITIES OF STAKEHOLDERS

The roles and responsibilities of stakeholders shall include the following;

13.1 Government

Government shall be responsible for:

(i) Ensuring a stable micro-economic environment, providing basic infrastructures (electricity, water, roads, telecommunications, etc.), Political and social stability;
(ii) Fostering adequate land titling and other property right sufficient to serve the collateral heeds of 'borrowers and financial institutions;
(iii) Instituting and enforcing donor and foreign aid guidelines on microfinance to streamline their activities in line with the policy; and
(iv) Setting aside an amount of not less than 1% of the annual budgets of state governments for on-lending activities of microfinance banks in favour of their residents.

13.2 Central Bank of Nigeria (CBN)

The role of the CBN shall include the following;

(i) Establishing a National Microfinance Consultative Committee
(ii) Evolving a dear micro-finance policy that spells out eligibility and licensing criteria, provides operational/prudential standards and guidelines to all stakeholders;
(iii) Evolving a microfinance subsection and institutional policies aimed at providing regulatory harmony, promoting healthy competition and mainstreaming micro financing with formal intermediation;
(iv) Adopting an appropriate regulatory and supervisory framework;
(v) Minimizing regulatory arbitrage through periodic reviews of the policy and guidelines;
(vi) Promoting linkage programmes between universal/development banks, specialized finance institutions and the microfinance banks;
(vii) Continuously advocating market-determined interest rates for government-owned institutions and promote the channelling of government microfinance fund through MFBs; and
(viii) Implementing appropriate training programme for regulators, promoters and practitioners in the subsector, in collaboration with stakeholders.

13.3 Micro Finance Institution (MFIs)

Microfinance services providers shall:

(i) Provide efficient and effective financial services, such as credit, deposits, commodity/inventory collateralization, teasing, and innovative transfer/payment services;
(ii) Undertake appropriate recruitment and retention of qualified professionals through transparent and competitive processes;

(iii) Adopt continuous training and capacity building programmes to improve the skills of staff; and
(iv) Strictly observe their fiduciary responsibility, remain transparent and accountable in protecting savers' deposits;
(v) Compliance with the rules and regulations as stipulated by the regulatory authorities;

13.4 Public Sector Poverty Alleviation Agencies

The MFB policy recognizes the rules of public sector MFIs and poverty alleviation agencies such as the National Poverty Eradication Programme (NPEP) in the development of the subsector. They shall be encouraged to perform the following functions;

(i) Provision of resources targeted at difficult-to-reach clients and the poorest of the poor;
(ii) Capacity building;
(iii) Development of MFIs' activities nationwide;
(iv) Nurturing the new MFIs to a sustainable level; and
(v) Collaborating/partnering with other relevant stakeholders.

13.5 Donor Agencies

Donor agencies offer free or subsidized funds, donations, or technical assistance for the development of the microfinance industry in Nigeria. They include Bilateral and Multilateral Institutions, NGOs and missionaries with a pro-poor orientation. The series provided by donor agencies include grants, donations, technical assistance, etc. The donor agencies, in conducting their microfinance activities, shall comply with the relevant provisions of this policy. The target clients for donors' support may include: MFIs, NGOs, Regulators and other relevant agencies. However, for the purpose of leveraging the evolving microfinancing initiative, donor have expected to direct most of their assistance to licensed MFBs' to ensure an orderly resource injection, transparency and synergy.

The MFB policy recognizes the roles of public sector MFIs and poverty alleviation agencies such as the National Poverty Eradication Programme (NPEP) in the development of the subsector. They shall be encouraged to perform the following functions.

CHAPTER 14
CONCLUSION

14.0 CONCLUSION

14.1 There exists a huge untapped potential for financial intermediation at the micro and rural levels of the Nigerian economy. Attempt by government in the past to fill this gap, through supply-driven creation of financing institutions and instruments, have failed, due to the poor capitalization of such schemes and restrictive regulatory and supervisory procedures, among other factors. The community banks were designed to fill the gap, but their low capital base and isolated mode of operation have not enabled them to made meaningful contributions to micro financing.

14.2 The microfinance banks being established in line with this policy framework shall be adequately capitalized, appropriately regulated and supervised to address the need of financing at the micro levels of the economy. The two categories of microfinance banks shall be microfinance banks licensed to operate unit banks (a.k.a Community Banks) and Microfinance Banks licensed to operate in a state.

14.3 Microfinance Banks licensed to operate as unit banks shall require a minimum paid-up of ₦20 million and shall operate branches and/or cash centres. A Microfinance Bank licensed to operate in a State shall require a minimum paid-up capital of ₦1.0 billion and shall operate multiple branches within a State, subject to satisfactory prudential requirements and availability of free funds for branch expansion.

14.4 The existing community banks shall transform to Microfinance Banks within 24 months of the approval of this policy, by increasing their shareholders' funds impaired by losses to a minimum of ₦20.0 million. Any community bank which does not meet the new capital requirement within the stipulated period shall cease to operate as a community bank.

14.5 The Central Bank of Nigeria shall supervise and regulate the microfinance banks. The Nigeria Deposit Insurance Corporation shall insure the deposits of microfinance banks.

14.6 The provision of this policy shall be subject to review from time to time at the full discretion of the regulatory authorities.

There exists a huge untapped potential for financial intermediation at the micro and rural levels of the Nigeria economy. Attempts by Government in the past to fill this gap, through supply-driven creation of financing institutions and instruments, have failed, due to the poor capitalization of such schemes and restrictive regulator/and supervisory procedures, among such other factors. The community banks were designed to fill the gap, but their low capital base and isolated mode of operation have not enabled them to make meaningful constitutions to microfinancing.

DISTINGUISHING FEATURES BETWEEN A MICROFINANCE BANK AND A UNIVERSAL BANK

APPENDIX V

COMMERCIAL BANKS IN NIGERIA
Access Bank Plc.
Afri Bank Plc
Bank PHS (Platinum Habib Bank)
Diamond Bank Plc
Eco Bank Plc
Equatorial Trust Bank Ltd.
Fidelity Bank Plc
First Bank of Nigeria Plc
First City Monument Plc
FIN Bank Plc
GT Bank Plc (Guarantee Trust Bank)
Intercontinental Bank Plc
Nigeria International Bank Plc (Citigroup)
Oceanic Bank International Plc
Skye Bank Plc
Spring Bank Plc
Stanbic IBTC Bank Plc
Standard Chartered Bank of Nigeria Ltd
Sterling Bank Plc
United Bank for Africa Plc
WEMA Bank Plc
Zenith Bank Plc

Mortgage Institutions in Nigeria
Abbey Building Society Ltd
Acclaim Home Savings and Loans Ltd
Accord Savings and Loans Ltd
AG Homes Saving and Loans Ltd
Allwell Savings and Loans Ltd
Anambra Home Ownership Co., Ltd
Aso Savings and Loans Ltd
Baico Building Society Ltd
Benhome Building Society Ltd
Centage Savings and Loans Ltd

City Code Savings and Loans Ltd
Consolidated (States Buildings Society Ltd)
Confluence Savings and Loans Ltd
Crop Savings and Loans Ltd
Comer Stone Building Society Ltd
Dale Building Society Ltd
Delta Building Society Company Ltd
Diamond Building Society Ltd
Dominion Building Society Ltd
Estaport Building Society
Estate Building Society Ltd
Euro-Basic Savings and Loans Ltd
FBN Mortgages Ltd
FHA Home Ltd (Savings and Loans)
Fina Corp Buildings Society Ltd
Fine Home Savings and Loans Ltd
First Amalgamated building Society Ltd
Foka Savings and Loans Ltd
Guardian Trust Savings and Loans Ltd
Gilt-Bond Mortgage
Global Trust Savings and Loans Ltd
Halmark Homes Ltd
Harvard Trust Savings and Loans Ltd
Imani Savings and Loans Ltd
Jigawa Savings and Loans Ltd
Jubilee Building Society Ltd
Infinity Trust Savings and Loans Ltd
Kebbi Stat Home Savings and Loans Ltd
Lagoon Home Savings and Loans Ltd
Lagos Building Investment Co. Ltd
Living Spring Savings and Loans Ltd
Leverage and Home Savings and Loans Ltd
Maegra Buildings Society
Margret Savings and Loans Ltd
May Fresh Savings and Loans Ltd
M & N Building Society Ltd
Mortgage Guarantee Savings and Loans Ltd
Multi-Bank Savings and Loans Ltd

Mustard Seed Mortgage
Mutual Alliance Savings and Loans Ltd
New Patriot Savings and Loans Ltd
New Prudential Building Society Ltd
Oasis Savings and Loan Ltd
Omega Savings and Loans Ltd
Owners Home Savings Loans Ltd
Perpetual Savings and Loans of Ltd
Pacific Savings and Loans Ltd
Peak Savings and Loans Ltd
Personal Trust Savings and Loans Ltd
Partnership Savings and Loans Ltd
Password Savings and Loans Ltd
Resort Savings and Loans Ltd
Safefirst Savings and Loans Ltd
Sakkwato Savings and Loans Ltd Stallion
Home Savings and Loans Ltd
Sky Reid Savings and Loans Ltd
Spring Mortgage Ltd
STB Building Society Ltd
Sub-Urban Trust Savings and Loans Ltd
Supreme Savings and Loans Ltd
Trinity Savings and Loans Ltd
TMC Savings and Loans Ltd
Union Home Savings and Loans Ltd
United Mortgage Ltd
Universal Trust Building Society Ltd
Yankari Savings and Loans Ltd
Yobe Savings and Loans Ltd
Adamawa Savings and Loans Ltd
Ahohol Savings and Loans Ltd
Gateway Savings and Loans Ltd
Intercontinental Savings and Loans Ltd
Kogi State Savings and Loans Ltd
New Central Savings and Loans Ltd
Platinum Savings and Loans Ltd
Solid Trust Savings and Loans Ltd
Taraba Savings and Loans Ltd

DISCOUNT HOUSES
Associated Discount House Ltd
Consolidated Discount House Ltd
Express Discount House Ltd
First Securities Discount House Ltd
Kekawa Discount House Ltd

DEVELOPMENT BANKS
Federal Mortgage Bank of Nigeria
Nigeria Industrial Development Bank
Nigeria Bank for Commerce and Industry
Nigeria Agricultural Cooperative and Rural Development Bank Ltd
Nigeria Export-Import Bank (NEIB) Ltd
Urban Development Bank of Nigeria Plc

Source: The Senate, Federal Republic of Nigeria Diary 2004.

APPENDIX VI

COUNTRIES AND CURRENCIES

Country	Currency
Australia	Austr. Dollar
Belgium	Euro
Canada	Can. Dollar
China	Yuan
Egypt	Pound
France	Euro
Germany	Euro
Ghana	Cedi
India	Rupee
Indonesia	Rupiah
Italy	Euro
Japan	Yen
Kuwait	Ringgit
Malaysia	Rupee
Nigeria	Naira
Pakistan	U Shilling
Saudi Arabia	Riyal
South Korea	Won
Switzerland	Swiss Franc
Tran	Riab
Turkey	Turkey Lira
Uganda	Afghani
United Arab Emirates	Dhirham
United Kingdom	Pound
USA	US Dollar
Zimbabwe	Zimbabwe Dollar

REFERENCES

Afolabi, L. (2005) *Law and Practice of Banking* 3rd Edition Ibadan Heinemann.

Danbazua, A. B. (2006) *Criminology and Criminal Justice*, Ibadan: Spectrum

Gamer, B. A. (1990) *Black Law Dictionary* 8th Edition P. 154

Gup. B. E. (1995), *Targeting Fraud: Uncovering Fraud in Financial Institutions* Chicago: Probus Publishing Company.

Halsbury Laws of England 3rd Edition P. 229 Para. 427.

Holden J. M. (1983), *The Law and Practice of Banking* Vol. London: Pitman Publishing Limited

Iroka, G (2003) *Pamphlet on Banks Law* Unpublished

Journal Goredema (2005) "Measuring Money Laundering in Southern Africa," *African Security Review*, Vol. 14 No. 4.

Magaji, B. M. (2010), *Principles of Nigeria Law: An Outline*, Kaduna Efsoon Print.

Magaji, B. M. (2007), "Constitutional Guarantees to Fair Trial: Scope and Limitations of the Armed Force Act No. 105 in Military Court.

Silberman, C. E. (1980), *Criminal Violence, Criminal Justice*, New York Vintage Books, Pp. 346-347.

UN Office Reports on Drugs and Crime, 2005.

www.ingramcontent.com/pod-product-compliance
Lightning Source LLC
Chambersburg PA
CBHW050524240926
51846CB00003B/681
9789786001203